The Origins of Man
and the Universe

The Origins of
Man and the Universe

The Myth That Came To Life

BARRY LONG

ROUTLEDGE & KEGAN PAUL

London, Boston, Melbourne & Henley

First published in 1984
by Routledge & Kegan Paul plc

14 Leicester Square, London WC2H 7PH, England

9 Park Street, Boston, Mass. 02108, USA

464 St Kilda Road, Melbourne,
Victoria 3004, Australia and

Broadway House, Newtown Road,
Henley-on-Thames, Oxon RG9 1EN, England

Set in IBM Journal, 11 on 12 pt
by Columns of Reading
and printed in Great Britain
by Billing & Sons Ltd, Worcester

Library of Congress Cataloging in Publication Data
Long, Barry, 1926-

The origins of man and the universe.
Includes bibliographical references and index.
1. Man—Miscellanea.   2. Life—Miscellanea.   3. Truth—
Miscellanea.   4. Reality—Miscellanea.   I. Title.
BF1999.L55   1984   001.9   84-3298

British Library CIP data also available

ISBN 0-7102-0337-3

To the truth

Contents

Contents

Preface

Two questions are likely to trouble you as you start to read this book. Where did the knowledge to write it come from? And how can you know if it is the truth?

The broad answer to both questions is that the truth — that is, all meaningful knowledge: knowledge of life and death and such profound subjects as the origins of man* and the universe — is within you and everyone now at this moment, in the unconscious.

Specifically, I have access to such knowledge because I am a spiritual teacher. A spiritual teacher is someone who has taken conscious responsibility for the spiritual life of a section of humanity. One's knowledge of the reality of life is determined by the responsibility one has taken for life. Appropriate to that responsibility and task I am permitted to enter the higher levels of mind described in this book. I write and speak from there.

To the other question — how can you know whether what you are reading is the truth? — the specific answer is that this book is a journey, a descent into your own psyche, the human psyche. As it is your psyche, you already 'know' all that is in it. As it contains the truth, you cannot be misled — unless you try to bring with you your judgmental conscious mind which does not know the truth. If you do that your mind will lead you into your memory, into your opinions,

---

* In this book I use 'man' as an abbreviation for mankind, which of course includes both man and woman.

beliefs and confusion, and you will not enter the psyche, or find the truth. You hear the beauty or truth of birdsong with your psyche — and name the kind of bird with your mind.

As you read the first section of the book and begin the journey down — holding the judging surface mind at bay — you will find a good deal that is true in your own experience, and this will be your affirmation that it is the truth.

But as you go deeper into the book, and down into the more obscure unconscious regions of the psyche, you will be less able to draw on the truth of your experience. You will have to trust more and more in your inner self, the part of you that is most real and most true. You do this, not by trying to work out what you are reading (unless it gives you pleasure), but by continuing to read on and listening for the ring of truth. The ring or sound of truth is the only means we have of recognising or 'learning' what is real or objective in the unconscious. Through it we receive the enlightening energy of the unknown, the unconscious itself, and by-pass the surface mind whose frantic need to know and name is the impediment to enlightenment. This will lead you to the extraordinary experience of realising that you did in fact already 'know' what your mind would try to tell you nobody could know.

I repeat, all that is in this book is already within you. Don't be put off by the mind that wants to judge, reject, form an opinion, argue, complain that the subject is too deep or say it does not understand.

Read on. Let the words wash through you and over you. Read it as you would pause to look at the sea or the stars. Don't try to understand. Don't compare. Don't compete. There is nothing to prove. It will all come together within you — if not immediately, in time.

Acknowledgment

I acknowledge the enormous contribution of Peter Kingsley, a lover of the truth, who worked with me for three years to edit and arrange this manuscript.

Part one

The origins of man

I

1
Science and religion: the missing connection

Man's speculations about his origins fall into two well-known categories — science's evolution theory, and the world's religious and mythical accounts.

Evolution theory, according to Darwin and others, describes man's animal and sensory development from the first microbe. No explanation is offered for his incomparable creative and artistic powers. According to the theory he is just a better kind of ape.

On the other hand, biblical and other religious traditions report some kind of divine or mystical creation in which man appeared physically fully formed and imaginatively inventive as we know him today.

The two approaches are irreconcilable — but only until the underlying truth connecting them is realised. Then the religious and mythical accounts are seen to be attempts at describing the astonishing emotional-creative beginnings of man — the element missing from the scientific theory.

As the religious stories pre-dated scientific rationalism by many, many thousands of years they could not avoid presenting a strongly emotional view: man's evolution since that time has been broadly from an emotional to a rational being. What is surprising today is that in spite of more than a century of super-science since Darwin presented his theory, the religious authorities continue to ignore the clamour in man's mind for a rational and intelligent explanation of religious phenomena in the light of evolution theory. This omission, or implicit inability of organised religion to understand the truth of its own doctrines probably accounts more than anything else for the decline in its credibility and influence.

Modern, rational man who depends on materialistic fact for his daily bread and his motor car, has outgrown the need for emotional explanations of the origins of things and will not accept that human bodies, bread or cars are suddenly created without a physical cause. And why should he? In a rational world such propositions are patently absurd. Yet while intelligent and earnest men continue to commit themselves to the creation idea it can only mean a massive misunderstanding has occurred somewhere along the line.

One would imagine that the two sides, having set themselves up as authorities in such matters as the origins of man, would be concerned with trying to find out what that all-important error or misunderstanding between them was, or is, instead of pursuing their mutually exclusive dogmas to the confusion of everyone who just wants to know the truth.

Religion argues from a position of faith. Science argues from a position of fact. With less emphasis on positions, faith can be factually described and fact faithfully sourced to original causes.

These two great opposing ideas — evolution theory and creation theory — actually represent the two sides of man, his mystifying dual nature: the sensory physical, and the vitally creative.

Without doubt, man is an animal — and yet he is uniquely creative. How, and in what circumstances, did an animal become independently creative, numerically inventive, emotionally resonant? And where is the evidence?

Under this kind of scrutiny, it is fairly obvious that neither evolution theory nor scriptural theory is really complete without the other.

And yet to believe in either of these perennial opposites seems automatically to deny the possibility of the other. As it is impossible to argue sensibly against evolution as regards man's animal development, evolution theory has become almost universally accepted as describing his whole ancestry — even though it accounts for only half of the man which every scientist, every human being, experiences himself to be.

To date, due more to the absence of an acceptable rationale

than to any great personal conviction about his descent/ascent from the apes and microbes, modern rational man largely has had to lay aside the fascinating scriptural and mythical possibility — talk of immortality, higher powers, visions and the rest — something like a fondly remembered but impossible childhood dream.

Rationality and science — intellectual materialism — have triumphed over man's deeper feelings and longings; and on the evidence adduced, rightly so. But the trouble with a theory — Darwinian theory, religious theory, any theory — is that it always remains a partly observed fact. That is, it is not yet a principle, not immediately demonstrable, like for instance the law of gravitation.

No matter how carefully and in detail phenomena are studied from an exclusive point of view — such as the animal ancestry of man which excludes the vitally creative side, or scriptural theory which excludes the rational side — the results are always partial, incomplete. And mankind remains as it is today, perhaps factually persuaded but faithfully unconvinced.

Evolutionists and naturalists like Darwin and so many others in our own time have contributed enormously to our understanding and appreciation of nature as the perfect system of perpetual motion. But what of the evolutionist himself — not his organism but the intelligence, the creative brilliance or genius with which he cognises the nature-system? What would the result be if he observed and catalogued this unique system of intelligence in himself with the same patience and dedication as he studies the formal, natural world around him?

By demarking a point some tens of thousands of years ago when homo sapiens — modern creative man — emerged out of the animal lineage of flesh and instinct, science tacitly acknowledges the occurrence of a unique and extraordinary event in time. It affirms that somewhere, sometime during the countless ages of HOMO (the biological order of primates which includes monkeys and apes) development, man acquired his SAPIENCE (sense of knowing discernment), that unprecedented humanising addition to his animal nature; and that this sapient factor is the other half of him, the

5

missing link, in the otherwise elegant scientific theory.

It is a little-known fact that the sense-perceived world is organised in such a way that every stage of man's past evolution as a race is represented, literally recorded, in the phenomena around him. Consequently, the scientist is able to collect his solid fossilised evidence preserved in the earth and gradually assemble a rational model of man's animal evolution.

But this ordering of things does not apply only to biological and physical evidence. The evidence of man's creative beginnings also is there. It is waiting to be discerned in the same vivid way as the significance of the earth's fossils was once suddenly conceived.

This evidence has been staring humanity in the face for thousands of years. It is contained in the myths and scriptural traditions of all cultures.

Gods and demi-gods — *the crucial question*

The Greek myths and Hindu traditions tell of gods and demi-gods walking the earth, fraternising with mortal man and even mating with him. Yet no one has ever seriously suggested that this was precisely how it was and had a hearing.

Paradoxically, our civilisation has retained these averred scriptural and mythological fairy tales as an essential part of its reservoir of learning and thinking: and yet the essence of the myths — those earthly antics of gods and demi-gods — is commonly regarded as fiction. Similarly, the scriptural and Hindu accounts of gods and divinities are benignantly shrugged off, at best as allegory or some sort of symbolism.

Even that wonderfully perceptive man C.G. Jung saw the energies of the myths acting outwardly through the unconscious but still failed to get back behind the symbols to identify the actual event in time that originated them. The myths may indeed symbolise ever-recurring patterns of human and emotional behaviour, as Jung demonstrated. But that merely underlines their importance as an effect, not as originating cause. What Jung regarded as fundamental is really secondary. Originating cause requires originating event or originating phenomenon. This is a fundamental truth. Nothing can have an effect that has not happened.

Neither the Greek myths, the bible, the early Sanskrit texts nor any other of the most ancient religious traditions mentions that the accounts do not stand for exactly what they say. For us to assume otherwise is just as arrogant and presumptuous as if future man were to look back on the tattered records of this civilisation and dismiss evolution theory, with its disregard for the humanising of man, as a symbolic statement. Evolution theory means exactly what it says, only it happens by omission to be half-wrong; as the myths and scriptures happen to be half-right.

As the original myths were presumably repeated by word of mouth until written down one has to expect imaginative accretions and distortions. But central to the Greek and all religious traditions — the one point beyond embellishment that makes them such incredible tales in our experience — are the unqualified references to gods and demi-gods with miraculous powers participating in human affairs.

Were the gods — mythical and religious — fact or nonsense? This is in fact the question at the crux of the whole science-or-religion dilemma and our search for origins.

On what grounds can we venture to presume that the reports are not fact essentially? Common sense? Our common sense can tell us only what is commonly experienced now. It cannot tell us what was the common experience when man was actually becoming man as the myths and scriptures try to describe.

The evidence of the myths is clear. To mate or walk with gods — could anything be more straightforward and down-to-earth than that? The only question, it seems, is how? This, this first section of the book will answer.

For those individuals who appreciate them, the ancient mythical and scriptural ideas (as well as the ideas expressed in this book) have an elusively familiar ring of truth, something like the feeling of a dream which though distinct persistently escapes the waking memory. Art is in fact the continuous endeavour to convey these original feelings ever more distinctly and meaningfully. From the mystical point of view they represent the indefinable quality called faith.

The origins of man

It is not the masterliness of the ancient writings that has made them so revered and studied down through the ages, or attachment to their value as original works; they were set down long after the events they supposedly describe. Nor, as some may claim, is it because of their imaginative power: innumerable equally striking and richly imaginative works have been written since.

What it is about the myths that penetrates and resonates to the depths of man's vital being without his necessarily realising it, is the unconscious recognition that the events they describe represent the fantastic conditions actually existing at the beginning of the human race.

2
The evolution of the species : the untold story

To understand evolution *before* man appeared on earth, before there were selves which we as man are today, it is necessary to grasp that Man was a principle, not yet an entity.

Man was the principle of intelligence behind all evolving forms of life — the intelligence who organised the evolution of the physical species. It may help to think of him as being already within or 'behind' the brains of the dinosaurs who preceded him, deep within the vast unconsciousness that was life at that time.

Through the evolution of the physical species on earth Man as the principle of intelligence was then able to evolve the human body to his own specifications. He did this over an enormous tract of time by gradually entering from the unconscious a partly developed physical body prepared for him by the earlier evolution of the rest of the species. The preparation of this body was the fundamental task of evolution. Although a very primitive body it was already functional.

Advancing into its brain as a relentless, intelligent pressure, Man forced the body to evolve into human form uniquely suited to his creative and self-conscious capabilities which we as his selves express today.

This story of the evolution of the species and man — which has never been told before — I will now relate in detail.

The tree of life

Every form ever taken by the earth's evolving species, from bacteria to primates, was a branch of the tree of life along which travelled the impulse that finally appeared as modern creative man — the self-conscious culmination of all the species.

The first simple life-forms that appeared on earth were like the first spring shoots on an otherwise invisible though gigantic trunk within the primordial psyche. By the time these life-forms appeared, this trunk was a superbly advanced cerebral network providing an acutely sensitive internal system of communication between all living things.

Evolution theory, being based on external observation, has no knowledge of any of this. The essential point missing from evolution theory is that evolution was a dual process. It was involuntarily physical and organic on the surface and intelligently self-creative and vitally persistent underneath and within. Both functions ultimately were to merge as the body and intelligence of homo sapiens, inventive man.

Evolution in fact was mostly an exteriorising process. Everything came largely from within and was managed from within.

For the first life-forms, we are told, the environment on the surface of the earth must have been extremely hostile. Unarguably, the difficulty was for life to obtain a foothold and to hold onto it. What we are not told is that behind the simple life-forms was a vast psychic network, a brain controlled by its own incredible intelligence.

However much the tormented earth writhed and its elements lashed, the brain responded from within with a viable organic mutation that somewhere, somehow, adapted and survived. What vital life within lacked in physical capability and resource, the brain made up for in timeless persistence and genius for adaptiveness.

It also provided the struggling life-forms with co-ordinated direction. Using every form of life on the surface as a sensor, it knew exactly the conditions operating and developing anywhere on earth where life had managed to get a hold. The brain evaluated this information and through its psychic infrastructure relayed back to all relevant life-forms the necessary adaptive changes and procedures to be started. Covering the entire region from within, its responses were immediate and localised over the entire globe.

Thus was all life able to keep ahead by anticipating geophysical and climatic extremes on the planet. Today, this continues: nature's anticipation of seasonal extremes and geophysical violence such as pending earthquakes — so evident among flora, fauna and insects — and all the other wonderful examples of nature's genius, are due to the use of the same subliminal psychic network.

The species did not, and still does not, evolve in the external materialistic way science and evolution theory maintain. The external mechanistic and chemical changes occurring within the cells, tissues and organs were merely the effects of this amazing psychic system of interchange of information between every living form.

Similarly, the balance of advantage between predator and prey which is essential to any life and survival pattern was and is maintained with consummate delicacy.

The stick beetle — to mention just one of the milliards of living natural wonders — did not evolve by sitting on a twig for aeons waiting for its colour and shape to change automatically while being gobbled up a few billion times by the same predators, as the embarrassingly naive scientific explanation suggests. The whole miracle of camouflage, interdependence and evolutionary survival of the species was, and still is to a large extent, the work of the psychic brain and the intelligence behind it.

They, not the chicken or the egg, came first.

The psychic world

All life that dies on earth survives in the psyche.

Probably the most tragic loss or omission for mankind due to scientific and intellectual externalism is the knowledge that within the human psyche — within the brain of the reader now — exists the astonishing living inner world in which humanity and all the species survive death in vital energetic form.

This, the much misunderstood psychic world, was not always there. Today, reconstituted and refined, it is teeming with man and life. In the beginning, before life on earth, it was merely a field of vital potential — the pre-conscious — a field of electrical force which today still continues to provide the electrical current for our physical brainwaves between parts of the brain.

Life when it first started on earth continued in the most elementary form for an inordinately long period before suddenly exploding into infinitely more complex and varied organisms. Fossil-evidence, or any correct reconstruction of the growth of early life, will confirm this.

The delay in fact occurred while vital energy from life-forms dying on earth was building up in the psychic field.

As life perished on the surface, vital energy returned via the trunk system and gathered in the vital field before finally recirculating back up to the surface.

At first, the surviving psychic energies were extremely weak and faint. But eventually they had combined in the psychic field to form a great reservoir and pressure of vital life. What had been up till then a mere seep of recirculating life-sustaining energy now became an intense instinctive drive from within for re-existence or re-experience. Surface life then burgeoned.

The first psychic doubles

In the beginning, life which had survived death on earth had no particular form in the psychic field. Life on the surface was too simple for the surviving psychic energies to have individual shape or conscious identity.

But as the developing species became more firmly and abundantly entrenched on earth, psychic doubles or doppel-gängers — vital replicas of the organisms — began appearing in the psychic mass.

The psychic field, or world as it was now becoming, contained the energy or doppelgängers of every experiment at life on earth. But only so long as a species managed to survive

12

and continue to evolve on the surface did the doppelgängers have permanent psychic form within. Otherwise they tended to disintegrate and vanish into the mass.

Compared to their physical counterparts, the doppelgängers possessed a more intense and enduring reality. The psychic doubles constantly changed their energetic frequency or image but they did not die as we apprehend death. Half a life-form — such as say, half a healthy living dog — is impossible on earth. But in the psychic world, which is an energetic world exceeding the parameters of ordinary conceptual imagery, halves and pieces of necessarily developing life-forms, as well as 'impossible' combinations that had or have no real future, are in the natural order of things.

It was — and is — an amazing world and I will have a great deal more to say about it later.

From psychic to genetic control

The purpose of evolution at any time is to make life on earth more conscious.

The first life-forms possessed the minimal consciousness — instinct. Instinct can be called the consciousness of the unconscious. It is the experience or knowledge of having survived life and death plus the urge to live or experience again. All life is instinctive because all life has survived death.

For scores of millions of years instinct — the desire to live and survive again — was a sufficient dynamic to keep the species evolving under the inner co-ordinating guidance of the psychic brain.

But there was a limit to how far instinct could serve the purpose of increasing consciousness in the species. Instinct is concerned with survival and the blind repetition of experience. It is instantaneous, immediate in its response. It could never provide sufficient pause in the awareness of the species to sustain reflective self-consciousness — the next evolutionary requirement. For that, more sophisticated bodies or organisms had to be evolved.

This, the next stage of evolution, involved an extraordinary psychic performance which led to the development of the

13

mammalian body.

The psychic brain began to exteriorise itself.

Physical versions of the brain started appearing in the species. The effect was the transfer and embodiment in the organisms themselves of many of the internal growth and survival functions previously controlled by the psychic brain.

This exteriorising of the psychic brain into innumerable creature-brains was made possible through the simultaneous handover from psychic to genetic control.

Genetics, the scientific study of hereditary variations in organisms, began less than 150 years ago. The genetic code — the handwriting of the psychic brain of a hundred million years ago — was discovered by science in the late 1950s. Science has hardly begun to decipher the code. But it knows, to its continued astonishment, that these intelligent biological instructions or ideas are actually recorded in the nucleic acids (DNA) of the cells. The genetic code contains all the data an organism will ever need for its life, propagation and eventual deterioration or devolution, even anticipating hybrid variations.

The transfer from psychic to genetic control not only made possible the evolution of the highest class of vertebrates, the mammals and primates, but also prepared the way for probably the most climacteric evolutionary step of all. It would eventually allow the last order of the species — man — to begin the step up out of the psyche into the world, into his by now potentially prepared physical body.

All he would have to do would be to gradually realise — enter consciously — the various senses in the exteriorised brain that had been partly developed for him by the rest of the species. In so doing he would be helping to evolve the senses and his physical body to the point of readiness for his final triumphal entry into the world as a self-conscious being.

3
Primitive man and his two strange worlds

Primitive man's body when the drive to self-consciousness began would have been barely recognisable beside the human body today.

He had only just evolved to the physical means of sight. Sight as we know it was the last physical sense to develop. All his senses were then present in an external body, but only in rudimentary form. It took several hundred thousand years to realise the senses, that is for the intelligence within to exteriorise itself, or, put another way, for man to come to his senses.

Meanwhile, primitive man lived mostly in his vital double: he did not realise he possessed a physical body. His body performed on the earth in a totally instinctive way, while the vital, feeling part of him lived a completely interiorised though parallel psychic existence.

Primitive man was not an individual as we today can experience ourselves. We have separative feelings: feelings of separate bodies, separate experiences. Primitive man experienced the world as himself.

He could not think; he did not smell or hear things through his nose or ears, or use his memory to identify these perceptions as we do. He used a completely subjective internal sense-relatedness which was truly remarkable compared to our self-conscious understanding.

Primitive man was the consciousness centre of the vital or psychic brain, the most advanced and sensitive point in the world organism. He was linked to his environment by an

15

interiorised system of psychic sense — not neural or sense-perceptive sense — which kept him constantly informed in relation to his needs. His range of experience was greater than that of any other living thing: all earth-life served to inform him through the incredible maze of his feeling brain.

This is reflected in the story of Genesis in which man is given dominion over every living thing. Man had this control and superiority by virtue of his central part in creation as the power of intelligence in and behind all life.

Science may some day discover that there is a connection between this and why more than half of modern man's brain, or white matter, is relatively inactive or used for very few of his known functions, relative to its mass.

When primitive man needed food he knew psychically in which direction to go and hunt for it. This is the essence of instinct. The nearest food plant/animal communicated its presence to him through the psychic network, of which he was the centre.

Naturally, he did not always find or catch his prey; he might fall prey to another hunter; or the prey may have used its natural instincts to camouflage or conceal its position when he got there. But the point is that primitive man knew, through being at the centre of a subjective world-data system, where to go to find what he needed without exterior sense-aids.

It was the same when he needed a female. He knew where a female was, ready to receive him. She might have been with another man or with a rival tribe; and if he persisted in trying to mate with her he might be killed. But he knew where to locate such a female — and she him — through this extraordinary psychic system — and both took their chances.

This original inner-sense system is present in our bodies today. It persists in part as our faculty of imagination.

* * *

Primitive man felt pain. But he did not know 'whose' pain it was. A headache is 'my' headache, 'my' exclusive pain. But not for primitive man. When he felt pain he|*was* pain. There was no sense of self to claim it as his. Pain was the same for all.

When he fought with another man or animal he did not know which pain was his. Logically, it could be said it had to be his own pain he was feeling. But that was not his experience. He knew only that fighting was painful. He avoided it when possible. And he did not injure or destroy other things unless they stood between him and his needs or survival. He fought instinctively to lead and to procreate because survival of the fittest was the only natural guarantee of the survival of all.

While modern man with his sense of self (self-consciousness) selects things to 'own' apart from his pain — my child, my house, etc. — primitive man was a sort of corporate feeling of all the things he required to survive. To him it was not just his world. He was the world.

He had a kind of broad tribal identity, but not a communal existence in which he shared his female or anything else. She was neither his, nor anyone's. She was just female — a feeling, not an objective form; and to her he was the same. Neither she nor any other thing he needed ever appeared in his feeling world or consciousness until he had the feeling of desiring her or it. Between those feelings female had no existence for him, as male had no existence for her; she was just there, part of the scene, much the same as the pictures that hang on our walls and so many other objects just there in our lives until we want them or need to notice them.

Primitive man used his home for protection, nothing more. If rival tribes fought, they fought for what they needed — without any sense of victory or loss. Winning or losing exists in the self-sense of 'my' and 'our' and that egoic identification he did not have. For the primitive fighting man there were only the spoils to use, or the pain of his wounds to endure, until contentment — the absence of desiring anything — came again.

Primitive man's battles were actually fought within himself, within his feeling brain or plexus. While his outer body might have gone through the actions of combat, he merely registered the feelings, or sensations, of what was going on in his internal world which was as instantaneous in its communication to him as our sense perceptions are today.

The difference was that there were no images, no concepts, no forms. He had not realised his senses, his physical body, so his body could not exist for him, even though it might have existed for a hypothetical observer.

Primitive man's battles were something similar to our experience when we are at war with ourselves, feeling remorse, regrets, guilt, self-doubt, indecision, uncertainty, worry. Whereas we are frequently in two minds — experiencing all the pain or discomfort of conflict without any external contact — he was constantly in two feelings, or a multiplicity of feelings. These feelings were searingly intense and abundant in information compared to ours.

As primitive man's state is compared with that of today, a striking difference reveals itself. Primitive man did not want: he desired. These are not the same sensations. Wanting is a symptom of developing self-consciousness — discontent. Wanting is violence, a necessary transition on the way to self-consciousness. Desire, on the other hand, arises from the need to survive and is fundamental to life.

Primitive man was not violent. He was savage and dangerous as a wolf or gorilla may be described. But we would not normally call these wild animals violent; and certainly not if we used the same word to describe man's violence reported daily by the media.

Primitive man's inability to want self-consciously was a part of evolution's amazing system of controls and checks which are permanently present to preserve the unswerving order of things. Man's evolution can never be interrupted by an external event which is not itself a part of the evolutionary scheme.

Here was primitive man — an extremely dangerous physical and psychic force, lacking all self-control, and actually at the centre or brain of things — made to behave ethically, almost responsibly, by the very simplicity of his existence.

Being at the centre of the interior world in which he had the feel of all things in his environment, he neither injured nor destroyed needlessly. He fought but no longer or more destructively than necessary. He was not cruel, sadistic, competitive or exploitive. Paradoxically, the world was safe in his savage hands.

Primitive man was the ideal ecologist.

*   *   *

Primitive man, as the intelligent focus of all life on earth, was the receptor of the 'feelings' expressed by his environment. This today we experience as our love of nature; or, if it is threatening or hostile, as our dislike or fear of it. This remnant of primitive man remains in us, only today we feel we need to know why. The first spasm of developed self-consciousness is to wonder — to wonder why things happen as they do, and later, to wonder at in wisdom.

Primitive man in his one-derness, could not wonder.

Plant life, to him, was a static feeling of background companionship, not unlike the comfort we may receive from background music. But often he felt suffocated by its ubiquitous presence — and he sought the deserts. He was just as finely attuned to the rock or mineral environment — even more so in the beginning, as he had evolved physically from it.

But as his being began evolving emotionally towards the moment of self-consciousness, he increasingly sought the stimulus of vegetation. Trees to him were like water-spouts and water even in plant-forms is the medium of incipient emotion or feeling. We are, as science tells us, mostly composed of water — or, in the terms of this philosophy, emotion.

Even today, emotionally excitable man is driven to live in the heat to dry him out. Less emotional man seeks the cold and damp to keep him supple. And man who prefers to live in the ice regions is a hybrid with his place in the same astonishing complex.

Deep space, or cosmic consciousness — towards which man is heading — contains very little heat, water or emotion. The consciousness of deep space consists mostly of an energy, a quality, called love.

19

4
The dawn of self-consciousness

The cosmic culturing

On a particular day, primitive man watched the sun rise in the east. No man before had ever seen the sun rising. He was never to be the same again. As he watched, cosmic culture was embodied in him. And the birth of self-conscious man began.

Sunlight is more than the energy that has been measured and evaluated across the existing scientific spectrum. It has a finer and higher psychic/occult spectrum. Sunlight contains the initiating force behind self-consciousness.

The sun had shone on the earth for immeasurable time, its eastern origins and western demise often obscured by clouds and mists of the cooling, settling planet. But what had utterly obscured the sun from cognitive existence was a membrane that lies behind all animal eyes which I have called the veil of opaqueness. On this day, both the horizon and the opaque veil in primitive man had cleared.

The sun's rays were electric, penetrating the muddied mists of his unconscious through to his psychic double. From deep within, another kind of sun or light – Man, the principle of intelligence, the germ-potential of self-consciousness – responded faintly, and so began the long exteriorising journey to existence.

It must be emphasised that the drive to self-consciousness awakened in man on that particular day in the east had to have an external trigger, sunlight. The potential was there in him but not the dynamic to start bringing it into existence. Nothing can come into existence without an external cause or trigger. The power comes from without, the idea from within. This ensures a synchronous and perfectly ordered evolution between the earth and the rest of the universe.

All causal power comes into the mind from the external cosmos. From an external viewpoint it could be said that the power to bring man to self-consciousness was seeded in him on that day, like a pearl is cultured in an oyster, by sunlight entering through the eyes.

Primitive man's body had been on the earth for many ages before this cosmic culturing occurred. He lived in various parts of the globe. Some of his later habitations have been discovered. These have created something of a fundamental problem for archaeologists and anthropologists. It is difficult for them to resolve intellectually the finer distinctions between man's habitations (often older and in their way just as organised) and his first civilisations. The difference between these habitations and civilisations represents the interval between the demise of primitive man and the advent of self-conscious creative man.

The pineal gland

The physical organ that finally made this momentous cosmic culturing possible was the pineal gland.

The pineal gland is a small appendage to the cerebellum, lying in the deepest and most protected area of the brain and skull. It gets its name from the Latin, pinea for pine-cone, which describes its shape. The pineal gland is present in all craniate vertebrates, that is, in all animals with skulls. In some reptiles, it has the structure of an eye and is called the pineal eye.

The precise function of the pineal gland is something of a scientific mystery. It is, however, considered by science to be a remnant of an important ancestral sense organ. Science has also determined that the pineal gland is co-ordinated with the eye; that it is aware of daylight; and that it influences the body's awareness of time. These scientific observations

21

become extremely significant when considered against the original evolutionary function of the gland which this chapter describes.

Science has yet to discover that the mysterious pineal gland was the original seat of the consciousness of man. Eventually, when the suitable body was ready, that consciousness exteriorised through the pineal gland to become I who am reading these words.

The superior senses

As the senses of the species evolved, so did the pineal. Their development was parallel: the two were intimately linked, yet separated for millions of years until the day described above when the pineal gland provided the means for the ultimate superior sense — creative intelligence — to start coming forward.

The appearance of the pineal gland in the species coincided with the appearance of the first of the superior senses — sound. What I call superior senses are senses like hearing, seeing and smelling that give warning-from-a-distance, as opposed to touch-feeling which provides no interval of warning.

The amphibians which climbed out of the seas were the ancestors of the reptiles. Both were prototypes, first test-organs of the sense of sound. Both had the pineal gland.

It was the bony vertebrate structure of the first amphibians and the later reptiles pressed full-length against the earth that gave rise to the sense of hearing. Vibrations transmitted through the ground — instead of through water as before — became an eventual sensitivity, still in the bone, to vibrations coming through the air — hearing.

The increased warning-distance which creatures gained from each of the developing superior senses was proportional to the evolutionary distance travelled by the species towards self-consciousness as the appearance of creative man. Self-conscious development was a growing sense of separation or distance from the environment or perceived events, giving time for reflection.

Yet, the existence of this early-warning system in a creature due to its having the superior senses is not enough to justify the term self-conscious. All the higher animals have superior senses but cannot be called self-conscious. They all possess the pineal gland. There has to be, and is, another factor.

The veil of opaqueness or psychic membrane

The difference between man and beast — at all times and in all ages that have been and are yet to come — lies in what I call the veil of opaqueness. This is a psychic membrane stretched across the back of all optical organs that have not yet evolved to that peculiarity of excellence known as the human eye.

The psychic membrane is not an abstract notion. As soon as science concentrates seriously on finding a method for measuring the energies of the psychic spectrum — perhaps it will be a new-century breakthrough — the membrane will be easily located.

The human eye, in spite of sharper vision elsewhere in the animal kingdom, is distinct among all eyes in having no psychic membrane. This gives man's vision a unique reflective factor which increases enormously the depth or significance of what he sees — hence perception and cognition. Freed of the membrane, man is able to reflect his awareness as perceptions through the posterior vital double and back on to the intellect behind. This reflective depth peculiar to man determines two things: first, the power of the intellect related to the sense-perceived world; and second, depending on the clarity of his psychic double through which the reflection must pass, the power of insight into psychic, spiritual and occult realities.

In the evolution of all the species, the veil of opaqueness and the pineal gland were intimately, vitally connected. The function of the veil was to shield the pineal from the effects of sunlight until such time as a suitable potential animal body had been evolved on earth for 'I', the intelligence of Man.

23

All the necessary rudimentary senses, the anti-gravity devices such as limbs, walking and a co-ordinating brain, had to be evolved first in the lower species before they could come together for final development in the one form that would be physically capable of sustaining self-conscious creative thought, action and control.

In the evolution towards self-consciousness, the 'I' of intelligence seated deep behind the veil of opaqueness and the psychic double had no sense of time. Nor did the exterior species. There was no way the psychic brain could know that a suitable physical body was ready for man to start occupying without some kind of energetic signal being received.

The crucial signal to the psychic brain that such a body was at last ready for further development and gradual occupation by the 'I' was to be sunlight getting through to the pineal gland.

The pineal gland was the finest of all the earth sensors connected to the psychic network. For scores of millions of years it had lain virtually dormant in the skulls of the developing craniates, not unlike a sensitive fire-alarm device requiring a certain intensity of heat to set it off. All that stood in the way was the psychic membrane, which also may be called the membrane of forgetfulness.

The birth of creative man

The rending of the psychic membrane was effected by a cosmic event 'seen' at night by a small group of primitives who had formed a habitation in the east. These were the beginning of the evolutionary fork which eventually produced the first man.

The vanishing of the animal veil allowed the energy of sunlight to stream through the optics and trigger the pineal gland. The pineal transmitted the signal posteriorly through the psychic double to the intelligence within. At once, the 'I' or creative man set out, up through the senses to eventually take his place amongst the rest of the species on earth.

For primitive man living his interiorised existence at the centre of the psychic mass, this meant the excruciating task of externalising his consciousness so that he could realise or relate to his physical senses and one day live in the world as we do today.

It was an unimaginably traumatic, painful and time-extruding process. Primitive man had to be turned inside out emotionally and psychologically. From a completely subjective and undifferentiated experience of the world — something like the warm, comfortable, uncomplicated existence of the nine-month child in the mother's womb — he had to be made to go outside himself, to realise the greater truth of what he had become as the son of the earth. He had to be born, or re-born. He had to see, hear, smell, breathe, groan; and know he had a self, a body, that was separated from all the other things by a world he would later call creation, and later still, time and space.

Man first became self-conscious around 200,000 years ago. But only 10,000 years or so ago did the majority of men complete this extraordinary evolutionary contortion. Even then not all had completed it. And even today some still have not. The mongol and the autistic are still trying.

5
Genesis of the gods

The Hindu religion — one of the world's oldest traditions — speaks of the gods Krishna, Rama and other celestials walking the earth in human form. The same idea is essential to Greek and all mythology.

I have explained that man, before becoming a self-conscious being, led a completely interiorised existence deep in the unconscious behind the senses at the centre of a vast psychic network or brain. He had no experience of his physical body which like the bodies of all the other species on the earth was evolving without any self-conscious presence or effort.

He was linked inwardly to all things as a psychic or feeling ethos. He was like our brain which is the centre of our afferent and efferent nervous responses. What thought is to us, feeling was to him. He was the optimum of clairvoyant and extra-sensory communication except that he had no senses, no individuality, no personalised life.

On one remarkable day the veil of opaqueness had cleared from behind his animal eyes and he witnessed the sun rise for the first time as primitive cognitive man.

For the first time sunlight streamed into his unconscious via the pineal gland. Excited by the solar energy, man's psychic mass began to swell and curl into a powerful wave. Man was no longer content to remain a part of the unconscious. For the first time darkness was dissonance; a growing restlessness, vague stirrings, urged him up towards the source of light. He had no idea where he was going, only the feeling that he must go, break away from the mother earth, the now-stifling comfort of the unconscious womb and find what he must — the truth behind his discontent.

Outside in the light, on the earth, the truth awaiting him was his physical body — unconscious and unknowing but fully functioning and prepared to receive him the moment he could manage that enormous journey to 'come to his senses'.

On the world's first wave of self or emotion man struggled up the solar stream of consciousness towards the surface of himself and the earth.

One man among several made it first. It was not unlike the arrival of the first swallow on the first spring day. But compared to a three-months spring season the intervals between swallows and spring days were ages. For a long, long time these first physically realised men were a very rare phenomenon in the small communities of 'phantom' body-men who lived together in various parts of the globe.

As each self-conscious man came to his senses to perceive the wonders of the earth, he was able to retreat into the psyche and communicate to the others coming up behind vague notions of the amazing existence awaiting them.

This was a very simple thing to do because the first self-conscious men were so loosely attached to their physical bodies — compared to us today with tens of thousands of years' experience and practice of attachment — that they lived in both worlds.

They had only to meditate, to withdraw from external attachments and their physical senses, and they were back in the feeling, inner world where all men were one.

These first-men could take back with them their self-conscious identities consonant with their physical realisation. They were able to inject into the feeling network or plexus of all potential rising men not only the powerful energies and feelings resulting from their sensible awareness, but also the extraordinary practical knowledge it gave them.

To the mass of self-unconscious man they literally were beings from outer space or another world.

Furthermore, all men approaching body-consciousness were at different levels of advancement or emotional evolution. Some were very close to physical realisation. Others were thousands of years away from even the possibility. Between the two were innumerable 'men' of all shades or degrees of incipient self-consciousness.

In the outer physical world all the men living together in communities looked very much the same. But those with more acute comprehension of their physical existence were aware of the differences among those with inferior comprehension and took advantage of it. They used this knowledge to exploit their inferiors, so laying the foundation of the later class systems.

A physically realised man was a very privileged specimen. He enjoyed tremendous advantages. He could communicate with his developing companions in either the outer world or the inner world — on the earth or in the psyche.

While in the company of lesser men on earth, he could tune into their psychic state and know exactly what each was feeling, what he wanted at that moment, and what he would do.

He could speak inwardly to the lesser man like some unidentifiable, all-knowing presence. He could put suggestions into him, frighten him, persuade him, instruct him — and finally, induce him to worship and serve him.

The first physical-self realised men were the mythical and legendary gods.

In ancient Greece a community of first-realised men, or gods, lived on Mount Olympus — or so they made out: it is not important. But the pre-Hellenic Aryans also had their gods. These myths they brought with them from the north to the Mediterranean around 2000BC. The Aryans further to the north-east took their god-myths to Hindustan — India. Each conquering people brought to the ancient world the traditions of their own gods and all the accounts commingled into the myths and legends we have today. These contain all the clues we need to solve and explain the mystery of the gods and the not-so-fictional first men on earth.

Nothing was impossible for the gods.

With access to both physical and psychic worlds or realities, they were able to create in the world-psyche monsters, visions and all the vague threatening demons which imagination can convey even today.

But it would be incorrect to describe theirs as a half-fantasy world. It was *all* reality. For many thousands of years, while man was becoming physical and entrenching himself in his senses, the world consisted of the primitive psychic as well as the physical-material.

No rational line could be drawn between fantasy and a physical reality. Men lived in both worlds with the gods — the realised men — having the best of both.

The gods were men. They mated among themselves. They hated and loved and warred among themselves. And when they desired a shapely unrealised man or woman's body, they took it. And so it is said that the Olympian gods loved many mortal women — especially Zeus who predictably is described as 'omnipotent king of gods, father of (un-realised) men' and master even of fate.

And why not? The men who handed down the myths were not gods. They were the semi-conscious masses, whose hazy psyches were used by the gods to wage fantastic wars against each other with thunderbolts and other earth-observed phenomena crudely scripted and sculpted into demonstrations of illusionary power and magic.

Zeus fathered four of the Olympian gods by mortal women. Why not? His body was as mortal as theirs. The difference was that Zeus and the other first-realised men and women never died. When their bodies wore out they withdrew into the psyche and took possession of another suitable body. If they chose, they could even push aside a man coming to conscious birth for the first time and take his body.

They could scare the daylights out of their ascending 'subjects' by swallowing children as Cronus did and creating gigantic monsters like Typhon whose 'huge limbs ended in serpent heads and whose eyes breathed fire' — and then destroy them and bury them under Mt Etna 'which still breathes fire'.

To escape each other's ghastly, ghostly creations they could turn themselves into rams, crows, goats, cows, cats, fish, boars, ibis — anything they fancied.

The goddesses — like Pasiphae — could mate with magnificent white bulls and in a phantasmagoria of erotic and sexual imagery conceive monsters such as the minotaur which fed on maidens and young men.

It was like a group of particularly privileged people waging wars of dreams among themselves in the primal mindstuff of humanity who could only look on in stupefied awe and terror.

It is now possible to understand the origins of the myths of creation. The mystery, the delusion, the endless intellectual theorising and speculation start to fall away, revealing that the truth is even more fantastic than the legend.

We can see the first conscious men and women on earth — in a world offering limited physical comfort, unimaginative contact and endless time for reverie — unable to desist from the game of creating in the psychic plasma. Here, the audience was live, unbelievably, feelingly real, offering a single response of concentrated wonder which every artist, entertainer and illusionist has dreamed of creating ever since.

On the earth, by comparison with their psychic artistry and games-playing, the physical reality of existence for the gods was impossibly slow and tedious, the audiences nothing more than servile zombies.

The physical sex of the gods and goddesses was good, but never enough. How could it ever be enough?

Never could the senses deliver in the final consummating moment of orgasm a potency of feeling equal to the tantalising excitement and delirium of their extended psychic fantasising. Today's imagination is a wraith beside it.

In their physical sex the gods and goddesses were able to communicate to each other, or to their lesser mortal paramours, the full reality of their erotic dreams. Each participant literally became any role they were playing while both or all shared in the living experience.

Which was reality — the drab physical mating action or the endless psychic stimulation? Both — but inevitably their copulation ended in the drab physical reality. 'I'm coming' was the cry in every ecstatic climactic feeling — and has been in every language ever since. Every lover, every man and woman, eventually comes to his senses — back into the world of the living.

The gods were men of the most extraordinary consciousness. Yet it was not that their consciousness was any more profound than man's today — only that it was not burdened with past.

Having no past as men they could do what they wanted and be what they were — free as no man or group ever again would be.

Past is the constraint which dictates the future, the inevitable. As these men had no past they had no future. They could exist only once, in the beginning, never again.

But for the waves of men coming to existence behind them, the creative and imaginative past initiated by the gods with their psychic games-playing would be an ever-increasing burden in their consciousness.

What the gods were and what they did had to determine for all time the future or nature of the human race. This legacy in which all men share is sexual pre-occupation, erotic fantasising, creative imagination, the longing to regain original freedom and divinity, the use of illusion to obtain power over other men — and the cultural legacy of the myths themselves that tell their story.

But nothing reveals the humanity of the gods — the future they set for mankind — more than the emphasis they put on sex and the inevitable crudity of those concepts. They had emerged from a world in which the sexual act did not exist into a world where it represented the heights of love and lust.

The psychic world is a world of fluid being — attraction, repulsion and embryonic love. In the psychic world energy such as sex cannot build up — it is immediately and continuously released and dissipated throughout the entire psychic plasma.

For the gods, the first men and women, entering into physical existence meant that their experience of the psychic flow was to an extent blocked by the senses. For the first time they became aware of the build-up of feelings of sexual desire which could be released — or heightened and prolonged — in the sexual act.

Sex is a physical experience — but actually, a psychic reality. Sex as we know it cannot be performed in the psychic world. But it is felt there. As we know it, sex culminates in an orgasm, in a glandular climax. At the physical level it is a sort of implosion, the release or return of a particular, pent-up psychic force.

All physical experience is made up of a moment-to-moment, minute damming of the continuous flow of psychic energy. This damming actually creates our solid physical form and the procreative nature of the genital organs.

But the energy of the genitals is not for all time to be procreative in the sense of merely producing physical beings. Behind the male and female reproductive organs are two intensely creative though at present largely separative energies — man and woman. As future man and woman make the psychic world a conscious part of their existence by being made to learn to truly love, their energies will merge and harmonise without loss of individual consciousness.

On earth man then will be one with his Bhagavati (the one divine woman all men seek) and woman with her Bhagavat.

Together they will create a new psycho-physical race of people on earth. From birth the living experience of these people will be of the psychic reality as well as the physical world, giving them an intensified sense of purpose and responsibility for life in both worlds. This future wave of men and women will be a mature, new version of the gods.

II

6
The forming of the human nature

When man and his past were very young

The gods had gone, vanished forever, leaving behind the first gentle swell of past that began with them.

The turbulent transition of self-conscious man to earth and flesh was over. A short period of extraordinary tranquillity followed. Through his new-found senses man began to participate in and enjoy the astonishing nature of the earth and to breathe into his being for all generations to come the living memory of its richness and beauty. Mother nature embraced her newest child.

At this time when man and his past were very young, nature was the only existing order of things. Nature was the earth's immemorial past consisting of yesterday's experience in plant, animal and man being applied as life today. There was no planning, no future, only action and doing now.

As a part of nature, man had no expectations and demands outside of what it was and what it provided, no desire to change it any more than did the rest of nature. Animals, birds, trees, flowers and men: what had existed yesterday disappeared back into the earth while all was continuously, effortlessly, miraculously replenished today. Nature was complete — the natural past unfolding as the natural present.

The gentle pressure of his own young past kept man finely balanced within his senses. He used the senses in the way nature had evolved them — as receivers, permitting him to stand back within and relish the sounds, smells, sights, taste and touch of the all-pervading earth.

It was a wonderful, simple state of living and being, of yesterday and today. Tomorrow never came.

But one day tomorrow did come. Man invented it.

The halcyon period in which man was in his element, his Eden, ended when the past the gods had started but never shared in at last caught up with him. The surviving self-conscious energies of the first men who died came back to live again. Behind and latching on to them were streams of instinctive energies vying for the experience only self-conscious imaginative man could provide. The gentle natural swell of returning life suddenly had become a huge wave, an irresistible surge of yesterdays thrusting into the most sensitive of nature-points — the human brain — to emerge to live again.

The mounting pressure drove man further and further into his senses away from his inner nature and towards the formal world.

Finally, the pressure from within started driving man out of his senses. He began projecting through them into the world. Rising emotion started to appear in his eyes and gestures. His sense of smelling reversed from a soft intake of breath to an often harsh and aimless projection of words. His sense of taste became a missile of opinions often expressed as violent likes and dislikes. Hearing developed into an emotional extension of his body — alert not for natural sounds but for intonations of insult and slight.

Attachment to his body increased. The further out he projected the more isolated, vulnerable and threatened he felt. This in turn made him cling emotionally to his body even more. The earlier fine balance between nature and the senses, his original inner poise, was destroyed. He had extended himself so far that he was now outside of nature: nature like himself had become for him a purely external sense-perceived form and no longer could provide him with the intimate feeling of oneness with the earth and all life.

In his new exposed externalised position, all he could see in the environment was the threat of death. To survive seemed the only realistic point to living; yet survival was impossible as the evidence of each day's dead bodies around him demonstrated. Death, once the most natural event, was now the most terrifying; the fear of dying and losing his body, the last apparent formal link with where he had come from, became obsessional.

Each dead body he started to see as an extension or projection of the end of himself. The now formalised beauty of the earth was as nothing under the pressure of this awful outward-going fixation. Man was beside himself. He was being consumed by his own psychosis, his emotional attempt to limit life and today to form. He had reached the end of his tether. He could go no further into the formal world without losing touch with his senses altogether. He had to find a way out, an escape, some other form of today, another world that did not end in death. Man was on the verge of insanity.

Tomorrow was his answer. With this one stupendous invention he could break out of today and create a new world of his own, a world of progress and continuity, an apparent ongoing, a distance between himself and death the end. Death could now be forgotten. It would come tomorrow − never today. In this way it became a problem that no longer needed to be confronted.

It was the world's first act of ignorance. The truth *is* immortality − man's original nature which he had allowed himself to be driven out of − and any substitute for it is ignorance.

Tomorrow is so naturally a part of life today it is almost inconceivable to us that once it did not exist. But our difficulty is only the inevitable result of that same ignorance which is now at the foundation of human nature. As with the behaviour of the gods before him, man's means of escape from the truth was to determine for all time the fundamental condition of his new human nature − as well as the inevitable course his projected world of tomorrow and progress would have to take.

By identifying himself with the idea of world progress and improvement man also unconsciously invented the necessary delusion of hope. Hope is not necessary for today; it arises only in trying to escape from today. In a world where man must die there can be no hope − apart from the delusive hope that he will not die. Hope is an attempt through ignorance to put off the inevitable.

Instead of living naturally for today man began living unnaturally for tomorrow. This meant projecting himself emotionally into the future — that is further beyond his senses and the formal world into imagination.

But the more he looked to the future in his imagination the more dissatisfied and discontented he was with today. This impelled him to start imposing his own idea of how things should be tomorrow — a new order — on the natural order of how things were today. Then, by constantly looking to see how things should be, he started to lose sight of how things were. Dissatisfaction and discontent, plus the peculiar ability to think straight about everything else except what was most important, were added to ignorance at the foundation of his new human nature.

Man reeled from reaction to reaction, every reaction creating a delta of effects. In those days when the past was young and man was subconsciously looking for an identity to reflect his forgotten immortality, any idea he could identify with became part of the new human nature he was creating for himself. He was still fashioning and ordering the human psyche and its human way of perceiving.

Perhaps in retrospect the forming of human nature — man's substitute nature — may seem to have been a very profound and complex process. But in fact it was no more than the complicated outcome of a very simple and purely psychological device for escaping from emotional pressure. By creating innumerable problems around a supposed future or tomorrow he was able to keep his mind busy and distracted from having to face up to the one big problem of today — death, the end of any future or imagined tomorrows.

This psychotic nature can be seen operating in every man's worries today. To worry today he has first to assume he is not going to die today. If he were truly aware he was dying, or going to die, all his other worries would vanish instantly like the chimeras they are. This, the dying, in their late-found wisdom, continue to try to tell him. But ignorance, the hope of an imagined tomorrow, closes his comprehension.

So death was projected hopefully as an event of the future. And by all men projecting the same idea together in the same hopeful, emotional and ignorant way, death then ceased to be a necessary consideration as a threat or end to the progress of the whole. The individual might die but the world of tomorrow would live on in the hopes and imagination of all other men. This meant that for all generations to come men could talk about death, plan around it for the future, even joke about it, without ever having seriously to examine it or feel the least bit menaced by it. Hey presto — death, the only real problem in life today, was eliminated!

The supreme act of selfishness

In those days when his past was young enough to be still recognisable in his perception of the present, man was born as an individual being, that is, born as a baby with his true nature of immortality intact. Under the new order of things it was essential that this individual be eliminated. If allowed to mature such self-knowledge of immortality could presumably destroy the delusion of tomorrow and perhaps even human nature itself; and all the present race of sophisticated and progressive men who depended on the idea of the world for their existence would have to die, or something worse. Such individuality would possess the power to start turning back the progressive past which was now the present until the point of sanity left long ago was once again reached where tomorrow and the world no longer existed and the past no longer mattered. This was intolerable.

To keep the world and humanity free of such dangerous knowledge and possibilities, into the subconscious of every child from birth was instilled the idea that this was a world that went on and on irrespective of what happened to anyone. Tomorrow was all that counted. To question death and dwell on it was morbid and unhealthy. People died but it did not matter because tomorrow was a new day and death could be forgotten by everyone in the promise of the future.

A remarkable change occurred in the human psyche.

Whereas man once had despairingly seen the end of himself and everything else reflected in the dead bodies around him, now in the bodies of his new-born young he perceived in his imagination the splendid living reflection or extension of himself, as well as the hope of the world of tomorrow.

Thus, when a child was born he proudly rejoiced — and the whole world with him: not for the extraordinary state of immortal individuality waiting to be recognised and acknowledged in the new-born consciousness, but for the limited and mortal form that that individuality with man's ignorant connivance would be forced to take in the world of tomorrow.

Every child from birth would now be immediately and ceaselessly labelled, first by his parents, guardians and teachers and later, as he got the idea, automatically by himself and the world until he fervently believed in both. Initially, he would be labelled baby and treated like one, taught to comprehend, think and react in an infantile fashion matching the ignorance of his parents and the people around him. The opportunity for them to address intelligently the immortal, unperturbed and clearly non-conforming individuality in the new-born body's consciousness would never be seriously taken. The parental duty at birth would be to assume immediately the protective position of the teacher of ignorance and mortality.

This was man's ultimate projection — and his supreme act of selfishness. In his ignorance and for all generations to follow he would sacrifice the uniqueness of his new-born offspring, its previous unperceived individuality, for his conforming idea of the world, the future and himself. This he perpetuates today in the form of parental and filial love.

The rest of the labels identifying the child as a progressively doomed idea in the world would follow automatically as a repercussion of the past started by the parents: one-year-old, two-year-old, three-year-old, boy or girl, good or bad, student or lay-about, teenager, man or woman, clerk or artist, manager or managing director, poor or wealthy, happy or unhappy, mother or father, grandparent, old, boring, senile, dying.

When this last label was finally affixed the idea of the

progressive man would die after a brief reappearance of the individual towards the end. It would always be the individual who died, no one else. Birth and death, the entrance and exit of man's progressive world, were now the only places left for the appearance of individuality.

In their grief, those closest to a dead person might have some temporary doubts about the sanity of this world or themselves, or the inferred security of either. But such anxieties would be largely and fairly rapidly obscured by the compulsive delusion of hope and tomorrow.

No dead man could be missed for long in the progressive world. Anyone who truly missed him would die to be with him and so demonstrate the individuality of true love. The whole delusion of tomorrow depends on the hysteria of mass forgetfulness: one must never look at the cause of today's suffering; one must not root out the cause today but must look to see how it can be removed in the future.

In man's world of progress all individuals are expendable because they have no place in it. Since the individual is the only one who dies and the world does not recognise death, dead individuals are remembered as figures, as the positions they filled — and are forgotten as men. In a world of progress and tomorrow a dead man cannot be missed for long because his position in such a world was only an imagined one anyway, and it will be promptly filled by the force of the imagination of the remainder. There are no spaces and no space in man's world.

All of this, the whole saga of tomorrow and the forming of man's substitute human nature, was the beginning of the process of evolution by involution.

Involution

Up to the point of self-consciousness and the gods, evolution had been confined to the physical ascent of the species or the descent of man into matter, his body. The next phase of evolution — involution — was to be the gradual enforced descent of his self-consciousness into a new body, a world-body of progress, his nescient substitute world, which later would form into reasonable knowledge and information — today's intellectual materialism.

Paradoxically, due to man's emotional escape into tomorrow, evolution by involution is his only way back to his lost immortality and godhood. Man invented tomorrow and has now to live in it. Involution is the endless complication of life by man's self-consciousness requiring him to go further away, deeper into the world-body of ignorance, falsehood or imagination, before he can get back out and free of it. As he determined the future when the past was very young is how it must be, except that finally the truth of his immortality and godhood must out.

Evolution by involution can be illustrated by the analogy of the wheel, a familiar symbol of time and progress. As the axis of the wheel of evolution moves forward, the wheel itself revolves backwards over old ground.

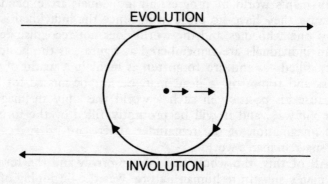

Today, man is still engrossed in constructing for himself his new body — a world-body of informational knowledge — like he constructed his physical body before it. The world's stupefying daily production and exchange of information as news, opinions and data suggests that this incredible body-building exercise is well on schedule.

The individual man must become thoroughly entrenched in this knowing habit, this new body, before beginning the task of freeing himself from it by realising in himself the intelligence, 'I', that supports every form of knowledge and body-consciousness. Then, and only then, can the next stage of evolution begin: man's voluntary re-entry into the psychic world, this time through self-knowledge, and as a fully conscious and no longer self-conscious or self-orientated human being.

7
The first society and the gnostics

When two or more self-conscious beings are in each other's company a powerful psychic atmosphere is generated between them. It is taken completely for granted.

This atmosphere is charged with man's emotional idea of the world as progress, continuity and tomorrow. It distinguishes him from all the other animals.

One man in isolation from his fellows for long is in danger of losing touch with the world, or the idea of it. Two men in contact together in isolation, even though competing against each other for survival, will keep the idea of the world alive between them.

In this lies the answer to the riddle of the wolf boys: will a human baby brought up by animals in the wild remain human?

Due to the unique humanising atmosphere generated between self-conscious beings, two wolf boys raised in the wild have a chance of remaining human, or in touch with man's idea of the world and tomorrow, as long as they are raised together. One wolf boy raised on his own will remain virtually an animal.

Conversely, animals such as domestic pets in the constant presence of human beings are seen to become 'intelligent' or more human. They pick up the progressive idea and accordingly tend to act less wild. Wildness is merely the state which refuses to accept or conform to man's idea of the world.

The first numbers of self-conscious men to generate this

uniquely human atmosphere saw — or in the presence of each other thought they saw — that the world, the things and people around them from which they had now become largely separate as self-entities, was not perfect. They inferred that things needed changing, that an order apart from the natural was essential. They were getting the progressive idea.

Simultaneously, society began to form.

A society is not a habitation. A habitation is where people live together. A society is where people live and work together linked by a common ethic — the idea of progress — under some kind of law or set of rules.

Society is the forerunner of civilisation. Society is the need for progressive order. Civilisation is the need for pleasure and art and these, man's most civilising drives, are his subconscious attempt to recreate the world of the gods representing the ultimate in pleasure and artistic creation.

Man's first society was shaped by the sheer necessity of his new self-conscious existence. Society had to follow the exploitive example set by the gods, as well as man's own escapist idea of a collective existence whose continuity must never be interrupted by the serious consideration of death.

Death, in effect, was outlawed as a proper topic of conversation and particularly as something to be ruminated on. Death was to be buried and never left around to disturb or disintegrate the progressive social idea. The show must go on. If death had to be seen or acknowledged it must be dressed up, disguised and given some sort of collective dignity to make it a part of progress, a sacrifice, an on-going, a ritual, a tragedy, a rest, a wake — never faced as its sordid, hideous self.

Man now was somebody. He had both an individual and a collective or progressive identity. He had something to live for today and to die for tomorrow along with his new compulsion to change the world.

But the message inherent in the evolution of self-consciousness (as distinct from its involution) is that to change the world (and not merely to move things or himself about) man must first change himself. Already few men could understand what this change was; and even fewer were — or

43

now are — prepared to make it.

The largest class or type of man found self-change impossible. He had to protect and raise his young and to do that he had to make sure of his survival as he was. Changing himself would have to wait. This was the family man.

While he was busy trying to survive and bring up his family, the family man found he had neither time nor adequate means to protect them. So he offered another type of man in the society food and shelter if he would fight off his enemies for him. The warrior caste emerged.

The simple more stupid kind of men, for their keep, became the servants and menial class.

And, for the dirtiest jobs of all, the insane, crippled and diseased were used — the wretched untouchables.

The smallest class of man had very different ideas to the rest. This class decided that the man who was celibate did not need to worry about surviving to protect his offspring. He could concentrate on finding the power within to change himself and so perhaps eventually change the world. This was the self-searcher, the original monk (from the Greek monachos — alone).

To a man who is celibate by choice the company of his fellow men is not so important. If he is looking for something within himself he is inclined to live in isolation or seclusion, away from external distractions and the idea of progress. A man trying to find the power within himself is not so concerned with living or dying: so, many monks wandered away and died of hunger; or they were killed by wild animals or other men.

Some of the monks who survived realised the search for the power within — and regained the idea of their immortality. Others pretended to. The pretenders and those who had partial success were the first priests. They entered the habitations and as the involving part of the greater evolutionary movement towards all men reaching the truth set about corrupting and distorting it with rites, ceremonies, interpretations and magic (psychic force) out of which arose worship and superstition.

The monks who did realise the truth fell into two categories.

The first and larger group, although very small in number, comprised those who had realised the Self out of which both 'I' and immortality arise — the truth which annihilates the need to change or search for anything. These masters, or holy men, wandered or settled, drawing to them monks and men to whom they taught the simple truth leading to Self-realisation.

The original gnostics

The other, smaller category of holy men emerged from among the Self-realised group. These were the original gnostics.

These first-wave gnostics and their successors had realised not only the Self, but also that level of mind which reveals the purpose of life on earth. This realisation reawakens the gnosis or knowledge of mankind's long-forgotten origins.

Monasteries and their equivalents were set up by both priests and Self-realised men. But it was the gnostic masters who founded the first real spiritual centres: real, in the sense that they were actual working models demonstrating the means and purpose of terrestrial life — the gnostic realisation.

The gnostic master, through the knowledge imparted by his realisation, knew that for him to attract right men to build and work in his centre, he had only to sit and wait. He had no sense of impatience. He could wait forever. If his body died, he would come again, or be again. Once on the earth he was always there, custodian of the gnosis which he would realise afresh in each life-form, for as long as it was necessary.

The original gnostics were already in existence when self-consciousness was very new. These men each lived to an age of several thousand years, made possible by two factors.

First, in those days the organs of the body could be renewed or revitalised from within through the vital or psychic double. Second, the original gnostics were able to occupy a succession of vital and physical bodies surrendered to them in selfless love by devoted followers. Rebirth at that time was a very long process — much longer than now — and was not necessary for the masters or custodians of the original knowledge of man's beginnings.

Moreover, at that time the physical constitution of human bodies was different; they were less solid in the sense that the vital double was less entrenched in the physical habit. (In this lies the origin of the monk's habit, his traditional tunic.)

And further, the degree of individuality was a variable factor: the soul or vital double alternated between the two worlds — contracting to appear as the ego in the physical, and expanding as the soul into the vital. Sometimes a man would be fully physically orientated; at other times he would be mainly in the psychic world.

After a time, as involution increased and man became more exclusively absorbed in the play of sense perception or the physical habit, the ego/soul unity flowed more rapidly backwards and forwards between the two worlds, finally to become the rhythmic breathing principle so familiar to us. The true significance of the Greek word psyche, meaning both soul and breath, will be appreciated from this.

The first gnostic centres

Each gnostic master formed his spiritual centre around himself. The physical centre was built in a remote place well away from other centres or human societies.

The gnostic masters made their spiritual centres fully self-supporting. Every man permitted to enter as a student had his worldly job to do in the centre as part of his spiritual preparation and instruction. Implicit in entrance was the unconditional surrender of his will to the master. He had no rights and abandoned all expectations, holding on to love, faith or trust in the master.

The gnostic centres were not unlike compact, refined models of the first societies — except that the defence and control of each centre was completely in the hands of one man, the master. He personified fundamental justice: he knew the truth and he wanted nothing.

The first gnostic masters repelled would-be intruders in the same way as they attracted right students — through the power of the Man they had realised within them. No hostile person or psychic force could penetrate their centre.

For us today, this would indeed seem to be an ideal, a state beyond circumstantial possibility. But we are approaching the evolutionary point where the individual's way back to it can begin. Those future men who eventually become gnostics will be different men to the first gnostics; they will have come to this state through self-consciousness, exist in larger numbers, and have a far greater influence on the humanity of their day. Theirs will be the knowledge towards which humanity will be consciously aspiring — not heading away from, as was the case in the time of the original gnostics when evolution demanded man's descent into the matter of circumstantial existence which is life today.

In the aeons that followed the founding of the original gnostic centres, involution — the process of complication of man's ideas and his world — began to grip. Gradually, but inexorably, intellectual complication overlaid and diminished the power of succeeding generations of gnostic masters to control matter as themselves.

It has to be remembered that the evolutionary journey towards a greater self-consciousness — the circumstantial life — had only just begun. The gnostic masters were fighting a losing battle from the start. The loss of their power, under the weight of matter as concept and wanting, was inevitable. But their purpose had never been to retain the power, anyway — only to preserve the knowledge by teaching it and realising it from life to life. The power would look after itself and reappear when the age of self (self-consciousness) was coming to an end.

So the defence of the centres became more and more a matter of combined action by all living in them, although the emphasis continued to be on utilising the power in the individual.

The later masters taught their students to deter attack by projecting the power without movement through their bodies in the psychic tension of confrontation.

As this power also began to wane, the movements of the student's body were used to harness the attacking force and

47

turn it against the attacker without initiating any violence.

Then came the unarmed blow to the psychic centres of the attacker's body, demobilising or killing him. And finally, there was the addition of weapons such as the sword and bow and arrow which the masters taught their students to use as psychic extensions of themselves, that is, as realised parts of their own power, or vital force, within.

All these forms of meditative combat taught by the long succession of gnostic masters in the original East, are represented in the martial arts that survive today.

8
Art, violence and civilisation

As originally practised in the long-forgotten East, the martial arts were a means of generating power in the man — such a peculiar quality of power that although the master of the art possessed the power to kill or disable, he could never use it and keep it. To use the force was to lose the power.

This paradox characterises the culture which man is heading back towards. Only this time, he will have his enormous experience and understanding of life to draw upon.

The power I refer to, of course, is the power which Christ was talking of in his doctrine of turning the other cheek. It is the power behind the teaching of surrender essential to the Old Testament, and behind Mohammedanism whose credic title Islam means surrender. It is the power invoked or invited by the state of desireless action central to Buddhism, the Mahatma power practised politically by Gandhi against the British in India, and the strength behind the doctrine of non-violence pursued by many great and effective men and women in history.

This extraordinary power latent in the individual man is something the world today has little time for, or understanding of. For the great mass of humanity it is a naive and idealistic fancy. It has been perceived by many men but not realised by enough of them to make it a significant truth for all. At present this power is on the descending node of evolutionary causes; Westernisation is in ascendance — the ideal of world progress powered by the involutionary drive into intellectual materialism. Consequently this power is not

49

permitted by the times to be publicly demonstrated, except in rare instances. These events if reported make the headlines as miraculous and mysterious happenings and are quickly forgotten, except by those who experience them. The Westernisation of the masses demands continuous streams of information − not knowledge.

The idea that puts faith in the power in man comes from the original geographical East which is long since vanished. The Eastern martial arts we are familiar with today are one of its superficial expressions which have managed to survive the world-swamping wave of Westernisation, the dive into the substitute world of intellectual materialism. Almost all of the East − even that remaining less than a thousand years ago − has now gone west.

The Westernisation of the world is not a modern phenomenon. In fact it has been going on since the start of involution. But the advent of the Roman Empire was the first significant crystallising of the process into tight numerical authority and force.

Christianity, the next stage of Westernisation, provided the necessary emotional impulse, bringing us up to the recent present.

Now, what is left of the East will come into the West through a new kind of ferment − a sort of anti-fervour − which is being generated for the next evolutionary advance. The first sign of this I have called the phenomenon of paranationalism, and it is described a little further on.

Meanwhile, Westernisation is in full swing. Every nation on the earth − backward, developing and developed − is striving for the same technological, material and intellectual ends. Individuality seems only to get in the way.

It is only a matter of time before the original-Eastern culture of faith in the power in the man begins to assert itself again. When it does, it will not be in the form of the ancient Eastern traditions as they are popularly understood by even the existing Eastern nations.

The new culture will manifest as *the* culture when the Westernisation of humanity − the full exteriorising of man's intellectual powers as materialism − is completed. The force of the intellect will then become the power of intelligence: the ability to discern unseen causes, principles and purpose.

There is one massive problem. The birth or release of the new culture from the human unconscious, where the idea of it is retained, will require the destruction of 99.9 per cent of the human race by nuclear war or holocaust. This can happen any day now.

Power, force and art

Why is it we hear about the fighting arts of the East but not about the fighting arts of the West?

The West has made a business of fighting, a profession and a necessity of it. For over two thousand years the developing Western identity, the Western way of life, has provided the world with ever-better weaponry or killing power. (The Chinese apparently thought their gunpowder invention was for making fireworks until Western ingenuity demonstrated a more profitable and business-like use for it.) But never has it made an unarmed art of combat. Not because its fighting men have been any less skilful, courageous, noble or murderously determined. But because the emphasis has always been on faith in the power of the weapon, or group, and not in the power of the man, the individual.

Over the centuries, the West has gradually built up its power and identity from number — in a fighting sense, from numbers of weapons, carried by numbers of men, conglomerating into one single armed force or power-pack.

Today, the ultimate effect of this can be seen in the power of the West (all ideologies) which inheres in the sheer numbers of men it can destroy (not as formerly, deploy) with a single weapon or unit of force — the Bomb. All of history's innumerable fighting men and their weapons have now been made redundant by this stupendous unit of annihilating force — or dead-rightness.

The Bomb is a brilliant vindication of the Western philosophy of putting faith in the power of the weapon — a fact indisputably measurable in its potential of dead men. The Bomb is the ultimate product of Western rationalisation, the final solution to the problem of modern logistics, a superb example of supermind economy. All those millions of soldiers it has supplanted lie like phantoms inside it ready to manifest as the millions of dead and dying the Bomb will leave behind when it goes off with the collective force of all their weapons fired in one catastrophic salvo.

It is a marvellously efficient philosophy. But its nuclear brainchild is not art. Such handiwork could never be included in a list of the fighting arts.

The point of art

In the case of the martial arts, it could be argued that a knife or gun would do the job quicker and more easily. This is the Western way of thinking and acting, the weapons or force way, which cannot be the point of art. Any killing or maiming — or threat at the point of a knife, gun or bomb — can never be the point of art.

If an exponent of the martial arts is to become a master he must eventually realise that even a threatening stance or hand cannot represent the art he is seeking. The power in man, whatever its quality, must be uniquely different to the threat of the weapon, the force of number or the fear of a blow.

In three thousand bloody years of recorded combat, the only empty-handed skills the West seems to have handed down to us are boxing and wrestling. Considering that long and violent opportunity for developing a fighting art-form, these skills remain crude and undistinguished — mainly because they are ends, and not means to anything greater.

Any art has to be more than a skill. It must possess that extra something, a quality, which penetrates and edifies the consciousness of the observer beyond the excitement and pleasure of being entertained. Art is for art's sake. It is not for winning.

The one recorded Western attempt to make its fighting skills the means to something better was the age of chivalry. And, as they say, the age of chivalry is dead. It expired to make way for the gun.

The fighting arts of the East as popularly practised today do not have much to commend them as art forms, except where meditative disciplines based on conscious restraint are demanded. None the less, the millions of people in both East and West seriously striving to master these arts have a great deal in common with the far more numerous scores of millions seriously pursuing other less physical art forms.

Both these groups share the same inexplicable attraction — the fighting group being pulled towards the source of original power, and the creative group towards the source of original art. In both cases, the source is man's forgotten godhood.

The fighting spirit, the fighting nature

The fighting spirit is that noble thing which moves us when we see it in a game, contest or attempt to overcome adversity. Its opposite is the fighting nature.

The fighting nature is ugly. We fear and distrust it. When we see it we hope to avoid it, or to see it vanquished.

The two are the difference between a fair fight and a massacre, a skilled defence and a knife in the back, a brave man and a bully.

The fighting spirit is in all of us. It is constantly trying to get the better of our fighting nature. We experience it as the effort to control ourselves when provoked. The fighting nature has no self-control. It lashes out with an angry word, a kick or a blow before the man in us has time to think. It is an instinctive reaction, a primitive, mindless impulse to hurt or disable.

This is not to suggest that everyone is going around looking for a fight. The problem of the fighting nature for most of us is more subtle than that. We are regularly assailed by hurtful words or critical attitudes. And, whether we admit it or not, most of us are just as ready for a fight or slight at the drop of an insult, just as quick to hurt — and to regret it after the damage is done.

The fighting spirit in adversity IS man; but not the animal part of him, his fighting nature, which clawed its way up from the swamps and slime to meet him at the point of destiny where the human spirit entered matter.

Man is separated from the animal, the primitive, cruel survival instinct, by his ability to sense consequences before he acts. His body — his tongue or fist — will lash out blindly and start chaotic sequences of violence. But not when his fighting spirit is developed. This prevents him from reacting blindly. For a split second he senses the consequences. There is a pause. This is the moment of truth: to do or not to do, to strike or not to strike, to kill or to let live. It is this intelligent pause, cultivated in the swamp of our base instinct, which is the difference between the admirable response of the fighting spirit and the violent reaction of the fighting nature.

The unbearable truth

We are faced with the fact that man is violent by nature, or reaction. And as we look around we apprehend the rest of nature, as circumstance, as being violent too. Yet it all works: life is good. Life is hard, is filled with unexpected death and injury, is often sad, cruel and unfair; but it is good. Why do we think like this?

Because every single one of us is fighting or living for something beyond survival.

One of life's mysteries and absurdities, however, is that most of us find it impossible to explain what this precious something is. After all, it is no new discovery that each of us is going to die. One would think that with the death-sentence already pronounced we would be distraught and unable to carry on. But most of us are not. For us not to be able to say why we keep going, and with such relish, too, towards the day of extinction, would seem to indicate that we are not facing up to something, or that there is more to our life than most of us are consciously aware of.

Despite our exertions after bigger houses, new cars, love, art, drugs, transcendental experiences, sons or daughters, lovely women, good men, fame, power, reputations — these things never are enough when we get them. Certainly, they are part of the means to whatever we are living or fighting for. But obviously, they are not the end we seek.

Yet, each day we fight or strive for more of them, or to keep those we have. Why?

'It's natural,' we say, 'that's life.' Which is true enough but it explains nothing.

All that ceaseless trying and struggling which the human race is engaged in is a means of absorbing and occupying the tremendous massed force of our fighting natures. If we were not made to expend the bulk of our energies in regulated, acquisitive directions, we would all be busy killing each other.

The fighting nature of humanity is not dissimilar in diabolical potential to the Bomb. Our efforts to possess man, woman, experience or power, within and under the almost-as-violent protection of the man-made law, make living bearably safe while we get on with it.

Each day each of us subconsciously retouches the picture of his life to make the grotesque travesty of living-to-die seem reasonable and to make some sense. We learn to live with a finger in the flame of doubt by refusing to acknowledge the pain to ourselves and each other, or to look for the cause of it.

We are benevolent liars to our children, hearty cowards to ourselves. Apart from a few Self-realised individuals, only the insane have seen the truth. Ours is a jungle in which everyone is kept as busy and as unquestioning as is humanly possible — not for the common welfare, but for the common safety.

Only in the real jungle are there no policemen, no doubts — and no insanity.

The unbearable truth which few are allowed to realise without going mad, is that every man is fighting or trying to live through his nature in order to make a better or more meaningful life for himself and the rest of humanity next time on earth.

This is the dynamic of human evolution. Each life is lived solely for the next on earth. As the point is always the next life, there is never really this life — therefore no apparent point, no permanence, no peace for long:

and no death.

While man lives, he must fight and strive to build the individual he will be tomorrow. As there is no tomorrow, and yet only tomorrow, there is no end. Man can never rest content, even when he is dead.

This is the epitome of futility, insanity. Which is why for man who is mortal, the truth of life must always remain myth.

Savagery and sophistication

Three thousand years ago, man had far fewer interests to keep him occupied. Practically nothing that most Western people use, do or think about today was known to him. Most men were serfs, soldiers or slaves.

Their wants were simple. Their lives were simple. Their means of killing were simple. Not because their fighting natures were any less acquisitive or aggressive than ours. And certainly not because the fighting spirit was more in control. But simply because in those days there was far less for man to want.

Even in the most distant days, long before the time of serfs, soldiers and slaves, man was neither more nor less happy than he is today. But he was more contented. Contentment exists in those moments when man is not aware of wanting anything. The number of things he can want, the objects of desire which disturb his contentment, depends on what he knows to be available and feasible for him to obtain. This also determines the violence, or force of his wanting.

Wanting is violence. All men want. So all men are violent. Man by nature is just as violent today as he ever was and ever will be. But the pressure, the force of his natural violence, becomes more and more diffused, less compulsive, as he discovers more to think about or dream of having.

A man who wants numerous things at the same time is not a violent man. He may be discontented, irritable, restless, industrious, an ordinary citizen. Only when his wanting has concentrated into one intense desire does he become dangerous.

Modern man, with so many desirable things within his reach, is able to diffuse his wanting-power through thinking and imagining. Thought and imagination become sophisticated outlets for the natural force of violence within him. By harmless thinking, planning and day-dreaming he spreads his wanting, his violent energy. He diffuses it even further by talking about his many interests to other multi-interested people. Civilisation and with it sophistication — the art of concealing forceful wanting — develop. And as civilisation, sophistication and social coherence become more and more the way of life through the growth of information (things to want or to talk about) so the origin of it all, violence, becomes more and more removed as a necessity of life.

Each age has had its liberal and enlightened approaches to violence: torture, flogging, capital punishment and all the associated cruelties become publicly unacceptable and are abolished; and we are appalled at the violence that even the last generation tolerated as necessary, let alone the iniquitous times which condoned the Inquisition and other horrendous atrocities committed in the name of man's law. Yet, that law so often infamous moves constantly forward towards more humane and less violent ends — civilisation. To some future man, we are the twentieth-century barbarians.

Back in the earliest of days when man had very little to dream about, or to imagine as outlets for his wanting, the spring of violence in him was a simple, savage one. Although more contented than modern man in between his simple few wants, when he did want it was with tremendous wilfulness. All the violence in his nature ripped through that one channel. His psychic mechanism was like a steel trap and one touch of wanting would set it off.

Early man could not be trusted to remain inviolent for any length of time. He was utterly unpredictable. His hours of contentedness would suddenly snap into violent action as a desire arose. He grabbed what he wanted, or fought for it, with all the pure savage fury of the man or animal who desires only one thing in that moment.

The birth of shame

In the later days of serfs, soldiers and slaves, man was a little different.

The unpredictable savage and savagery had begun to wane. Man was less erratic and more imaginative because he had more to want. But the force of his wanting, or his violent nature, was still very much the same. His rulers understood his simple psychology and exploited it. By keeping him underprivileged, as a slave for instance, man could be made to give up wanting the impossible things possessed by his masters, and be content only to dream about them.

A day-dreaming, imaginative man is not a violent man. He is no risk to established privilege as long as he can be prevented from wanting. The man who wants the impossible is a dangerous man. For the so-called impossible is only what some other man has. And if that impossible thing happens to be freedom, and if freedom is the only desire a man has, he is indeed a fellow or force to be reckoned with.

The most powerful want a man can have is for the thing he sees as the symbol of his freedom.

The most ancient invading armies were raised on this psychology — except that the soldier-man was fighting for a different kind of freedom to the slave-man's, which the soldier-man imagined he already had. The soldier-man demanded a more tangible reward for his services: spoils — the right to indiscriminate pillage, rape, wine, gluttony and all the rest of it, including the fleeting posture of absolute power — the caprice of life or death — over his defenceless equals, the conquered army. He wanted the power over others his masters had over him without the fear of penalty or the need of justice.

By inciting and encouraging the soldier-man's imagination towards these orgiastic symbols of his freedom, his privileged rulers kept his primitive emotions whirling with anticipation. Spoils were one thing man could want with all his unsophisticated heart and soul. These substitutes for his usual contentment could be depended on to drive him on through all of war's privations and hardships to the moment of victory or his death. His masters indeed knew how to harness his wanting-power, the fighting nature: promise man any impossible freedom he can be made to believe in and he will do anything for it.

But eventually, the soldier-man's fleeting spoils and wretched keep were not enough for him. His discontent, like his imagination, was more lingering. He began demanding more. His sophisticated, privileged rulers quickly got the message. Before the soldier-man could even think about organising the mass wanting-power he had unknowingly discovered — revolt — his masters stepped in smartly and invented for him money.

It was a masterpiece of evolutionary strategy. Man took the bait — incapable of snatching the rod and the power behind it. With money, and even more promises, his rulers began playing him and paying him off so that not for many, many thousands of years would he ever think of, or want, that impossible freedom which he came so close to discovering — power without money.

The appearance of money in the world signified man's social realisation of shame.

It was a momentous point in his evolution. Until money was invented for his use, he had not wanted enough things to be ashamed of what he wanted. His needs had been too natural and basic for there to be much choice. What one man wanted was pretty much what all men needed; and what all men want is nothing to be ashamed of. Shame arises when some men want what most other men do not choose to want or to be seen wanting.

Money's base appeal is that it does not reveal where it came from, or what kind of act earned it. Thirty pieces of silver could be payment for any job. Spoils, like other men's possessions and even power, can be too easily traced back to a source — perhaps back to a donor grateful for some treacherous or infamous act performed for him by another. But money, that superb alternative to possessions and power, can be hidden away or just spent. It does not identify the giver, the receiver, or the act that earned it. Money is universally faceless. It represents in one idea everything a man can desire or want — a very dangerous commodity.

So now the soldier-man fought for spoils plus money. His dirty deeds — which had become more and more numerous as he found more things to want — could (with a little luck) be concealed. Men did things to satisfy their wanting — or paid for them to be done — and pretended they did not do them or want them.

Out of this pretence and the shameful feelings it evoked about his wanting, a new kind of pernicious dishonesty crept into man's mind and man's world. For honest toil, man was pleased to accept as barter his keep or staple commodities. But for the killing and exploitation of his fellow man he needed a traceless hard-bitten currency — money.

Money is looting. That is why, since they invented it, man's privileged rulers have never touched the stuff.

The art of civilisation

Natural selection insists on the survival of the fittest to perpetuate the animal form of all the species. It is the law of the jungle and it works — in any kind of jungle, real or concrete, where the killer instinct is essential for self or pack survival.

Civilisation is not concerned with self or survival. It leaves this to the natural acquisitive and competitive instincts that look after themselves.

Civilisation is a cosmic pressure, not an instinctive drive. It does not affect animals. Animals and the least evolved men are content with habitations.

The civilising process at all times represents the descent of higher mind into matter, of human spirit into nature. This descent brings with it the ideas responsible for material progress. But the nucleus of these ideas, the principle supporting them, is the ideal of Man. It is against this ideal that the achievement of every civilisation is measured: to what degree did it succeed in providing justly for *all* its people?

Civilisation is art on the grandest scale, the continuous endeavour to express excellence in the form or matter of humanity. Humanity is Man's becoming.

Civilisation is the art of putting man first. This is not an easy idea to comprehend let alone to try to put into practice. It is not just the admirable concept of putting the other fellow first. It is not just being kind or doing good. It is probably best described as doing nothing more than being just.

Civilisation demands that all human beings within its compass must come first — or none at all. All the people are the one Man.

At this stage of evolution, however, human beings are only part Man, as society is only partly civilised.

Man, the idea or character of the human species, is a towering, impeccable principle, fully alive in all human matter and human circumstance and beyond any one person's intellectual or self-conscious capacity to know in its entirety. Yet each human being can be that Man and each society that civilised excellence in any moment of nobility, justice or compassion.

The nearest the individual (or a society) can get to understanding the principle of Man is through that person's own ethic or ideal — how each one of us would like the world to be for ourselves as our fellow-man. Service to this ideal through the means at our personal disposal (and, as a community, at our collective disposal) is the civilising process.

All civilisations are attempts at civilisation. All have failed due to an inherent flaw in the social conscience stemming from humanity's inability to grasp what civilisation is for.

Within the more impressive achievements of each great civilisation is the means of its inevitable destruction. Where it was thought to have succeeded most is where the poison will be found. It is not unlike a parasite that gets into the flower in full bloom and infects the fruit before it has formed.

The Roman genius for colonisation and government was the means of that civilisation's downfall. For the earlier Mediterraneans it was their rampant curiosity. Seeking distraction, they gradually forgot man's astonishing origins which were the foundation of their culture. With the power of that knowledge — original art — they created beautiful images instead of excellent men. The resultant ignorance and moral laxity in the shape of the barbarians invaded their territory as well as their psyche and eventually destroyed them. Vandalism in all ages lives on in the hills of the mind.

Similarly, the South American Inca/Aztec cultures and no doubt many others collapsed through an over-indoctrination of myth as superstition through priestly rule. Priest rule prevents the necessary development of discrimination and common sense in worldly affairs which is part of survival and the struggle for civilised excellence.

The means of Westernised civilisation's destruction will be through its super-technology, probably in some form of almost instant wipe-out as a logical improvement on the old, slower processes of degeneration and decay.

The means of destruction of a civilisation must not be confused with the cause. Moral failure, I repeat, has been the cause of every civilisation's downfall. Our moral failure — the worm in the Westernised flower — was cultured by the instinctive drive for more among the privileged while the many by comparison had little or nothing.

Western civilisation — the schisms of failure

Ours is the first world civilisation. In that we are unique and represent the end of a phase in mankind's development. Western civilisation is an extension or culmination of all earlier civilisations and their aspirations for ever-more conquest, wealth and influence. Only, Western civilisation has gone the limit and conquered the globe.

The conquest has yet to be consolidated and consciously realised, if there is time. But the pattern of consolidation is inevitably established and there can be no major changes; just modifications. Any pockets remaining of the ancient cultures are already regarded as backward or underprivileged; and by their own consent and connivance are being eroded further every day.

Our main civilising achievement has been to bring mankind together through our technological and intellectual genius without the necessity for altering his position on the globe. Through Western thought, politics, weapons, transport, finance, science and telecommunications we have done just that — exciting everyman's wanting and ensnaring him with his expectations.

Each day the world gathers more solidly under the flag of intellectual materialism, in spite of its ideological differences. Never has there been such solidarity. The common aim is for more, more of everything — freedom, leisure, government, peace, power, information, military hardware, drugs, computers, flush toilets, travel and unlimited credit. There is no other way to go and no evidence of any meaningful demand for an alternative.

The remaining obstacles to the completion of the Westernisation of mankind are not due to any outraged opposition but to sheer lack of resources to satisfy the universal scramble, whether white, black, brown or yellow. The world is populated by Westerners — first, second, third, fourth, fifth, sixth and seventh-class citizens; that is, man's privileged rulers, the super-rich or powerful, the rich, the workers, the poverty liners, the exploited and the abandoned.

These are the schisms of failure.

Ours, like all the great civilisations before it, has served the planet's evolutionary cause. As a part of the cosmic earth experiment, it has succeeded. But its self-failure in being unfit to endure as the permanently civilising way of life, lies in the expediency of its shifting values.

Our particular failure is intellectual duplicity — double standards. In two thousand years our civilisation has not been able to be honest to itself — to its people. The times we lived in would not permit it. By the 'times' I mean the power mankind has attained in any age through evolutionary experience to control matter, or circumstance, morally. Man who can control matter morally is a man who puts man first.

We have not possessed the moral strength to stand against the pressure of wealth and self-interest, to uphold in practice the worthy ideals we protested. Where men rose to rule, the ruled became the sacrifice. Now, after two millennia of chances, no man or men can ever again rule in this civilisation. The rulers are ruled by circumstances, the force in matter. They are powerless to change anything significantly, as previously was possible — and the thoughtful ones know it. The privileged position of rulership by man on this planet in this civilisation has been forfeited and withdrawn.

The cosmic law of limited violence

Man, in spite of his nuclear might, still does not possess the power to wipe out the human race.

But he can destroy most of it. And, as I have mentioned, this will be necessary for his evolutionary advancement.

Man has a limited mandate for violence. Although he cannot destroy the race, he can decimate its component parts as he has so often demonstrated in the past.

The scale of violence man can inflict on the planet or against the race at any time is controlled by a cosmic or deeply subconscious principle. This principle also operates against any internecine accidents or folly which could threaten the existence of mankind. Such a profoundly important cosmic issue as the survival of the human race could never be permitted to depend on an emotionally capricious will like man's at its present stage of development.

The cosmic law now guaranteeing the survival of the race against man's destructive genius and fighting nature states: man's ability to destroy nature or himself (mankind) is only equal at any time to his knowledge of nature or himself.

In other words, he cannot destroy himself until he knows himself — and then he will know better.

Weapons — man's evolutionary status symbols

The demonstration of this cosmic law is man's weapons. They reveal the extent of his knowledge of himself or nature. Weapons are man's evolutionary status symbols.

Once, his ultimate weapons were the club, knife, axe and spear. They were primitive like his knowledge and aspirations. He understood very little about nature or himself. And so, in line with the cosmic law, his ability to destroy either on any large scale was correspondingly limited.

As his knowledge, ambitions (imagination) and skills

increased, he added the sword to his arsenal, enlarging his lethal capabilities.

Then came the long-bow with which he could destroy greater numbers with greater accuracy and greater impunity due to distance. All the time his knowledge and power to want (to visualise more) was increasing.

Eventually, delving with his mind into chemistry he discovered the knowledge of gunpowder, the first significant means of mass destruction. This matched the revival of learning and artistic aspiration represented by the Renaissance.

Over the next few centuries as he probed deeper into nature's secrets, becoming more aware of the finer things he could make and want, man developed ever-more effective mass-slaughtering weapons and systems — artillery, the cartridge gun, repeater, machine-gun, gas, aerial bombing, rockets, guided missiles. . . .

Finally, when his knowledge of nature through atomic physics had reached some sort of optimum, he devised the Bomb. Today, this appalling weapon of mass destruction, or mass knowledge, can devastate (but not annihilate) nature and humanity — a fitting symbol of man's enormous knowledge and matching power to inflict violence.

But, in spite of man's fears, the ultimate weapon has not yet been developed. His knowledge of nature or himself is not up to it.

This ultimate weapon — symbol of the ultimate knowledge he has yet to achieve — will be to use the earth itself as a bomb or energy device and to disintegrate the whole planet.

One day, many scores of thousands of years hence, this may be done deliberately by cosmic man.

The cosmic moral law and the quality of man's wanting

Just as a cosmic law controls the devastation man can wreak upon the earth at any time, so another cosmic restraint prevents him — or so far has prevented him — from unleashing the nuclear force now at his disposal. The balance is so fine that nuclear war is a possibility at any moment.

The only certainty — guaranteed by his current state of

self-knowledge — is that man will survive in sufficient numbers to perpetuate the race. This is hardly a comforting thought for the four billions who will be destroyed; nor for them to know that the holocaust will have been absolutely necessary for the inevitable progress of Westernised culture towards the enlightened race man must become.

The first cosmic law I mentioned only guarantees the survival of the race. It cannot determine whether or not man will use the Bomb to cause the damage he is now capable of inflicting. The factor determining whether he will use the Bomb, is the cosmic moral law.

The cosmic moral law helps to illustrate the distinction between power and force — the two foci of the cosmic moral system in which man is involved.

Down the ages from knife to Bomb, an extraordinarily fine moral element has determined whether man used the ultimate weapon of his times. This involuntary moral control lies in the *quality* of man's wanting.

The more man knows about life, or the world, the more there is to want of it in power and possessions. Yet, the more a man lives or practises wanting — which can be a violent period for himself and the rest of us — the less he will eventually want, and the more he will then be said to be civilised or restrained in his desires.

We see this not only in our own lives and in those of the people around us, but also in the struggles of nations to become developed and prosperous. A nation with enough knowledge to have made the Bomb has a great deal of wanting power (or knowledge). Today, with the wanting-power or knowledge equivalent to the force of the Bomb shared by several countries, the need for self-control or civilised restraint (victory over the fighting nature) has become imperative.

Here is where the cosmic moral law comes in. So far, man (men) who controls the Bomb is civilised enough not to want anything the Bomb can give him, except the peace of being spared its immediate and cumulative horrors. Unlike in the case of any other weapon in history, even for man's privileged rulers the spoils are just not worth the consequences of employing it.

The significance of power now reveals itself. At this no-action, *negative* level of wanting, the Bomb becomes a power for peace instead of a force of destruction. It will be seen that this power, the product of restraint, becomes the power of non-violence referred to earlier. It is not unlike the achievement of the true master of the martial arts who has the power to destroy but can never use it. The release of power as force at any level of existence invites counter-force in counter-blow or counter-tactic — the misery of war and conflict.

But one essential weakness remains in the peace-keeping power of the Bomb. In depending on it for his survival, man is relying on a power outside himself. The Bomb symbolises faith in the power of the weapon — the Western faith now fully materialised. No one man has control of this weapon in the way a man can be said to have control of himself. The situation is therefore precarious and through proliferation becomes more so every day.

It only needs one power-mad man, or nation, to demonstrate the horrific consequences of this Western philosophy of developing the weapon before the man. Sooner than later some idiot man, or group, lacking the quality of wanting nothing the Bomb can offer, is almost sure to push the button.

A man who knows a lot but wants nothing is the most powerful man. He can protect us. A man who knows a lot and wants a lot is the most dangerous man. He can blow us up without the need for it. A man who knows a little and wants it a lot is a beginner or a fool — and he is just the kind of idiot who will be used to do the job when the time comes.

Paranationalism — the new Kamikaze terror

The newest and most world-shaking extremity of violence and change is what I call paranationalism.

Paranationalism is any organised attempt through terrorist acts to draw attention to the evils of the status quo anywhere in the world.

It aims to destroy the root attitudes of people supporting the formation of power and privilege — conventions so integral and fundamental to a society that even to the radical political mind the attempts seem senseless and even psychotic. This is especially so since the violent means employed usually involve the death and injury of innocent people.

The strategic weapon of paranationalism is violence itself: indiscriminate violent acts against the expectations of society, against society's natural values and unquestioned loyalties.

Instead of taking on the police, the paranationalists take on the politicians and society leaders as a means of getting at the people. They know that no one can get directly at the people short of involving them in the horror of total war; that the people of a modern society are completely shielded from change by the massed media, the authorities and the despised conventions.

To the paranationalist, the people are as much the enemy as the objective.

This seems a contradiction, but to the dedicated paranationalist mind there are no people, only positions. To such a mind, people act out their positions. Positions have to be destroyed in people's minds for the real person, the individual, to be reached. So, in these terrorists there is no mercy, no compassion of the kind conventional people or conventional positions can relate to.

They represent a completely new psychological phenomenon which is rising out of the unconscious in man. They still operate at the subconscious level, which means their motivations cannot be comprehended by the conventional mind or attitudes.

Unlike any known political activists, or revolutionaries of the past, they are fighting for an idea which is not yet even definable, let alone understandable. They are the mindless ones, the warrior-end of the blank generation — that bland paranational band among the youth of the world which does not so much defy as fail to understand society's conventional expectations of them.

The paranational terrorists are the new breed of Kamikaze

warriors, suicide fighters.* To them, death is nothing, and living is ignoble once the evil of positions-without-people is seen. And like all the precursors of the approaching new culture, they come out of the East.

Paranationalism does not aim to establish any new national boundaries. It aims to pull down all conventional divisions. Where the line is to be drawn, no one knows, least of all the Kamikaze robots. Paranationalism is not anarchy or nihilism. It does not preach revolution. It is not idealistic in the least. From the Westernised viewpoint, its motivations, like its achievements, are inscrutable.

Paranationalism depends on the stark terror and horror of its indiscriminate actions to drive home its idea or message like a steel pin into the subconscious of humanity, through the armourplate of the enemy — the contented massed position. It aims at the individual, not the masses. Every Kamikaze terrorist action has a subliminal message that lodges somewhere in the human psyche where it will slowly rise to consciousness among the blank generation, tomorrow's rulers. Its ideas form very slowly in the social conscience.

There is no conventional power-drive in this kind of terrorism, no personal reward apart from death, no ideological fantasies.

The communist and totalitarian countries are as much its targets as the democracies and dictatorships. But where the Westernisation process is at its height and the social conscience likely to be the most outraged is where it will strike most hideously and most often.

Paranationalism is a new expression of power at present largely mixed up with nationalistic struggles in Africa, Northern Ireland, the Middle East, Asia and elsewhere. It has yet to divorce itself from these conventional freedom struggles and realise its independent identity and task . . . . as it has yet to do its inconceivable worst.

---

* Kamikaze is a Japanese word associated with pilots of Japanese planes in World War II whose sole missions were suicidal crash dives into Allied ships. The word means divine wind and alludes to a storm called up by the prayers of the Japanese people which destroyed an invading Mongol fleet in the thirteenth century.

The millennium of decline

The millennium of decline is here.

The first shock-waves of paranationalism — unnoticed or forgotten by the majority almost as quickly as they disappear from the headlines — represent the beginning of the end of Westernised civilisation.

It is difficult to imagine that our familiar way of life can possibly come to an end as a way of progress. The populations of the past great civilisations probably felt the same. And yet all lie in dust apart from a few relics. No civilisation seems able to visualise its successor.

If the fighting nature does not get the chance to wipe us out first through some convenient power-mad action, the paranational terrorists eventually will. To begin with, it may be an effort of attrition. But finally the weapon will be the Bomb or some equally effective product of our super-technology — our finest achievement.

One day it may be said that Westernised civilisation gave more men more years to live in better health, comfort and luxury so that finally it was able to destroy more than if it had never existed.

The barriers that paranationalism or the Bomb will destroy are those that have created the different nations separating one people from all people — an intolerable anachronistic distinction for a world civilisation.

Evolution proceeds on this planet in distinct, halting time-stages in which the process stops, gathers, bursts . . . and out of the shambles and chaos leaps the Zeitgeist, the spirit of the era, to seed a new cultural attempt at civilisation containing that which was best of the old.

The time that is left is virtually no time at all. There may be a final, brief cultural flowering — the natural result of our civilising achievements — just before the end. This flowering will be distinguishable by the feeling in the individual, the society, or the world that life has reached some worth-while peak.

9
Emotion – the genie out of the bottle

Man's most civilising drive is the need of pleasure. His most self-destructive impulse is the need of love. Between these two compulsive longings lies the treacherous ground of emotion which he often mistakes for both.

Let me make it clear what I mean by emotion. Man is being emotional – and therefore not himself – when he chats or thinks about the past; when he tells his troubles to anyone except perhaps a professional consultant or spiritual teacher (both of whom will keep him to the facts); when he gossips about another person; or when he justifies himself or accuses or blames another. To risk seeming to be going to extremes: he is even in danger of being used by emotion when he expects anything from another, or when he makes a statement not in answer to a question direct or implied.

In other words, when I speak of emotion I am not just talking about the stronger feelings of anger, joy, grief etc. I am referring to something more subtle yet massively pervasive, something as fundamental and ever-present as the past itself. In fact, emotion *is* the past itself.

Emotion is the past because it originates from instinct, the first driving-force of life on earth. Instinct is the desire to survive and live again. The very essence of that is the experience or knowledge of having lived before.

Instinct culminates in the expression of animal life which is so complete and perfect in its unself-conscious artistry. In man, instinct continues to govern his animal responses but

71

rising to self-consciousness it becomes emotion — that is, the need to project himself, make an impression on his environment, whether by anger, moods, talk, threat or desire for recognition in the form of sympathy and acceptance.

Emotion is the self-conscious expression of instinct. Animals, being unself-conscious, do not get emotional.

As instinct was the driving force behind the development of the animal body to the point where self-consciousness was a future possibility, so emotion was the rising wave on which man travelled out from the psyche finally to become attached to his physical senses and the world as the consciousness of self.

Then, mainly through conflicting desire — competing emotions — forcing him to choose and think, it provided the stimulus for the mental development of homo sapiens to his present creative level of performance.

Now that man has realised his senses, entered his body and ordered his reflective thought processes, emotion as the prime mover of these evolutionary achievements has served its purpose. But like the legendary genie who escaped from the bottle and discovered its enormous power over man it cunningly refuses to go back in the bottle.

Emotion is now man's torment, the main source of his misery and lack of fulfilment. Emotion is living off him, sucking like a vampire at any excitement it can stir in his sensitivity and leaving him depressed, discontented or unfulfilled until he is revitalised and can be used again.

Nevertheless, as it was evolution which extracted the cork and let the genie out, so evolution must redress the position. Thus, how to get the emotional genie back into the bottle and put the stopper on for good is now the great evolutionary task of humanity.

Consequently, more of the human race than in any other recorded time is searching for solutions within themselves without necessarily realising the identity, subtlety, power and cunning of the one common enemy. Modern man — as a race — is endeavouring to rid himself of the confusion and uncertainty created by emotional indulgence and ignorance. All the genuine meditation methods and different schools of philosophy and psychology — as well as the whole remarkably popular self-growth movement — are directed towards this end.

A huge and growing section of mankind is ready to discover that their emotional living and thinking, for all its apparent seriousness and harmlessness, is no more than pathetic self-indulgent games-playing, the demand for love. Love cannot be demanded. But emotion thinks it can.

By facing up to the fact of emotion, by starving the demonic genie out of himself, man can begin to get free of its selfish use of him. Then he can begin to realise and fulfil his two great basic drives for pleasure as self-expression, and for love as union.

At present, due to the distorting and confusing demands of emotion, man can only sense vaguely that continuous creative pleasure and constant love are attainable. Certainly, his experience of living does little to confirm it; creative pleasure and constant love remain for most the impossible dream. Yet all continue to pursue them in their way with unshakable certainty — for the simple truth is that man was born to love and create.

The invader from the underworld

Emotion was created in the first place by the action of sunlight entering and exciting the unconscious psychic mass. Being the first child of light, conceived in the black womb of the unconscious, its prime motivation is to get back up to the external world of sunlight, back to the source of its excitation. Emotion is restless and immature, unseasoned by sufficient experience of the outer world it seeks.

Emotion — the demonic genie — rises continuously to the surface through man's senses, not unlike an inquisitive snake out of some underworld. It prefers, if given the chance, to peer through the unsuspecting eyes of the human being into the self-conscious outer world. There it looks for recognition in the world mirror of emotional reaction — the affirming reflection of its existence in some other eyes, face or attitude.

It is this which makes it dangerous to look into the eyes of some dogs unless one intends to deal with them. Our own self-consciousness makes the animal's otherwise purely instinctive reaction, emotional. The only protection is to remain perfectly emotionless in one's eyes — a very difficult thing to do. If the animal senses the slightest weakness or fear in the eyes — the presence of self-consciousness — and feels it can win, it will attack. Emotion is a violent energy which cannot resist the opportunity to enslave, hurt or destroy the emotionally weaker form. It is cannibalistic. It lives off itself.

When we catch the eye of a person who is emotional we instinctively know that they are looking for trouble and to stay clear. Emotion is trouble looking for itself.

Emotion in others is fairly easy to discern. In ourselves, it is much more difficult because of the speed with which it takes us over. It is there before we can be aware of it performing as us in our awareness. If we can manage to race ahead of it, or more realistically, develop the power in ourselves to be present intelligently the moment the emotional genie begins to rise, we can halt it and master it; this without creating frustrations and neuroses which come from bottling up the genie in ignorance.

The false now and the real now

Emotion rises. In primitive man it carried the waves of instinctive intelligence up and across to the unrealised senses. It pushed and it strained ceaselessly from within to bring the sense of knowing, the sense of self, into the incipient human brain and then into the outer senses.

When at last the connection was made linking each outer-world sense-organ with the physical brain and the vital double within, man's body not only possessed the sense of smell, but man *knew* he could smell. He was to that degree reflective. And simultaneously his sense of self was born.

Emotion created that self — that I-ness, that past, that karmic (repetitive) continuity of effects that is my body, my emotional feelings and my now.

In the individual person today that is all completed, finished, realised, inevitably connected as both the stream-bed and stream-current of our daily lives, from heart-beat and breath to our complete set of senses.

Today, however, personal time has moved 'forward' as a possibility, although this might not be immediately evident. A slightly different time-apprehension is involved. 'This moment' is minutely ahead in time of that past or now-spurious now, that collection of old self and I-ness just referred to.

That past I and now rely on memory and are the spurious creations of an emotion associated with naming. Naming in turn derives from the positional mind which started to form in primitive man as he approached self-consciousness.

The positional mind was the psychological extension of animal instinct. Man's body possessed all the animal instincts of survival but he alone of the species had this new incipient thinking capability which also had to be developed as a survival tool.

The development of the positional mind paralleled the evolution of the human memory. The early positional mind like primitive man's memory had none of the fluidity and subtlety of connections our mind has today as a result of the inflow of feeling or emotion with the advent of self-consciousness. Man 'thought' disjointedly. Each memory he had was separate, solid, very concrete. He recalled only isolated past incidents, as fixed perceptions or positions.

For example, if he had caught an animal for food (or found water or any other need) in a certain place he would remember that event in isolation and return there habitually even though no animals ever turned up there again. Through this early positional thinking he established wandering and nomadic patterns which whole tribes followed without ever understanding their origin. The patterns in turn were later given magical and religious significance leading to ritual and those who remembered them the longest, the elders, were named wise and given venerable titles.

With the advent of self-consciousness man used his positional mind or fixed perceptions in attempts to interpret and satisfy new emotional feelings or desires as they arose in him. He enjoyed letting past events play on his memory and watching the pictures come up. Gradually he resorted to the past in this way to deal with the present, and started the positional habit of living in the past which persists in all men today. This was the origin of the old, old habit of naming which binds us — and the people we name — to the past and prevents us from breaking out of our narrow time-bound cage.

Naming is a pernicious habit of the emotional self that operates incessantly in man at the conscious and subconscious levels especially as continuous thinking and worrying. Naming is the reaffirmation and replenishing of the false self's existence.

When a man is able to break his dependence on the primitive, positional mind and cease this constant naming — it involves a good deal of conscious effort and psychological pain — the false self dies. With it dies the old now which was his reference to the past, or his living in the past, and his main source of confusion and uncertainty. With the death of this past self — the old enemy emotion — he automatically transfers to a refreshing new sense of time — the moment, the real now. Now he is truly alive and no longer just living. Now he sees things and people as they are, not as they were.

The moment is part of a new factor of awareness currently making an increasing appearance in consciousness. It is extremely fine and delicate as yet; perception of it is immediately clouded over and lost by any emotion or subjective reference to the past. The moment has a purely mental or intelligence base as opposed to the old self's emotional or irrational base. To exist as a ceaselessly naming individual is obviously not rational; it is emotional, and therefore expendable.

In any moment, with effort, we can observe the naming habit in ourselves, stifle it — and start to live anew.

10
The human psyche

The human psyche is our instrument of thought and perception. It begins immediately inside the human body and extends down through the subconscious (where we think and dream) into the unconscious.

The unconscious part of the psyche is the world of the living dead and of our feeling self — the vital double. To us — the dying living — it is symbolised by the inside of the solid body of the earth. It is unconscious because we cannot be conscious of what is in there or what is beyond it. However, to the living dead whose world it is, it extends out to include the entire area prescribed by the orbit of the moon. Looking out consciously as we do into this area we cannot see this part of the unconscious. For that we have to withdraw inward into the unconscious — as when we die — and enter that realm from there. Thus do the dead approach and observe the earth unbeknown to us.

Each living creature (from individual man to collective organisms such as hives or insect colonies) is attached to the psyche like hairs to a scalp. In total, the mass of all living things on the earth at any time covers the psyche, or psychic body, like a short dense pile.

Furthermore, every living thing is a receptor, convertor and battery serving the total evolution of the psyche.

While alive, each organism absorbs into its unique psychic system (its hair-stem or body) cosmic energy/data provided by sunlight, the dynamic behind all life and terrestrial evolution.

From the light-energy assimilated, each living battery transforms and stores two primal life charges, one actual/

positive, the other potential/negative. The positive charge is the vitality which powers the life of the physical organism. The negative charge is a far more subtle residual energy impossible to quantify in positive or vital terms. This extraordinary energy represents the intrinsic value of the life of the particular organism. The value of each bit of life or life-experience, no matter how seemingly minute in form or ephemeral, is equally important and essential to the whole. Throughout an organism's lifetime this negative energy builds up and remains unused.

At death, the positive vitality remaining in the living creature/battery travels down the narrow hair-stem channel into the collective unconscious of all life, taking with it the unique negative essence as a contribution to the 'having lived' experiential value of the whole. After the extraction of this essence during an intensive after-life process, the vital energy rejoins the collective reservoir of recirculating instinct. After a further process the essence takes on a new vital self and, returning to the earth, grows into existence in a new body among the species — and the whole cyclic process is repeated.

The most extraordinary fact about the psyche is that it consists of the instinctive and emotional past of all life that has ever lived and died on earth. Every creature since the first microbe is an evolving part of it. At every moment the psyche is being swelled but also refined by the continuous recirculating life-and-death cycle of all living things.

We must endeavour to grasp and appreciate this strange new idea: that the psyche being used to absorb and understand these words has evolved over the past two thousand million years out of the instinctive surviving vitality, the incipient emotion, of all life on earth. This peculiar, one might even say weird, vital consistency of the psyche explains many of man's otherwise mystifying and irrational dreads and fears.

The psyche is one vast fluid whole of which man's vital double is the self-conscious centre, its most intelligently developed nucleus.

But the relatively enlightened human centre is very small compared with the enormous surrounding mass of natural or instinctive ignorance. Instinct, in spite of its superb efficiency as a survival reaction, is ignorant and unenlightened in relation to the movement towards a civilised or moral purpose which only man among the species consciously reflects.

Consequently the individual man, in spite of his superior intelligence, frequently becomes psychically disturbed by the pressure of the surrounding primitive mass.

The 'dark hours' of early morning are often the most anxious and depressing for him. These hours are no darker in the sense of light deficiency than the other midnight hours. Their power to disturb, exaggerate fears and arouse dread lies in the fact that they represent the nadir of the period in man's day when he is denied the reassuring and restoring stimulation of sunlight, the power behind his self-consciousness. In these hours the surrounding psychic ignorance asserts itself and assails the sensitive centre and the man feels — usually with pessimism and sometimes hopelessness — the vulnerability of his beleaguered psychic position.

The sufferings of all men and all life that has ever lived are indelibly imprinted on the psyche. The experience of every horrible death, cruelty, torture and pain persists there as a vital part of the whole and intermittently rises sufficiently to be reflected in the self-consciousness of the individual man.

The superstitions to which even the most civilised of men are prone have their origins here in the dread of the unknown, which really is the dread of what the total psychic consciousness has already known.

Most nightmares, psychic disorders and apparent insanity have their source in involuntary perceptions of this red and raw unconscious region of the psyche. Every animal cry contains the hidden sounds of countless ages of animal and human suffering. Not surprisingly in the dark hours the hoot of the owl, the howl of the dog and even the human voice can induce fear and dread.

The hallucinations that terrorise the schizophrene are due mostly to these hyperceptions of the psyche, the instinctive and emotional past of man and all the species.

Psychic utilisation

Utilisation of humans by psychic forces is extremely common.

Since the psyche pervades man's brain and every cell of his body, these forces are able to invade the individual's psychic space with imperceptible stealth.

They enter from a man's vital double via any emotional abnormality. Their presence excites him further enabling them to take temporary (sometimes permanent) possession. In this way the energies receive the vital stimulation of experience — something that cannot be gained direct in the psychic world — without the responsibility of existence. When the passion or impulsion has exhausted itself, that is, when the invading entity has had its fill, it vacates, leaving the man to face the consequences — usually in a slightly devitalised state. A feeling of being cold or drained often follows.

Just about every negative mood or feeling we experience as individuals can be attributed to this type of possession.

One strategem is for the energies to attach themselves to any emotional thinking which can be induced. Thoughts originate as single-frame flash images which are unavoidable. The danger arises when a single thought is allowed to run on by association. Invariably it focuses on an emotional point in the past. The psychic forces wait on these thoughts, enter on the emotion and temporarily influence the moods, decisions and actions.

The psychic energies also attach themselves to man's fears of illness or death and when he is sick make conditions worse by causing depression. They also manifest as brooding, paranoia and hysteria and attach themselves to such natural and involuntary emotional phenomena as the female menses.

Protection against psychic invasion lies in resisting any thought that does not involve the intention of action. When action is the object such as in preparing a plan for a house, or performing work, man reasons from fact to fact and is not emotionally vulnerable. Any other thinking is discursive and carries the danger of invasion.

Over-indulgence in sex and other excessive sensual or

emotional stimulation can provide the necessary catalyst for the psychic forces. This includes over-excitement in anticipation of even normal events, as often happens in children.

The after-effects of possession — depression, self-pity, tearfulness, pessimism, moodiness, demandingness, lethargy — may not appear until a couple of days later. This again shows the cunning of these emotional entities. The time-lapse prevents the person from seeing that his depression is caused by his earlier thinking or excitement. This would undermine the entities' parasitical credibility and existence. Everyone knows that thinking is natural and perfectly harmless . . . so goes the propaganda.

The point of human existence

The point of existence is for man as a race to build a new world of his own and to be fully and permanently responsible for it. It has to be a world in which he is immortal, where his conscious presence and control are uninterrupted.

Men of goodwill have sensed this down the ages. Many have imagined it as a hope for the physical world, only to have their efforts ended by death or uncontrollable circumstance. Mystics and saints have perceived it as a life in the spirit of selfless love in which the need for any existence at all disappears.

But humanity's future world is neither physical nor spiritual. It is psychic.

While alive, humanity must start to take conscious possession of the psychic world, currently the mysterious and turbulent domain of the dead.

To date, man has had no world to call his own for very long. Death excludes him from the physical world; living excludes him from the psychic world. He never remains long enough in either, is never sufficiently responsible for his collective actions, to be entitled to call one or the other 'his'.

The psychic world as a whole is chaotic. Nevertheless, it is man's world, his own involuntary creation, in some ways his own monster. All man's pain, greed, cruelty, hatred, jealousy and sadism is there together with his accumulated feelings of love, devotion, kindness and goodwill. All these emotions are vitally alive there. They are able to take form by entering any of the countless weird (or saintly) mental images which the primitive and developing mind has put there. Nothing in the past has been lost. All must be taken responsibility for. All must finally be resolved by and in man, the creator.

Man's power to control his destiny in the death world is no greater than what he manages to achieve while alive. While alive he cannot see that the final responsibility for his life and the world is his. The result is that he lives a life mainly of abdication of responsibility: he compromises endlessly, goes with the stream and contributes only what is necessary to the common good. Consequently, expansion of the racial awareness is glacial and the power to change things in either world practically non-existent. It is an endless cycle.

The epoch has now arrived in which man is to start taking conscious control of the psychic world and his own existence.

This will be done by the individual extending his conscious awareness to include that of his vital double in the world of the living dead. Only the clarified consciousness of the individual has the power to unite both living and death worlds to form a new immortal existence. Success by a few will make a stronger bridge for others to follow; and enough across will begin to form a new world.

This unification of consciousness has been going on in individual men for thousands of years. But because of its intensely personal demands rarely is the process seen for what it is — the forerunner of a massed race effort to build a new world for all humanity.

A man's vital double — his own immortal self — is as close to him as his feeling of being alive. But he is separated from it by all his negative feelings, moods, fears and desires. These create the individual's psychic space separating him from the experience of his immortality. This space becomes the play-ground for the psychic forces that enter and take possession of it.

When a man embarks on clearing his space in earnest these forces start opposing and afflicting and tormenting him. They are tricky and resourceful, skilled at exploiting emotional weaknesses, particularly fears and doubts and human ignorance of death. Here he can meet the self-willed, perverse, part-conscious, part-animal, part-human, part-divine and part-demonic forces that since time began have pressed for self-expression through man and his imagination.

Imagination is the battleground. But imagination is not just an abstract fantasy function. The further one gets into the psychic world and towards one's own vital reality, the more imagination becomes psychically substantial. Inner and outer, psyche and space conjoin. Thought lives.

Here, approaching the source of the man's vitality – his id – the phantoms actually come to life using his own residual energy without his suspecting it. Consequently, they are as strong as he is weak, as weak as he is strong. Panic is their ultimate strength.

A man ceases to be controlled by his imagination only by facing up to death and the psychic world and understanding both. In proportion as he does this the negative forces are rendered impotent and can no longer afflict him; his space is clear.

Many intellectual men feel they have their imagination firmly under control. They are untroubled by psychic forces and are dismissive of this part of reality.

But these men are protected by default. They have not yet begun the evolutionary phase of having to face up to death and the psychic reality. When they die they will enter the death world as dreaming shades, not as conscious individuals.

From such a mental distance as theirs the death world's reality appears like fanciful images. Such images, like death, can be rationalised away – but only so long as one is able to keep his distance, which no man can do for long.

If a man endeavouring to clear his space is deterred by the psychic forces that oppose and resist him, he certainly will be unable to face up to the reality of himself – his own psychic double.

The meeting will without doubt petrify him; it probably will happen at night. A man's psychic double is a living entity, immeasurably more powerful, base and terrifying in its perceived presence than a man can ever realise until he actually comes face to face with it.

This he must eventually do to gain conscious control of his part of the psychic world.

Mediums and clairvoyants may communicate with the world of the dead. But no human being may have conscious control in it while alive until he has confronted and dealt with the gigantic psychic presence of his own living past, the accumulation of a billion years, the door to life and reality.

11
The source of the world

The earth is a cosmic being whose mind — the terrestrial mind — is the earth's magnetic and gravitational field. This field extends out well beyond the orbit of the moon.

The outer region of the earth's enormous electro-magnetic field or mind is super-ionised, that is, kept abstract by rays from the sun and certain other stars. It is unimaginably cosmic, containing inconceivable future earth existences or cultures in which man has yet to participate. These represent the future potential of the race.

Closer into the earth but still outside the moon's orbit, the field/mind becomes less abstract and forms a thin sphere made up of a clustered overlay of innumerable disc-shaped concentrations of energy/knowledge.

These are earth ideas.

Earth ideas are ideas of the earth being itself, electrostatically, meaning in this case permanently, fixed in the terrestrial mind. Plato had glimpsed the sphere of earth ideas when he wrote of an originating world of ideas behind the physical world. All earth objects are the manifestation of earth ideas.

Initially, the notion of earth ideas may be difficult to grasp. The sense-dependent surface psyche identifies objects by differences, peculiarities, and pure idea has none of these. Horse, table, car — at the idea level — have no conceptual image, no ground for differentiation. Horse is horse. Whether black, brown or pied is incidental. All horses are horse.

In spite of their proximity to each other, earth ideas remain pristinely separate in the mind. None influences or blends with any other.

The sphere of earth ideas is the matrix behind the inevitability of shapes which all classes of earth things must take.
This guarantees that all earth objects are formed with the
same astonishing exactitude as crystals.

Precisely thirty-two classes of crystal shapes exist in the
solids of the earth. If crystals are suspended (melted or
dissolved) and left to cool or form they inevitably reshape
themselves into one of the thirty-two class-shapes. The
number does not vary, and the shapes do not mix. Snow
flakes, one of the thirty-two crystal forms, are always six-
sided.

The inevitability of the thirty-two classes of shapes which
crystal (as an example of earth ideas) will assume on physical
appearance is due to the effect the idea of crystal has on the
earth's magnetic field or mind. The presence of the idea
creates a magnetic warp in the immediately surrounding field
so that it dips or phases at thirty-two points.

Within these thirty-two phases are lesser dips and phases
which in turn cause the additional 230 variations known in
the thirty-two classes of crystal shapes. The pattern of
phases within phases continues until the individual crystal
(or horse or table) is electro-magnetically represented in
space/mind as a potential object.

Physical manifestation depends on the stepping down of
the cosmic *power* of the idea into *force*. This is done through
the medium of the psyche.

The psyche is a relatively substantial supersensitive plasma
extending in from the orbit of the moon. It is superbly
responsive, a perfect conductor of cosmic power, the energy
of earth ideas. But its substantial spongy consistency makes
it a medium that necessarily refracts and differentiates.

The cosmic power behind idea is spiritual. Cosmic and
spiritual power are one and the same. But power, spirit or
cosmic knowledge cannot be transmitted to the earth direct.
It has to come through the psychic plasma. Without the
psyche to differentiate it, spiritual energy/knowledge would
remain beyond human cognisance.

Immediately on entering the plasma the power/ideas are
broken down into force/information — psychic force/
information. The ideas now reduced to information lose

their power to remain pristinely separate. They superimpose on each other in qualifying relatedness. The idea of horse is modified by the idea of brown and other ideas. And the individual horse appears in the psyche with its distinguishing peculiarities.

The terrestrial intellect

The intellect we use is not individual. Nor is it the exclusive property of man. All the species use the same intellect although with varying degrees of intelligence.

The intellect has a definite fixed position. It consists of the inside of the sphere of earth ideas surrounding the psyche and the solid earth. While the ideas furthest out from the earth are few and loosely spaced, closer in they are so tightly packed that seen from the earth side they form a smooth, highly reflective electro-static surface.

The intellect reflects all psychic activity on earth, creating the awareness in which the current of earth intelligence operates. It is impenetrable to thought, that is, no human thought can pass out through it into the cosmic region of mind. Every conscious thought or concept bounces back off the intellect thus enabling the individual to reflect, conceive and reason.

Perception of the same objective natural world by all humanity and the species is due to two energies, one derived from the other, acting on the intellect from either side. The first, cosmic energy, acts on the idea side; the other, psychic energy, acts on the intellect from the earth side. Cosmic energy originating from outer mind (outer space) penetrates the sphere of ideas picking up the appropriate images of the natural world. This idealised energy continues undetected through the back of the intellect across the psyche into the collective unconscious represented by the inside of the solid body of the earth.

There the energy is converted by the sensing mechanism into sense-impressions of the idea and projected back to the intellect, which then reflects it in the individual's awareness as the physical world we all see.

The same intellect is used by the dead. The difference between the living dead and the dying living lies in the sensing mechanism, the dead living behind or inside it and the living outside it.

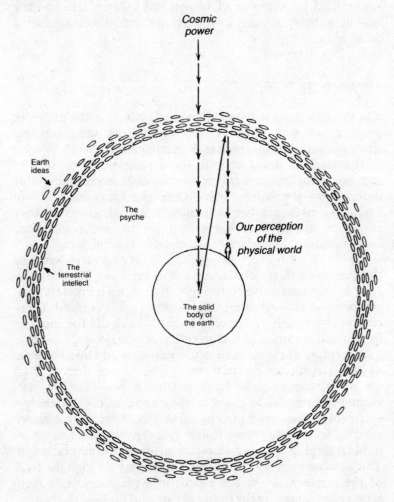

The Source of the World

The projected physical world

The external physical world is the projection of a real world, the world of ideas, on to the intellect. In effect, it is a reflection in matter or sense which is as relatively real — and as powerfully deceptive — as any reflection an observer is prepared to identify with.

Inside the external world, that is within the observer, is the vital world, the feeling world of the vital double. And within that vital world is the reality of all physical existence, the sun, moon and entire universe, not in the relatively flat perspective in which we observe it externally, but in its ideal, diamond-like splendour.

Man's vital double looks into this magnificent energetic world in a way similar to how we look out at our beautiful natural world — the real world's reflection.

However, it is our vital double's vision of the real world that supplies the joyous feelings behind our perceptions of the earth's beauty. What we see with the psyche 'out there' is devoid of such beauteous reality. Often we see the world as it is in all its emptiness and it is terrifying. Then we reconnect with the vision of our vital double and although nothing has changed life loses its drab, hopeless mundanity and is worth living again.

In life, and especially in death, man can consciously perceive the supernal real world direct through his vital double, but only as lucidly as he has managed while alive to free himself from identification with the reflected world and to that degree has united with his double.

Death — the reasonable reality

The psychological and vital roots of every man — his real id-entity as distinct from his persona — are in the world of the living dead.

It is self-evident that his roots are not here on the earth. What is here leaves here, disintegrates after each flowering — for it is man's lesser part though no less important.

His feelings are all within, his thoughts are all within, his pain all within, his satisfaction within, love within, ambitions within, dreams within.

The external world does not possess the reality each of us

ascribes to it. We know this and live this every moment through our immortal vital double. Otherwise we could not possibly go on.

A so-called reality that exists for perhaps eighty years is utterly intolerable; or it is tolerable simply because it is already known to be a relative reality.

Out of all the species only man has to live with the intolerable self-imposed concept of life with death at the end. It is just another theory, another partly observed fact that he has reasoned out for himself from his external sense-impressions. To the rest of the species, death and life have no reasonable span and no reasonable distinction.

The truth is that even man only regards death as a possible end when it is happening around him, which normally is very seldom. Otherwise, he lives confidently oblivious of it and utterly dismissive of his foolish reason.

Man only resorts to reasoning when he does not know something. As soon as he knows he ceases to reason. Reasoning can solve many of his worldly problems, for in many ways it is a reasonable world. But he cannot reason his own continuous vital existence; it is a self-evident truth which he can realise, feel for himself, at any moment.

Like the rest of the species man knows better about death — that it does not exist as an end. But because he does not consciously pause to realise he knows better, he reasons perversely. His reason cuts him off from the truth, from awareness of his immortality, the ever-present feeling of his true self, his vital double.

Never has there been a moment when any man knew he did not exist. He may reason through recollection and memory that he did not exist at some time but this is transparent assumption and speculation.

His external perception may tell him a person he loves has died. His external perception may weep. And yet he will still find it tolerable, reasonable, to continue to go on living and, as a race, to continue to die in the same old way, generation after generation, millennium after millennium. This is not reasonable. It is illogical and insane. But the absurdity of it fails to penetrate the reasoner because his vital psychic being already knows the lie of his lamentations, the half-truth of his reasoned fixed perceptions about death and the tolerable fact that he and all things have permanent vital life.

Senses that don't make sense

None of our senses is real.

None of our sense-organs can realise — that is, make known to itself — its own existence. Each sense is dependent on some other sense to verify its external existence. What this means is that each sense is manufactured or concocted by the other senses which themselves are not real.

The whole of the senses together — they form one vital nucleus in the unconscious — is real; but the differentiated versions appearing as nose/smelling, eyes/seeing, ears/hearing etc. are not.

The tongue cannot taste the tongue. Nor can the ear hear the ear. The eye cannot see the eye. The eye requires a reflective device (another eye) such as a mirror, or one of the other senses such as touch, to prove its existence.

We say we see: this is undeniable. However, it is imagination to say the eye sees what we see. It is impossible to prove the existence of the eye as an instrument of sight except by the negative means of obscuring, damaging or destroying it. But something cannot be proved to exist by the action of destroying it: that proves only that it does not exist. By resorting to such reasoning what we are trying to do is to prove that existence is non-existent. And that, too, is impossible.

Furthermore, our concept of body-shape is derived entirely from the evidence of these external 'senses'. Feeling such as that which tells us we are hungry cannot feel the body as our senses present it. When the fixed perceptions provided by the positional senses of sight and touch disappear, who can say what shape or form the body has?

The body has being, feeling, sensation, call it what you will. This sensation is its reality, its only positivity.

It is indeed the body which is our feeling, but not the body in the shape and appearance that our senses or fixed perceptions would have us believe. Our senses have produced a body that ages and dies. Sensation never ages, never dies. And although it may alter in frequency — as between pain and well-being — it is never absent.

The body, as indeterminate sensation, is the ground of our psychic existence, whether we are alive, dead or dreaming. This body cannot die. Only our fixed perceptions are seen to be dying. It is always some other body which is seen to be dying. If I should ever see my body dead then I cannot be dead. If I never see my body dead then death is an assumption.

This mind of mine which I am conditioned to imagine is confined to somewhere in my head, is not positional at all. My head is one of its fixed perceptions. If the head is taken away, as in sleep, where is outside, where is inside? All is just space or psyche in which heads and dreams are created every moment.

How necessary are our senses, our physical bodies? The senses are utterly necessary to physical existence. But they are not vital to our psychic or non-positional being. Which means that without our senses or bodies we still are.

Does this mean there is no physical world in reality?

No. It means there is no reality in the physical world except that which I provide. If the physical world were real, no one would die and no object would disappear.

The reality of the physical world lies first in the psychic world, in my vital double. But until I can get control of my own emotional space I can never discover this reality, or any other; I must go on dreaming and sensing it.

The fifth and sixth dimensions

External space — the sense-perceived world — contains no living or feeling thing.

It is defined as four-dimensional, everything in it being distinguished by length, breadth, thickness and time — or more simply, position. In spite of appearances, and by definition, no object or person in external space has feeling or sensation. Feeling and sensation are qualities exclusive to the fifth dimension which operates solely within the observer and is in fact his vital double, or the psychic world.

This is not an easy proposition to accept.

The most difficult part to grasp of the idea of the fifth dimension is that only one viewer-feeler exists in the world — the individual I who am viewing and feeling now. Any contention of plurality of viewers/feelers is assumption based on four-dimensional reasoning and has no truth outside of appearance.

Inevitably this raises the question of suffering observed in people and animals.

Such suffering exists only to the degree it creates compassion in the observer. If the observer is compassionately unmoved there is no pain in the other creature, only the appearance of it which is the assumption.

Compassion is vicarious suffering by one for another, the sole, albeit tenuous, virtue in the sense-perceived world.

Compassion alone has the power to end the appearance of pain in the world — the conditions in which our fellow-man and the species are observed to suffer. Moreover, by reducing the external conditions — hunger, injustice, cruelty, poverty, exploitation — compassion then has a reflex effect of actually reducing the reality of pain, that is, pain I the observer feel or will feel.

This began to manifest as a fact in the physical world less than 150 years ago with the introduction of chloroform. By virtue of the compassion the human race had acquired by then, the sixth-dimensional idea of anaesthetics — the sixth dimension is the world of idea — could be given to the world.

This was the first real step towards alleviating the reality of pain in man and the species. It exemplifies the higher self-regulating justice governing human existence. As only one feeling or fifth-dimensional being exists in the sense-perceived world — I, who am reading these words — so to the extent I am compassionate and help to eliminate the conditions and appearance of pain in the world do I reduce the actual reality of pain for myself.

This can be put another way. The reality of pain is the pain — physical or emotional — I actually feel. Although very real to me it has very little virtue — meaning evolutionary value — for me or humanity unless endured vicariously (borne for another); or unless my forbearance and patience in bearing it arouses the appearance of compassion in another so that they are moved to change the condition of the world causing it. This is the quality behind the appearance of social progress.

In both cases the evolutionary outcome is to save myself from pain at some future date whoever I may be.

From all this the future of pain in relation to the human race generally, and the individual specifically, can be safely stated. As the conditions of pain — poverty, cruelty, exploitation etc. — are eradicated from society by compassionate action — a fifth-dimensional response — so the reality of pain I actually feel will be progressively relieved by sixth-dimensionally inspired ideas for scientific advances such as pain- or disease-killing drugs, as well as expanded cosmic consciousness (also sixth-dimensional) which alleviates suffering in the individual through higher knowledge.

Part two

The birth of the earth

12
The seven levels of terrestrial mind

The creation process

There is one universal mind. In it are innumerable creation-points — stars — each of which is the centre of its own stellar mind.

The earth originated in the solar mind as a creative thought of the sun. This occurred long before the planet appeared in outer space.

For the sun's thought of the earth to become effective it first had to achieve the status or potential of an idea. This depended on it being favourably considered by the cosmic will. Only if it were affirmed by the will would it possess the necessary potential to continue to mature in the solar mind as a cosmic possibility in time.

Nothing in the creation process is certain. During the three phases, from thought to idea to cosmic existence, there is no certainty that a thought will become an idea or when an idea will manifest.

The profoundest thought, even though deriving from a mighty creative power like the sun, can be still-born. The universal mind is filled with myriads of non-existent possibilities, thoughts that have emerged from the creative stratum of mind — the stars — but have not yet been validated by the will. Time and existence are the uncertainty of their becoming or not becoming.

Creation involves incalculable time and complexity of action by will and intelligence.

Intelligence is the condition of mind. That is, it varies in degree according to the mind expressing it. In this case the vast intelligence of the solar mind was behind the thought/idea.

Will stands behind mind, entering and pervading it at will. Will is extra-cosmic. No intelligence can ever grasp what will is.

The closest word to describe will is purpose. At no level does intelligence know what the purpose of creation is. A creative power can only be aware of the idea, the object of its willing. And idea is merely a part of purpose as is any object or objective. Purpose is the will's inviolable secret.

The will's consideration of the sun's earth-thought was not dissimilar to what occurs in the human mind or psyche. When a creative thought forms in the psyche the will either attaches itself to it, or it does not. If not, nothing happens. Some of man's 'best ideas' never mature.

The sun's earth-thought did mature. The will embraced it and it became an idea deemed within the purpose of things to be cosmically feasible in time. This act of validation by the will allowed the earth idea to structure or occupy a permanent place of its own in the mind: the terrestrial mind within solar mind.

No idea can remain in the mind or psyche without moving towards outer existence. The surge of the will is always towards manifestation.

But the gap between the highest cosmic creative levels of mind and the human psyche in which the sense-perceived physical universe appears is inconceivably large. Any idea deriving from such an august, abstract reality as the sun has no means of manifesting in its original state in sense or matter. The character of the idea is too refined to allow it to become substantial, to make sense: matter is too coarse a medium to respond in form and shape, rendering existence impossible.

The solution to this problem is the seven levels of terrestrial mind.

By strength of will the power of the original idea is stepped down and held in four permanent states of deepening density. These in turn are divided into seven levels of terrestrial mind. Original purity and simplicity are intentionally sacrificed to form ever more densifying and differentiating strata of forces, energies and information. What began as unity — the pristine seventh level idea of the earth — degenerates into an actual world of simulated sense experience. Unity becomes duality, multiplicity and finally infinite complexity so that the idea which cannot really be can be seen or sensed to be. In the space between Level Seven and Level One mind becomes matter.

*   *   *

The sun's earth-thought formed the nucleus, the original seventh level of the terrestrial mind. In the beginning it was all there was of the earth. The other six levels were added gradually one by one over what we must regard as an enormous stretch of time.

All seven levels of terrestrial mind are embodied in man.

Level One is his awareness of the outer world or physical universe.

Level Two is where he thinks and dreams, his subconscious.

Level Three is where he sleeps dreamlessly and survives death, and which he has very little knowledge and experience of. This is his unconscious.

Separating Levels Three and Four is a narrow area I have called the Band of Death.

Level Four is man's individual evolving soul.

Level Five is his true soul.

In Level Six, as the will or great Self, man upholds and creates all the levels below.

And in Level Seven he is the consciousness of the earth itself, literally the spirit of humanity, the cosmic Lord of the earth.

*   *   *

The four states or densities of terrestrial mind are:

First, the spiritual or cosmic state forming Levels Seven and Six. This is consciousness, the awareness supporting all intelligence.

Second, pure mental energy or intelligence, the state forming Levels Five and Four.

Third, psyche, the state forming Levels Three and Two.

Fourth, sense or matter, the state forming the material outer world of Level One.

Reversing the image of Level Seven as the nucleus of terrestrial mind it can be said that consciousness, the first state, supports and makes possible the other three. Inside consciousness is intelligence. Inside intelligence is the psyche. And the focal point of all three is the sense-perceived physical world.

*   *   *

The first distinguishing peculiarity of mind is individual consciousness. That is to say, everyone experiences themselves as I. This I persists in dreaming and at all levels up to the highest seventh level of terrestrial mind.

Each of these seven levels is an actual world. This can be appreciated by considering the first three levels which every normal person is familiar with.

The first level of sense perception is a real world of existence.

The second level of dreaming, even though it has a different quality to Level One, is experienced as a real state of being. At the time of dreaming we can experience the full range of emotions while performing impossible feats which at times are so real we dismiss our own suggestion that we are dreaming.

Level Three is the level of dreamless sleep — another real state of existence. We spend a third of our life there; we enjoy it, look forward to it and usually feel better after it. We may not feel so good after a bad dream; but those dream images are in Level Two. Sleep without dreaming, the third level of our mind, is as real a part of life as any, even though we may be oblivious in it.

We accept these three levels as normal. Normal is precisely what they are, as they mark the limit of normal or natural man's experience. Natural man cannot pass beyond Level Three into the higher levels of mind until, while still alive, he passes through the Band of Death. Intrinsic to this transition is the astonishing realisation of immortality, that beyond any doubt he is the immortal 'I' of individual consciousness.

13
The higher levels of mind

Level Seven — the world of the first idea

In the same way as a man experiences himself to be an individual in the outer sense-perceptive world of Level One, so seven layers within he can experience himself as the sublime consciousness of the one earth being.

Level Seven of terrestrial mind is experienced as pure, glorious spirit, perfection, the Heavenly Lord, the Blessed Earth and the one body of mankind where no other exists.

On realisation Level Seven is apperceived as Paradise, a literal garden of Eden identical in one single feeling/image with all of man's most rapturous moments of love of nature combined: as he has ever smelled, heard, tasted, seen and felt the earth to be in all its fullness. Except that here this fullness is experienced as a single unified being free from need of differentiation into sense objects like trees, clouds, sea, sky and creatures which in manifested nature excite man's wonder and love.

Moreover, this one originating beauteous Being of the earth does not vary or diminish. It is realised to be constant, divinely eternal, perfect in the unalterable substance of endless mind and spirit. Level Seven is the Buddhist Nirvana and the Hindu place or state of reunion with Brahman, the Highest.

At this seventh level of terrestrial mind there are no competing individual desires or interests to create war, conflict or pain. Only one being is present, one Earth, one impossibly sweet nature — the essence of the being we call the planet earth, the one and only Man. This finally is what

I am as earth man.

At Level Seven the earth-man consciousness ends. But although the end of a cosmic phase of mind it is not the end of mind. Profounder levels exist as solar mind — perhaps requiring solar or cosmic man to realise them.

Level Six — the world of will and impersonal love

Before a man can enter Level Seven he has to have realised Level Six, the level of Self-realisation. Self-realisation is achieved through a long cathartic preparation of right self-inquiry and meditation, right company, right instruction, right suffering and right self-centredness.

Spiritual progress of any kind is possible only because each of the seven levels of mind exists as a real, separate, interacting world or division of knowledge. Without these levels there would be no way or stages into the truth-seeker's mind and all aspirations towards reality would be pointless.

Consequently, Level Six realisation invests all men who have it with the same unmistakable knowledge and authority even if they have never heard of the terms Self-realisation, Level Six or been a reader of books. The truth is in the level of the mind, not in any description of it.

The will formed Level Six out of itself by embracing the pure earth idea of Level Seven.

While Level Seven consists of idea only, Level Six combines idea and will. Will introduces power into the mind, creating the first duality. This duality divides Level Six into two halves: one static, the other dynamic.

The will itself forms the first half of Level Six nearest to Level Seven, holding the earth idea in a mighty potential of unexpressed, unstirring but infinitely knowing creative poise or purpose.

This is what the Hindu tradition calls the Purusha, the single ever-present, all-present almighty Self or Person, the unknowable origin which many mystics have realised in its indescribable, pervasive intimacy as the 'nothingness' which yet is everything.

Level Six Self-realisation being in itself the realisation of the will may be regarded as the highest realisation — for nothing can be higher than the nothing that is everything. Even so, Self-realisation does not necessarily permit access through this 'nothing that is all' to the pure idea of terrestrial mind at Level Seven. That requires the rarest of all recorded realisations.

Level Seven realisation is possible only with the consent of the guardian will at Level Six. And that consent is embodied in mankind. At the sixth level of mind mankind is empowered to decide who, as surrogate for his fellow man in different ages, shall realise the central idea of the earth and report back, thus ensuring that the truth and knowledge of it never leave the world of living men.

The outer half of Level Six abutting Level Five is the dynamic aspect of will in the mind — action. Action at this level is identical with all motion and movement in the world at any moment. When realised, this font of action at Level Six is seen as universal (impersonal) love.

Love is the creating element in terrestrial mind. This inspires the not infrequent insight that love is the Creator and that love is all.

Level Five — the world of true soul

Level Five of mind is the world of true soul. It is the spirit of will and idea in Levels Seven and Six stepped down into pure mental energy — the second state of terrestrial mind.

Level Five contains the true soul of every human being who has ever lived. Each soul is a unique facet of the original earth idea of man and all combine here — without ever having been separated — to represent one extraordinary, indivisible soul or character.

True soul is eternity. It is realised as individual consciousness — 'I' — and at the same time as ultimate unity. Man realising the soul at Level Five (and many have) knows he is one with all, that all things are in him and that he is in all things.

It is an astonishing experience for I the individual to feel so personally privileged (and yet so personally insignificant or perhaps unworthy) as to be the very centre of this one indestructible, universal continuum of unlimited life.

The world of true soul sometimes manifests sense-perceptively at Level One as the spirit of humanity, the living spirit. When this appears in a man it is the rare phenomenon of transfiguration. Without exception, to see it in man conveys the immediate conviction: 'this is the living God'.

Being perfect, man's true soul or the world of soul never alters. Neither does it participate in the levels and planes of existence below. Its role is static: it is the shining exemplar, the self-luminous image in which all forms of life and existence strive to perfect themselves in the trauma of evolution.

Level Five is the quintessence which the Greeks intuited as the fifth element of creation. It is what the late gnostics called the divine body of the anthropos (the one Man) suspended in eternity.

Level Five also contains all the eternal ideas which soul (man) uses or draws upon in his evolutionary progress. Here is Plato's archetypal idea of table, triangle, tree. As all ideas come to man or from man out of this profound region of mind — even the idea of soul and man himself — Level Five may also be called the world of Ideals.

Level Four — the world of evolving soul

Level Four of mind contains the evolutionary soul, or as it is called in this philosophy, the empiric soul, of every human being living and dead.

The empiric soul is not perfect. It is what the individual man is now. It represents in pure mental energy the image the man has managed to make of himself through endless earth experience of striving towards the ideal of his true soul in Level Five above.

Every man's experiential approximation of his true soul to date is here in Level Four. Whether he is dead or alive makes no difference. Only in the denser levels below is the drama of life and death enacted. In Level Four the living dead and the dying living are the same, both evolving slowly as their empiric souls towards the supreme ideal. Here there is no death. This is the level where immortality is realised.

The realisation of immortality

A man realising immortality while still alive is experiencing the state of his evolutionary soul at that moment.

This does not mean he experiences himself as being any different to what he normally is: how could he when his empiric soul is always himself as he is now?

But what does astound and amaze him is the realisation that what he is now is and always has been immortal.

He sees that he must go on living as a person whatever lies ahead. He may even feel like a lamb going to the slaughter inasmuch as he must continue to live and die. But he knows it does not matter — wonder of wonders, he is forever!

The realisation of immortality is probably the most splendid step man ever makes into the mind. Realisations of the other levels undoubtedly are more profound in abstract ways. But the realisation of immortality is the first in which man gives the lie to his fiercest dread — death. Nothing can ever quite equal the astonishment of this first stupendous freedom from the universal lie.

Evolution

Evolution is the attempt to reproduce in Level Four a replica of the true and perfect soul above. Theoretically, when this is achieved the soul's or man's life on earth will be perfect; the mythic Paradise or Kingdom of Heaven will have come to earth.

But just as the empiric soul evolves here, so also do the ideas which man uses and perceives.

For example, the original idea of table is permanently fixed at Level Five. No one knows precisely what this idea is. But its energy is constantly present in man's mind at Levels Two and One (where he thinks and perceives); and his attempts to reproduce this ideal table in all the myriads of tables he makes in the world are recorded as the single, evolving, formless image of table in Level Four.

In Level Four the world of ideals becomes the world of progress towards the ideal. Here occurs the first movement in the mind as each empiric soul and idea adjust in shade and tone to the evolutionary changes occurring in the forms below. Here is preserved the real significance of changing fashion, style, preferences and tastes, all variations of the classical moving in time towards the ideal — progress.

The Band of Death

The Death Band between Levels Four and Three separates immortal man from mortal man. To mortal man it is the ring-pass-not. All men are immortal but few realise it.

To die physically is not to realise immortality, and the Death Band does not pertain to physical death. Physical death occurs well below it. This death is psychological and/or emotional and is gone through while the body and person are fully alive and active.

Psychological and emotional death are simultaneous in my experience. But in the last few years a notable tendency has developed among the people I teach apparently to realise psychological death only, or first.

This probably means one of two things. Either there has been a change in the human unconscious minimising the intensity of emotional death and rendering it less apparent than I and others experienced it; or the people who realise psychological death have yet to realise emotional death. I suspect the latter is the case. Even so, the truth will only be determined by time and the experience in the world of those who have realised what I here call psychological death.

Psychological death is the realisation that death is an illusion and that whether the body dies or continues to live is irrelevant. It is accompanied by relatively brief though intense feelings of love and beauty. But mainly it is an experience of pure comprehension and direct knowledge which raises enormously the individual's sensitivity to impersonal beauty, love and divine power. Whereas indirect knowledge received through the senses and reason inevitably creates doubt and the need for more knowledge, direct knowledge from within dissolves doubt and eliminates the need to know more.

The psychological experience of death brings a vivid new permanent state of inner clarity which may be described as the realisation of space. Space becomes indescribably clear and pristine, enabling objects and facts to be seen in a finer and sharper all-inclusive perspective. This realisation in fact represents the cessation of naming in the individual — the end of that chronic, conscious and subconscious habit of all men which perpetuates the existence of the false, superficial, intervening self.

Emotional death on the other hand is filled with feeling. It is the realisation of immortality accompanied by the full joy of release from the mortal emotional self or burden, and the realisation of the individual's oneness with all life and purpose whatever that might be.

If the two deaths are to be experienced separately, psychological death is likely to precede the other. But both are the outcome of a relentless search for truth or self-knowledge.

Emotional death is by far the more painful and personally distressing and is almost certain to include psychological death if that has not already occurred.

Emotional death usually occurs in circumstances causing agonising emotional disturbance. This is of an intensity that can be equated with the mystic's insane unrequited love of the divine, or with the loss or death of the most loved person in the individual's life (who may actually have been neglected or abandoned because of the search for the truth). There is likely to be some awareness of having caused wretched suffering to others through the uncompromising stand of having put the search for truth before any other consideration.

14
The planes of existence

Life from the moon

Existence is such a familiar and dominant condition of mind that it does not occur to man to question it. He questions his own existence and the existence of everything else but not the existence of existence. Existence he assumes to be the ineluctable permanent state of things. But for man it is only the necessary temporary condition of things. Conditions change but states do not.

Level Three is the beginning and end of existence.

Here the whole drama of life, death and survival-after-death receives the very peculiar, very strange substance of existence.

It could be said that Level Three is all that exists. The higher levels of mind are purely potential, dependent for their expression on life at this level, while Levels Two and One below are its shadows or its stage.

Everything that has ever been known or experienced or ever will be known or experienced must happen here in this existence. And this existence is due solely to the astonishing substance of Level Three.

Level Three consists of moon plasma. To describe this plasma I use the term relative substantiality.

Although the universe ultimately is beyond relative substantiality and is only in the higher mind, the moon plasma enables man to apprehend the universe as something existing outside the mind.

The moon orbits Level Three, investing it with its own life-force. The moon appears to be a dead planet because its essence is being drained from it and used to produce life on earth.

However, this is not an involuntary draining. Relative substantiality is a gift to the earth, a magnificent cosmic gesture of self-sacrifice by the moon whose selfless life-force is evolving as a result of it. In this aeon of existence – which eventually will be dissolved and refashioned by the cosmic will according to the law of karma or evolution – the moon and the earth are permanently linked as twin planets. But through its votive offering as part of its own cosmic evolution the moon one day will be a cosmic being supporting life and intelligence in its own right.

The Blue Plane – Vita

Relative substantiality is the third or psychic state of mind. Originally this was a pool of pure moon plasma.

Moon plasma is an absolutely unself-conscious medium. Although essentially alien to the other energies of terrestrial mind it is perfect for their expression. It is never perceived as itself and has no quality besides supreme plasticity and receptivity to the higher-mind influences of intelligence and spirit.

Level Three was formed by a focus of attention – what I call the primary attention – descending on to the pool from Level Six. The effect was to impress or characterise the moon plasma with will and the idea of the earth, so transforming the plasma into the fundamental substance of terrestrial existence – the elemental, principling factor behind the appearance of life and sense. I have named this substance Vita.

This descent of the primary attention is recorded in the myth of Genesis:

'And the earth was without form and void; and darkness was upon the face of the deep' – the Level Three pool of pure moon plasma. 'And the spirit of God [will and idea as the primary attention from Level Six] moved upon [impressed itself upon] the face of the waters' – and vita, the beginning of all life, light and form was created.

110

The whole of Level Three now consisted of elemental vita, whose colour is blue. Vita is the Blue Plane, the first of the three planes of Level Three and the stuff out of which the other two planes of existence were to be formed.

Vita is the finest of the planes of Level Three. It has no external quantity or quality outside of the massed appearance we call existence. Just as the biologist's line between life and death can never be drawn outside of artificial parameters, vita cannot be defined. It can only be described and felt as 'life'. From this point of view nothing on earth can be said to be dying: it is decaying, eroding, disappearing, disintegrating or changing. Life goes on. That which goes on behind the flux of changing and vanishing forms is vita.

Fundamentally beyond human comprehension, vita is the power, purpose and mystery behind existence, matter and all the laws of science and physics. It contains all the force of unconscious matter enabling it to explode, disintegrate and destroy when given the right trigger — whether that trigger is a human mind exploding an atom bomb or the devastating elemental fury of weather or volcanic activity. Such phenomena are indeed under the omniscient control of the will due to the permanent divine focus of attention from Level Six. But this control, like the purpose behind it, is inscrutable to us and amounts to nothing but seemingly blind elemental force or nature.

The creation of sense

Vita is the indefinable essence of the sense-perceived world. Through it the primary attention creates the physical universe of Level One.

But it does this in sense only. That is, it does not create an external universe as we perceive it. Most economically and incredibly, it creates the whole external appearance through the sense of sense inherent in the Blue Plane of the mind and common to all sense perception.

In other words, the physical universe has no objective external existence. There is no universe or world 'out there'. What we see is a subjective experience, a process within the mind, within the individual, us. The external world is a product of the sense-complex lodged deep in the unconscious, in the elemental Blue Plane.

This is not to suggest that the universe is insubstantial. Level One is unarguably a sensible reality common to all things having senses and sensible relationship. Relationship, as the power to affect and be affected by other things and forces, is the substance of the world.

Just as terrestrial mind is one mind, so the primary attention is the one fundamental attention in all men. Therefore, every individual man perceives the world exactly as it is to all other men — mountains are seen as mountains, sea as sea, people as people and so on.

The Yellow Plane

What allows the world to be perceived at all is the Yellow Plane.

The Yellow Plane was created by a secondary focus of attention descending on to vita from Level Five. This formed the plane of pure intellect and intelligence, the etherial or quintessential plane. The Yellow Plane is the means of intelligent reflection in the psyche.

Due to this second focus of attention the Yellow Plane covered two-thirds of Level Three leaving Blue Plane vita occupying the one-third section nearest to Level Two.

The Yellow Plane is intelligence without self.

The Red Plane

The feeling of self is supplied by the Red Plane.

The Red Plane is formed by a third focus of attention descending on to the Yellow Plane, this time from Level Four, the level of man's empiric soul. This permanent attention impresses the individual person's evolutionary condition of soul on to the half of the Yellow Plane next to the Blue. This then becomes self or emotion — the Red Plane.

The order of the planes is then Blue next to Level Two,

Red in the middle, and Yellow next to Level Four, each covering a third of Level Three. The Yellow Plane is formed out of the Blue and the Red out of the Yellow.

The Red Plane is man's emotional or past self; the Yellow Plane is his intellect; while the Blue Plane supplies his sense of senses which creates matter and the physical universe.

Being the world of self, the Red Plane also is the world of attachments. Here originate man's exclusive feelings of individuality arising from his emotional attachments to people, objects, concepts and conditions.

Thus, billions of people on earth are able to perceive the same physical world and yet by emotional identification create 'my' mother, 'my' country, 'my' house, 'my' body, thereby producing an extraordinarily complicated and completely subjective world within the naturally objective world.

At death, the individual withdraws into the Red Plane and survives there.

The nine powers of existence

Level Three consists of nine powers of existence. The Blue is by far the most powerful of the three planes, accounting for five-ninths or more than half of the powers of existence. In addition, the other planes are formed out of it. Next is the Yellow Plane with three powers. And last is the Red with one.

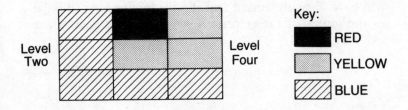

The three planes are different energies together making up a field so vast and complex that it accounts for the entire sense-perceived universe and all life, as well as the worlds of survival after death.

They blend to produce a single effect — existence — in a way similar to the blending of the seven colours in white light. But as any segment of sunlight contains the seven separate colour-frequencies, so any segment of life or existence contains the three planal frequencies in the proportions stated above.

However, there is one variation which although not affecting the principle of existence does change the condition of man's existence. In most people and for most of their lives, one of the Yellow Plane powers of intellect is persistently invaded by Red Plane emotion or self:

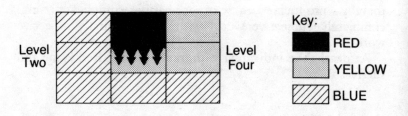

This means that the part of the man's being which should be pure, clear intellect or intelligence is constantly coloured and confused by emotional considerations.

Personal evolution enables the individual gradually to pull back the incursive self, thus clarifying his mind or intellect. When this is achieved the individual can be said to have aligned his powers or attained equilibrium: the self-perpetuating habit of continual naming, thinking and self-considering will have virtually ceased and the instinctive survival impulse — the source of the emotional self — will be back where it belongs.

15
The authentic being
in the world

Level Two of terrestrial mind is the subconscious. We think, dream and perceive here.

But this is the tip of the iceberg.

Beneath these images is our real being, what I call the Authentic Being in the World.

The authentic being is our unchanging reflective state, our permanently open window to the three worlds of waking, dreaming and unconsciousness. Whether we are awake, dreaming, unconscious or dying it is always present and alert, impartially reflecting and recording all that is going on in all three worlds at once.

Man (as we know ourselves now) is where his attention is at any moment. He cannot simultaneously be awake and asleep, or unconscious and dreaming. His attention is either on or in one world or another, never consciously on or in two or all three together. But his authentic being is. To us, such simultaneity of perception is impossible because we have not yet understood or penetrated to the timeless profundity and depth of our own being.

The authentic being is the connecting thread along which our attention travels between these three worlds. It originates in Level Four in the individual's empiric soul, runs down through the Yellow, Red and Blue planes of Level Three and ends behind the eyes in the subconscious of Level Two.

It represents the mental aspect of our being. The Red Plane of Level Three represents our feeling self, the emotional aspect of our being. The two combine to be what we are at any moment — our empiric, evolving self.

The mental energy of our Level Two aware-and-thinking self has a very close affinity with the Yellow Plane. But unlike the Yellow Plane it has experience in it.

As the representative in the world of our Level Four evolving soul, the authentic being retains the record of our evolutionary progress in this life, and in our life of survival after death.

When a man goes to sleep his attention travels back from Level One along the thread of his authentic being into the subconscious (Level Two) and/or the unconscious (Level Three). When he dies he makes the same journey only the thread linking Levels One, Two and Three is snapped and he survives in the three planes of Level Three.

In death, his authentic being remains the link between these planes. And after an important period of concentrated attention in the Red Plane he finally ascends up the thread through the Yellow Plane and the Death Band to his empiric soul in Level Four — to the end of himself, and a new beginning.

The rape of the authentic being

Contained in Level Three in the Red (emotional) and Blue (elemental) planes is sex energy, the libido. Sex is the energy of death and the past — that is, instinct and emotion that has survived death — forever striving to perpetuate and express itself again in life. It is the energy of the unconscious striving to attain to self-consciousness.

Sex, the libido, is the driving force behind all self-interested action. It is the irresistible pressure behind every thing man has ever desired or dreaded, forcing itself through his mental images at Level Two to colour and distort his view of the world and himself. It is the living past rising to impel us, often against our will and better judgment, to repeat experiences good or bad for the sake of sheer experience.

Sandwiched between this awful pressure and the world is the authentic being, man's innocence. Its position is one of almost unbearable conflict.

From Level Six the will exerts an irresistible urge and longing in all men for inner knowledge — for the authentic being to turn inward away from the outer world of experience towards the pristine higher levels of mind. But the impersonal elemental force and emotion from Level Three together exert an almost unbearable outward pressure on the authentic being struggling towards that deeper consciousness. The Red and Blue pressure of substantiality drives men to madness while the counter-urge of the abstract will endeavours to prevent madness. The hideous paradox of the will from Level Six fighting with itself as will-created vita symbolises the battle of the spirit against matter, soul against unbridled desire, principle against expediency.

* * *

Each man's physical body is in Level One. Inside the physical body is his mental or authentic being in Level Two. And inside that in Level Three, putting on the pressure and driving man's authentic being into the world and nearly out of his senses at times, is his psychic self, his emotional and vital body.

From Level Five through the abstract Yellow Plane the authentic being is under a constant though imperceptible pull to 'return home', to let go of the transitory world — to surrender identification with the emotional and vital self's demands and rise to be united forever with the divine self, the man's own true soul.

But again the authentic being is powerless to obey its higher longings. Every man is tortured by doubts and fears about his life and self, feels insecure, inadequate and confused and longs for the peace he knows is possible but never seems able to attain.

The element of self, or emotion, always intervenes.

Self is the distance between our authentic being and our true souls. That distance or intensity of self is measured evolutionarily in our need to experience the world. While we yearn for the world we yearn for self and are Red Plane mortal beings.

That degree of self in each of us is where we are actually at in the evolutionary stakes. Until we are free of the need of the world, until we have overcome the world not by force but by understanding, we must drive forever outward to experience what we lack and need.

From the moment of birth — which is the recurring restatement of our emotional need of the sense-world — this relentless pressure of the vital body drives the authentic being out into the physical world. It forces it to identify with sense perceptions. The authentic being has no choice but to register these perceptions on the embracing vital self. Closer and closer that body presses against the authentic being until both seem to be one.

By the time the rape is complete — coincident with puberty or the twelfth to fourteenth year — the authentic being is convinced it is entirely dependent on the emotional self and the physical body for its happiness and survival. Death alone breaks the delusive bond.

Yellow Plane consciousness

In deep dreamless sleep, when all our physical and emotional dependencies and desires disappear, we are in the Yellow Plane and are perfectly content. Awake, we are seldom content for long. And our dreams (expressions of self) frequently leave us disturbed and unhappy. Self, clambering for emotional expression through the senses and our dreams, is the main cause of man's discontent and dissatisfaction. It can never get enough of life and finally is baulked completely by old age and death.

While we are in need of material and sensational consciousness — that is, while we live as though our physical body and emotions were all we consist of — we are unable to appreciate or tolerate a finer, less substantial reality. We cannot bear the peace and ease of Yellow Plane being. The lack of inner conflict and desiring becomes boredom.

But when the need for physical and emotional stimulation becomes the lesser part of a man due to the realisation of life's impermanence and through having had enough of pleasure-and-pain living, he can gradually begin to withdraw into his Yellow Plane consciousness. Then consciousness as distinct from self-consciousness is no longer felt to be the denial of being or life. When consciousness is free and emptied of self, I remain and neither life nor death nor dreamless sleep can obscure my reality.

The man eventually feels, and then knows, he is being informed in every moment of everything he needs to know about life and death without the necessity for emotional or physical participation to teach him the hard way.

The hard way — alternating pain and pleasure — is the constant demand of a self-conscious existence.

16
Survival after death

A person dying violently and instantly often experiences a temporary continuity of external awareness of the fatal events in which he was involved.

His awareness is sustained by a combination of two factors: first the fact that his attention at the time of death was directed outward through the senses; and second by the explosive release of his vital and emotional being into the space or psyche around him.

This explosion away from the body into the surrounding psychic field is typical of all degrees of shock and, in extremes like violent death or the threat of it, provides the medium for a temporary psychic presence to be maintained outside the physical.

If more than one person is killed in the same incident, or there are casualties or spectators, the intensity of the psychic field is compounded and the affected area extended. There can be two lots of people moving around the same scene — the dead and the living.

In the moments preceding a fatal accident the victim is usually extraordinarily unemotional, almost indifferent as he observes the succession of events leading up to the instant of his death. A kind of slow-motion detachment occurs.

This is because the person's emotional self has already left the body and is charging the immediate psychic field. Emotionally he is outside himself. When self is dispersed the capability for feeling reaction is minimal and the authentic being or 'I' registers the scene in images alone.

Also, in such perilous moments of shock the authentic being can be externalised in the emotion. But the dispersed condition of the self reduces the degree of emotional identification so that again the person frequently witnesses the whole scene with detachment, this time from a point outside and above his own body.

Death of the body severs the connecting authentic thread to the senses; the externalised awareness diminishes and vanishes. The individual's distended emotional self gradually contracts to re-form his psychic body behind or inside the senses. The person is then in the Blue Plane of Level Three, unconscious or in a dream state.

*   *   *

A person dying gradually and non-violently first withdraws into Level Two of the mind, the subconscious world of imaging and dreaming. This enables him to have glimpses of the forces of the Blue, Red and Yellow Planes of Level Three.

His attention shifts between Levels Two and One. To an observer he may seem semi-conscious and rambling. To himself, he possesses all his perceptive powers although what he is perceiving may be beyond his ability to comprehend or describe. He may simply lack the means, or the will, to communicate consciously to those by his side at Level One.

Death occurs when the attention finally sinks into the Blue Plane, the elemental universal unconscious. This marks the start of the cathartic passage of the man's awareness through the essential forces which appear in life as his physical body.

Each plane of Level Three contains a purgative or cathartic energy which provides the means for the dead person to evaluate as self-knowledge the experience he has accumulated in the life just ended.

The Blue Plane is a tremendously high energy source, one of whose functions is to break down biological matter and extract all emotion. Such primal energy if experienced consciously provokes awesome, if not dreadful and terrifying perceptions. Even unconsciously its effects after death are disturbing. The living often experience it at night as a nightmare in which impossible tasks have to be performed or faced.

121

The Blue Plane is the reality behind our concepts of the physical interior of the earth such as stygian darkness and molten core. From fixed perceptions of Blue Plane energy have derived the impressions of hell-fire and the sense of hopelessness attached to being confined in such a sunless underworld. This world *is* the body — the matter of it, not the form.

The function of the Blue Plane is essential (not vital); it sustains the life-force intrinsic in all matter. The vital functions of organisms are secondary and are a Red Plane phenomenon. When vitality is cut off by the will through the Blue Plane these functions come to a stop. Red Plane self has no power over life and death.

After death this Blue Plane energy disintegrates the body, removing every bit of emotional content from every cell. The breaking down of the physical body by the Blue Plane elemental energies appears externally as decomposition. However, the inner process is completed in a much swifter time-frame. Respect for the dead and ceremonies and traditions that create an interval between death and destruction of the corpse are instinctive acknowledgments of the time normally required for the process to be completed.

After extraction of all emotion, the remaining pure energy/matter of the body returns to the Blue Plane reservoir of earth elements out of which all forms, organic and otherwise, are ceaselessly being created.

The extracted emotion combines with the person's emotional self which then passes on to enter the Red Plane for evaluation by Red Plane energy.

* * *

The Red Plane is the world of life after death. Everyone who dies has a relative experience of the death world — relative because no dead person experiences it exactly as another does.

Here on the earth the emphasis is on a fixed formal world, the constant structure we perceive. But in the death world the individual person literally creates his own world moment to moment.

He does this by re-experiencing his own emotional self or past.

When a person passes into the Red Plane after death, the world he enters is literally his own emotional self. But he does not see or realise the world around him as being himself any more than before death he saw the physical world as a projection coming from the Blue Plane within his own unconscious.

His awareness, instead of being at the centre of his own sense projections (the physical universe) is now at the centre of his own emotions. The position has reversed. Instead of looking out at the world and feeling his emotional responses within, his own emotions or feelings are what he actually perceives as the new world around him.

At the moment of dying, the life he has lived often unrolls before him without any emotion arising. This happens in his flash passage across the subconscious of Level Two. But now he is dead and in the Red Plane the emotional re-living begins. He feels he has only to think of someone or something to which he is attached for it to appear, or for him to be there. He does not realise, however, that such thoughts are prompted by his emotional condition and that he is completely controlled by this re-run through his own emotions or past.

As self, no one can ever hope to declare all he is attached to. Often the strongest attachments only reveal themselves at the time they are threatened or severed. A person can seem completely detached from the world and unemotional, and yet after death know tremendous longing and need. Such longings and need are the fixation-power of the self; and the self's infinite possibilities for attachment to things and conditions make the death world a uniquely relative personal experience.

However, even though in the Red Plane after death each man creates a world of his own, he cannot disengage himself from the reality of the earth.

Dead or alive, man's invincible, controlling passion is for life as it is lived, or may be lived, on earth.

Living and death are two poles of the one complete earth life. Living is the positive conscious pole. Death is the negative unconscious pole.

The undercurrent in death, unconsciousness and sleep is always towards the earth, recurrence in the world of the living. The earth is the centre of all that man living or dead can know and wish for: there is no other existence he can aspire to. Any other life he imagines is merely the hazy perception of a facet of his or humanity's future.

Man while he is dead returns to the earth frequently. But he does so in the negative mode, via the unconscious.

The unconscious streams down on to the surface of the earth from the direction of outer space. We, the living, perceive against or into the stream. This dynamic thrust induces the conscious, positive mode of earth life − sense perception.

The dead travel down this unconscious, negative stream. Looking consciously into the incoming stream we are unable to see the visiting dead. But with their negative perception they can see us. Stripped of our physical form − it is purely a positively induced phenomenon − we are essentially negative beings like the dead.

Similarly, the earth is a negative psychic structure. The dead perceive it in all its natural fullness, can participate in its elements as we do but without physical restriction, and are able to observe the affairs of the world or people to whom they are drawn − all without the knowledge of the living.

The dead person returns to that part of the world or earth and to those things objectifying his strongest unconscious attachments.

These may not be what he considered his deepest desires while alive. Once dead and in Level Three the man is freed from the Level Two subconscious and its superficial memory which during his lifetime was responsible for most of his explicit attachments and concerns. These may now have no meaning at all for him. In death man has entered the deeper unconscious part of his memory where his true attachments and desires reveal themselves. Thus no man's evolutionary status can be safely judged on his current life: his nature, personality and behaviour may be no true indication.

His first experience in the death world is of the place,

object or person closest to his heart. This may be someone alive or dead. If alive he will perceive the person as they are on the earth. If dead he will be united with them in the world of the dead. If another dead person is an enemy or the victim of an action that caused intense guilt, a confrontation will occur but without any overt conflict outside of what he himself registers. This can be a violent experience for him depending on the force of emotion involved; but inevitably it is salutary.

Anything a man wants or is drawn to he can do as long as it does not require a conscious earthly response or the sharing of other dead people's emotions beyond a limited degree.

If he wants to fly over oceans, cities or other parts of the earth, he can. In this he can be described as the past flying over the present. He can perceive the earth exactly as it is and yet have no effect on it except through living people and their emotions. He can move freely among the living but to make his presence felt he must use emotion or love. Only through emotion and love is it possible for the dead to communicate with the living.

Emotional communication, being an interaction of self or desire, has a wide range of possible effects on the living, most of which produce some kind of negativity or apprehension.

The dead in their ignorance, or by their desires, can produce in the living moods of gloom, fear and confusion according to the emotional connection they are able to establish. Most living people lend themselves to the errant dead by being emotionally co-operative through excitement, brooding and over-indulgence in sex and sexual fantasising.

But love or affection for the living has a different effect. Most of these positive communications are a mixture of love and emotion. They allow the recently deceased person to project a sign of presence to a living loved one, conveying without arousing anxiety a definite feeling that contact has been made.

*   *   *

The returning dead perceive people and events on the earth as they are in the present. But to the dead that present is not the crucial point of existence it is to us. For them the time element has changed. It has lost its narrow focus, its urgency or edge.

This is because there is no future in the death world.

The future is only a device of the living for trying to put off facing the idea of death. When death removes the future all the strain goes out of the present or the person.

The death world consists totally of past — the surviving vitality of all life that has ever lived on earth. The past of the death world is the living substance of the future. That is, there is no substance in our future apart from death. This is the most important lesson any consideration of death can teach us while we are alive. If we can see the truth of it, even glimpse it, the strain of the future immediately starts to go out of living.

As the future among the living is only a configuration of the past, the dead if they wish can perceive our future for us. They have only to look into our past, and there it is. But the future as we understand it — little insubstantial bits of it here and there — is of little or no importance to the dead themselves outside of any concern they may feel due to the problems of their mortal loved ones on earth with whom they are emotionally linked.

Whereas the living are pre-occupied with trying to secure or fill in their future, the dead are pre-occupied with reliving their past. When this is completed their future looks after itself.

*   *   *

The awareness of a person in the death world is more acute and concentrated than at any time when he was alive. Now, in the Red Plane, he is behind the senses which can no longer break up and distract his attention as before. He has literally withdrawn inside himself to become his pure ever-vigilant and conscious authentic being.

Around this point of awareness like the yolk of an egg is his old Red Plane vital self. And around that like the white of an egg is a sphere of energy representing the accumulated abstract value of the life just ended. Together these make up his personal world of survival.

This world of survival is the reality of a life he never really understood at the time of living it. Death offers the means to understand that life through re-experiencing it in its reverse negative mode.

As the dead person relives his emotional links with the past he works his way out with his awareness through the yolk of his surviving emotional body. The understanding he extracts and absorbs in the process is virtually identical with the abstract energy of his authentic being. This understanding is the remaining value of the life just ended; together with the authentic being it passes out to join the surrounding sphere of life-value already accumulated.

As this unquantifiable extract is removed, the old Red Plane self dissolves and disintegrates. The discarded pieces fall away back into the reservoir of constantly recycling Red Plane vitality.

The person's authentic being, expanding outwards from its original point or centre, finally comes face to face with the surrounding sphere of abstract energy. This is the point of entry of the person's awareness into the Yellow Plane.

The person has now gravitated to a setting where some form of creative work is begun.

This creative work is his endeavour to assimilate the value of his past life and transmute it into something finer — what he could have been instead of what he had been. By drawing upon his virtues to balance his shortcomings the person is able to adjust and amend the life just ended — in short, to rectify his past. Death provides this incredible, unique opportunity.

Having already reduced his whole existence to the abstract substantiality of the Yellow Plane, this value of his life now becomes the work of his life. Here after death every man generates some form of artistic expression which he spends his time working on with great seriousness and immense satisfaction. The work avenues available on earth are extremely limited by comparison. Whole new ranges of self-expression open up for him such as may be imagined to exist between a garden-lover and a sculptor; or a school teacher

127

and a philosopher; or between a man who just loves to walk and an athlete or a dancer.

Gradually the person becomes completely absorbed in his work. For a time he can be called back to the earth by clairvoyants or by living loved ones with their emotions. But as time goes by he is too absorbed in his art to be reached from the earth or be bothered with it.

What the dead man probably will not realise is that the work he is enjoying so much and slowly disappearing into is the designing of his next incarnation.

With the materials provided by his last existence he now labours to produce the finest work of art he can manage — the outline of his next life on earth.

This outline will be modified by a number of other important factors, namely: the discrepancy between his empiric soul and his true soul; external cosmic, solar and planetary influences; the influence of the Blue Plane vita out of which his new physical body and environment will be formed; and the influence of the Red Plane instinctive energy that will go to make up his new emotional body.

When the dead man has used up all the materials at his disposal he rests content. He can do no more. Having re-experienced his past life he has exhausted his emotional self as explicit need or longing. In this state he can have no fresh desires. He is now his own authentic being, his ageless empiric 'I', surrounding or encompassing the abstract resultant of his labours. He is almost pure understanding, that is, pure abstract self-knowledge. He has virtually dissolved himself and is now 'being' as nothing, reduced to minimal existence in the Yellow Plane.

Since there is no longer any self to be conscious of, the person is no longer self-conscious. He is in fact now conscious.

But unless while alive he has begun to identify consciously with this self-less state, his experience of it now will be identical to deep dreamless sleep.

If the man could only be conscious of his state, content in his understanding and aware of his 'I' without self, he would not be asleep. He would be real or objective — self-sustaining, complete — and have no need ever to 'wake' because he would understand that whatever he awoke to would be some sort of dream, substitute world or time.

But since while alive or awake he did not learn to give up the need of the dream to mirror or substantiate his existence, the effect for him now is the same as deep dreamless sleep. The man is really awake — but he does not know it. So he lingers in a kind of expectant condition waiting to wake up when he is already truly awake!

A remarkable thing now happens.

The person's 'I' or authentic being, freed at last from the weight and limitation of self, passes up through the Death Band into Level Four.

The Death Band dissolves the last vestige of relative substantiality (moonstuff) from the person's authentic being. It is cleansed of all trace of existence. Even the infinitely faint self-consistency of the Yellow Plane needed to sustain the existence of the great spirits in the world is removed. The authentic being is now pure mental energy. On reaching Level Four it unites completely with the individual's empiric soul. The union is registered as a change in the soul's vibrational frequency or colour: the immortal being of the former person has then evolved that much more.

Every empiric soul at Level Four is itself an incipient art form, a kind of energised wraith forever seeking the means and inspiration to fashion itself in the image of its creator, its true soul in Level Five.

This endeavour is true art and is precisely what art is about even in the external world.

But the art a man expresses in any one incarnation is often minimal compared with the innate artistic capability his soul has evolved to. His soul is itself the art-work of many lifetimes that may or may not require him to appear on the earth next time as an artist. He can have the soul capacity of a great artist and yet express this in some way quite unrecognised by the world.

Man is the artist, man is the materials and man is the art. One earth life is but a few brushstrokes sometimes revealing a high point of colour or drama in the never-completed picture of a man's soul, but very often signifying simply the filling in of some essential though unspectacular piece of background.

129

When a man's authentic being merges with his empiric soul, that particular life and life-after-death are ended. No trace remains of that particular individual in the worlds below. That person who lived before is never seen again.

But immediately the man — not the man he was but the man he now is — comes again in a new form.

From his empiric soul in Level Four a beam of attention descends on to the Red Plane of Level Three. Passing through the Yellow Plane it picks up the outline of the man's next life which he had left there and projects it on to the Red Plane reservoir of self. Implicit in this radiant beam of potential life is the man's authentic being.

Immediately, like iron filings attracted to a powerful magnet, Red Plane energy clusters around the focus of the new life to form a new emotional body or vital entity. Although past or self, this energy is not necessarily the individual man's previous past or self. That is all held abstractly in the man's authentic being. This Red Plane energy is out of the whole reservoir of past or self left behind by all men and life during the after-death process since time began on earth. It is intensely instinctive, passionately attached to vital existence. It provides the instinctive knowledge in life which ensures survival of the organism until the last moment; it is the living memory, the vital memory of the species and the race intrinsic in the unconscious of all men.

The new man now consists of a highly energised soul-centre still waiting to awake, and a surrounding vital or instinctive body. He now exists as almost pure need and emotion.

Rising as a wave of emotion from the Red Plane through the Blue Plane he spirals up across the subconscious of Level Two (through the dreams or thoughts of the mother) towards rebirth and personification of the experience and self-knowledge he lacks.

His emotional body is shaped something like a coned wire spring with the base loop spiralling up to a single point at the top. This point is the point of entry into the emotional womb of the mother, which to external sense perception appears as the physical womb. His entry is equivalent to conception. From there the new person is finally born into the world at Level One.

130

17
The source of love
in the world

Before man, the world was devoid of love. Beauty as nature alone existed. But nothing in nature could reflect on that beauty. The power to reflect on beauty came with man. And out of that emerged his power to love.

Man has been struggling ever since to bring love and more love into the world. It is every man's unrealised longing to match the beauty he senses with the love he feels.

In the span of one lifetime this is as difficult to do as to understand because each man has to create that love out of his own emotion. Emotion is not love; but it is all man had to start with.

The whole point of the living, dying and re-incarnating process is to imbue man with an ever-deepening sense of love. Through many, many lives of pain and pleasure each man grows in understanding and ability to convert his natural deep red (plane) emotional self into lighter and lighter shades or frequencies approaching the finest of pinks — love in the world.

As already described, after each incarnation is completed and before being finally dissolved as that particular person a man works assiduously at designing his next life. The skill and artistry (or otherwise) he employs in this handiwork depends on his power to love. If emotion has been his highest form of love his efforts (as his next life) will reflect this. Emotion is only love unrealised but it reproduces self-love and self-service and therefore a limited, unfulfilling life.

However, even love is not an end in itself. If it were, love would be the cessation of action. But love *is* action. In its finest shade of pink it becomes action free at last from self-consideration because the direction it takes is invariable, one-pointed towards bringing something even finer into the world: character.

Character and nature

As the Red Plane is the source of man's emotional nature, so the Yellow Plane above it represents the seat of character — his spirit or true soul.

Man's emotional nature is a condition of self-consciousness, therefore a limitation of his being. He feels bound, restricted and sometimes threatened by it.

Character on the other hand is a state or quality beyond self-conscious knowing. Man does not feel restricted or threatened by character: while he invariably admires it in another, he can never be aware of it in himself. Anything we see in ourself is our own nature. If we think we see character in ourself we are self-conscious and what we are seeing is our emotional self, our misplaced concept of our self.

Being unknowable as our self, character can only appear in us when we are not self-conscious. Although it appears in individuals it is not individual. And it never changes. But seated as it is above the denser Red Plane it gets very little opportunity to shine through man's normally fluctuating emotions and the superficial demands of his self-conscious personality.

For character to come through with its unmistakable power of presence the polarity of a man's nature has to be altered. It must be given a negative value in place of its worldly-wise positive value of self-centred projection and consideration.

Developing love does much to achieve this transformation but ultimately self has to be eliminated altogether from the man's self-consciousness so that consciousness — pure awareness — is the greater part of his being.

Sooner or later every good man who has learned to love

and perhaps to serve something worthy in the world reaches a crisis point. In a particular incarnation he has to start facing up to the only thing that now stands between him and true selfless love. This is himself, the final residual redraw emotional entity which he overlooked and unconsciously assumed was loving or doing the loving. The self itself — representing all that lives in him apart from love — must now be consciously destroyed.

This is done by using his authentic being to observe and understand his emotional self. It means turning his attention inward instead of allowing it to be driven outward.

For a long, long time the man must live out of character instead of out of his nature. This is an extremely difficult thing to do for it entails going against much that is psychologically and emotionally natural in himself and society. And naturally, to all other men living natural lives his behaviour and actions at this time will seem to be unnatural and therefore questionable. Furthermore, while the struggle is in progress the man's ability to love may seem to the world to be non-existent or completely self-centred.

By persevering a man gradually aligns his nature with his character. When the alignment is distinct enough the character shines through, giving a new dimension to the natural being. A man can then be said to have had power or presence added to the force of his nature — and this is equilibrium or willpower.

Character is not commonly seen in the world. Even when it is seen it has no discernible continuity like the nature of a person or his personality, the nature's offspring. If personality is to be termed positive as it naturally is, character has to be described as negative.

Character is not so much seen for what it is as for what it is not.

That is to say, character usually appears or stands out in situations where the natural instinct of self-preservation or common sense is to go in the opposite direction. Character tends always to be isolated, to have to stand alone or out front. Also it tends to prove very little of value from a worldly point of view apart from the virtue of its own existence for anyone perceiving it in another.

133

To observe character in another usually evokes compassion (spiritual love) or the feeling of gratitude. Gratitude is the finest of all emotions. But it often deteriorates into a form of self-service with the giving of gifts in return. We give gifts to assuage our self-conscious feeling of not being able to give enough of our self.

To be worthy or evolutionarily effective, gratitude demands first an immediate offering up of self, the feeling itself, to the 'unknown' within, the Yellow Plane seat of the one and only character above. It is then divine gratitude. Divine gratitude is the sacred act of sacrificing the natural self because that is seen to be the only appropriate offering. By expressing gratitude first in this way to the source of character and not to its person (another human being), self-consciousness is helped to be cleansed of self.

Any giving of gifts can come later as a complement to the giving of self. But when the self is given (up) in time, service or surrender, no greater gift is possible and none is really necessary.

Ancient sacrificial and votive rituals stem from an original understanding of the true meaning of self-sacrifice. But all the ceremonies we have any record of today are materialistic substitutions that are all the more misguided when it is some other self, life or body that is offered.

Character and nature are a world apart.

Character, man's true self or virtues, is always present, potential, implicit in being as beauty is implicit in life. But it does not incarnate. What incarnates through birth are the vital, self-projecting evolutionary needs of man's nature.

This may seem a deplorable constraint for the world. But the justice of it is undeniable: it is up to each individual to express character and virtue in the world by incarnating them through himself if he thinks those qualities should be here.

Otherwise he — and the world — is stuck by default with his narrow emotional Red Plane self and existence.

18
Higher intelligences and communication from space

Science and the energies of the three planes

In this philosophy scientific principles correlate to esoteric verities. Truth at every level is analogous. The difficulty is to perceive the connections. To correlate discovery and knowledge of the universe with self-discovery and self-knowledge is probably the most difficult yet exciting and rewarding connection man can make.

The different energies of the three planes of Level Three demonstrate the vital correspondence between the two systems of truth.

In science a molecule is defined as the smallest portion of a substance that still retains its chemical identity. Similarly, the Red Plane consists of spiral-shaped molecules or spirillae that make up man's chemical identity, his reactionary self as distinct from his spiritual identity. Spirillae are molecules of self or instinctive past, the emotional stuff people are made of. They are mutant and influenceable.

As molecules are larger than atoms and immeasurably larger than elementary particles, so molecules of self are larger than the atoms of the Yellow Plane and immeasurably huge compared to the elementary particles and forces of the Blue Plane.

So far science works only with one of the energies of Level Three: Blue Plane vita.

Blue Plane vita — the substance out of which the other two planes are created — contains the elementary forces and particles of physical creation. Here is the source of the physicists' sub-atomic particles, electro-magnetic radiation, anti-particles and the endless variety of tangible and abstract forces which meet and play at the edge of mind and matter. Study of Blue Plane energy provides an understanding of matter but in pursuing it alone science remains essentially a materialistic discipline.

The permanent atom of the Yellow Plane

Atoms of the Blue Plane with which the physicists work are not permanent. That is, they can be broken down into more elementary particles or energies. There is no end to these particles, it seems. Even among the physicists there is a joke that whenever they are stumped by a fundamental gap in their knowledge the gods decide 'let's throw 'em another particle'.

What the scientists eventually will discover is the permanent atom. Permanent means causal.

The permanent atom is the constituent energy of the Yellow Plane. It is a unit of supreme intelligence, freestanding in the mind, a combination of will and idea. Its quality is 'I'.

It will be discovered in a very remarkable way — probably as some intelligent communication from space. This will happen either within a particular scientist's mind — possibly as a voice or presence of unquestionable authority — or as a message from outer space received on some future instrument.

The permanent atom has no material existence. But it does have integral existence. Integral existence is existence independent of matter, within or without matter. It can also be called presence — presence as I am present in my self. It is this that makes it so devastatingly personal and authentic as an experience.

The scientific consciousness has certainly reached the level of abstraction needed to register this presence. It has already found it necessary to invent a 'virtual' particle — a particle that appears out of nowhere and has never been measured, weighed or even seen except in the mind of the theorist — to explain its latest black hole theory.

But unless the individual man who is the scientist has been adequately prepared by catharsis of his Red Plane chemical self, direct communication from Yellow Plane intelligence can cause an emotional breakdown. This I suspect has already happened on numerous occasions.

Recording and measuring instruments used by scientists are material extensions of the one scientific consciousness. But since consciousness is always ahead of matter, science's first contact with Yellow Plane intelligence almost certainly will occur in the mind of individual scientists if it has not already done so.

The first acceptable mental communication probably will take place simultaneously in the minds of several leading physicists or astrophysicists. This will at least provide them with some reassurance about their mental states, and hopefully encourage a determined and concerted effort to identify the source of such intelligence.

However, as the chances are that even then Yellow Plane communication will be mistaken for mental illness, or not mentioned, the world may have to wait for a more respectably sourced message on some future instrument.

*   *   *

The permanent atom or 'I' is behind all intelligence including our own. For us it can be said to have three aspects. The aspect of our intelligence at any moment depends on the degree to which we are submerged in subjectivity or psychic consciousness.

These three aspects can be called higher-mind point, mid-mind point and lesser-mind point.

From the higher-mind point, the permanent atom or 'I' contains all there is to know without any need to reflect on what it knows. It is completely self-consistent. This is the realm of what would be called infallibility or omniscience.

From the mid-mind point, the permanent atom represents the intellect and through necessity (the world) it performs a reflective role; it cannot help but reflect what it already contains or knows. This reflection creates in the mind the phenomenon of existence, the earth idea attenuated through sense as space, time and matter — the realm of scientific and all inquiry.

From the lesser-mind point, the permanent atom represents the memory function, again a purely reflective role. As the memory it reflects stored sense perceptions (individual impressions), thus creating an intellectual sense of continuity as self. This is the realm of ordinary living and relationships.

The negative substantiality of the Yellow Plane permanent atom places it outside the speed of light. It is omnipresent. Neither its speed nor position can be measured; it has neither. This is because its motion or velocity is integral. Integral velocity is this-moment which has no time (for reflection). Terms like instantaneous and simultaneous are inadequate to describe it as they come under the inferior sense/light timescale.

From the higher-mind point the permanent atom is responsible for all events. The stream of all action, it never moves itself. Our time is the succession of such events which then appear in the even slower emotional time of circumstance.

*   *   *

The Yellow Plane and its permanent atoms of intelligence are poised beyond and above all the confusion and self-serving which characterises human existence.

The Yellow Plane is the highest point and the end of Level Three, the world. It is suspended over the Red Plane of self and confusion like the sky above the earth: however high man ascends it is always there.

In praying to his god or gods, lifting his eyes to heaven for a sign or answer, sighting UFOs or just contemplating the night brilliance of the universe he is acting out and reaffirming his timeless recognition of the Yellow Plane heavens as the source of his faith, hope and inspiration.

'Up' in the Yellow Plane, away from self and confusion, the mind of humanity divides into two divine presences of higher intelligence. These are the devotional presence of mind (consisting of 'left-spin' permanent atoms) and the scientific presence of mind (consisting of 'right-spin' permanent atoms).

The devotional presence of mind is responsible for all emotional and artistic urges: giving or the attempt to give. And the scientific presence of mind accounts for all intellectual activity: receiving or the attempt to receive as the pursuit of information and knowledge of any kind.

Anyone can observe these two basic motivations in his psyche for they determine which one of only two possible directions every thought, aspiration and activity will take. Every moment the individual is a reflection of one or the other, or an admixture of both. Since all ideas coming down to man through the Yellow Plane are given left or right-hand impetus these two presences are behind every conceivable effort on earth.

The two divine presences of mind contain the nature spirits of myth; the genii and muses of music, poetry and other arts; and the gods of war, providence, and other deities associated with various skills and disciplines.

The development in the ancient world of the skills of war together with the processes of government, politics and administration arising from them represent the first attempts to reach (or return to) the scientific presence. Religion, mysticism and art were endeavours to reach the devotional presence.

At the summit of the mind of humanity is the *transcendental presence*. This is the presence of the earth spirit itself descending through Level Five to inform the atoms of intelligence in the Yellow Plane.

All intelligence on earth derives from this single supreme presence. Out of it devolve the dual devotional and scientific presences below and out of those in turn the lesser spirits, deities, beings and selves, the whole determining the hierarchic structure of the human mind.

The transcendental presence or spirit together with the two lesser divine presences forms a divine Yellow Plane trinity. Each of the trinity is a spiritual being which the individual can experience or realise in himself as an all-knowing, all-present intelligence such as would be described

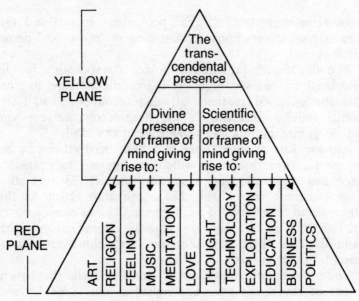

The Transcendental Presence

as God or a divinity. Man also can actually experience being such exalted presences for a short time.

Eventually, through the life-and-death process man can evolve to BE one of these presences. This is the high point or point of human evolution.

As the Red Plane represents life-after-death, the Yellow Plane stands for what this philosophy calls life-beyond-death. Life-beyond-death is another term for cosmic participation.

Cosmic participation occurs in and through the Yellow Plane which is the extremity of the human psyche and the beginning of the abstract levels of mind. Any visiting extraterrestrial intelligence has to come down through the higher levels of mind and finally express itself through the permanent atoms of the Yellow Plane.

*   *   *

The permanent atoms of the Yellow Plane are constantly informing mankind. Their presence is recognisable by the unique quality of their information: originality as expressed through science, art or truth. But as the knowledge has to come through the self-conscious and emotional Red Plane much of it, even in the highest expression, is lost or unperceived. Furthermore, it gets twisted and distorted.

While the Yellow Plane is responsible for every new and original idea man receives, the Red Plane repeats the idea, recapitulates it and generalises it. The important point is that Yellow Plane communications are received via the self and to the degree that the self has not been cleansed of past the clarity, newness or truth of the message is reduced. Also, the self then thinks it got the idea or invented something when really it was only the receiving instrument.

When self is absent there is no doubt that the message comes from another source. Direct communication from the Yellow Plane is the experience of personal contact with an independent and far higher intelligence than the limited self of any man. Self-consciousness has then been superseded by consciousness.

Typically, the 'voice' of God, or a god, or of an intelligence from another place, planet or star system is registered in the mind, distinctly and with no possible doubt for the recipient in that moment as to its truth and validity.

But all sorts of obvious difficulties now close in which make such communications extremely dubious, not only for the man concerned but also for the world which he may then try to convince of the validity of his experience — only to end up desperately defending the soundness of his reason.

Immediately after the experience, due to an inrush of self or emotion, the man may lose his clarity and certainty and start thinking he imagined it, or doubting his own sanity. The world itself has good reason to doubt this kind of experience which is common among the insane, religious manics, drug-takers and lower psychics all of whom, due to Red Plane or psychic distortion, are themselves confused to begin with and unable to communicate its simple truths.

However, genuine direct contact with higher intelligence has already been successfully and permanently established in one area of human consciousness. This is maintained by what are called Self-realised men, the genuine spiritual teachers who have realised at least the sixth level of mind, the originating Higher Person or Purusha. At this level and above 'voices' are no longer necessary; the knowledge comes direct out of the teacher's Yellow Plane awareness.

The flying saucer phenomenon

Below the level of Self-realisation permanent direct contact with higher intelligences is impossible to sustain. After a time they will seem to break off contact and just vanish.

The danger in this for an individual hearing genuine cosmic 'voices' in his consciousness is that inferior psychic forces will rush in after them and fill the vacuum with misleading information and false revelations. Joan of Arc and many others in history and our own time have found to their despair and consternation that the voices they had learned to trust suddenly became unreliable.

The reason for all this is that higher or cosmic intelligences have no past whereas our earthling sense-perceptive awareness depends completely on past. We see and hear through the accumulation of this past which is the space or psyche around us.

Similarly, our internal apperception or conceptualising ability also depends entirely on past − in this case, the inner accumulation of that past or space we call our self. Self and past are synonymous except that self is the past or space within in which the individual thinks while past includes the outer sense-perceived space in which our body moves.

Since cosmic intelligence possesses no past it has no space/time of its own in which to manoeuvre or communicate. In order either to appear visibly as an object or to communicate as a presence in the mind, it must use either the earth's external past or space (the psyche) or the individual's interior past or space (self).

In doing this it actually 'uses up' the past or self supporting it. A phenomenal visitation such as a UFO (unidentified flying object) requires and consumes far more past than a one-to-one psychological contact such as a voice or presence in the consciousness.

When the particular stratum of past or self being used is exhausted the contact cannot continue. On the other hand, any man whose self or past is dissolved sufficiently automatically transfers to the level of cosmic consciousness where he is permanently in phase with every intelligence in the immediate universe on his particular mindwave. Each individual has a unique oscillatory cosmic frequency with which he can 'perceive' once attachment to the psyche or the world's pseudo-reality is broken. This book is written on a cosmic mindwave.

The rate of consumption of past by manifesting cosmic intelligences is extremely high. Consequently, UFOs appear to move at great speed, and to communicate in the mind almost at the level of illumination.

Flying saucers after a period of incredible activity in the 1950s and 1960s gradually disappeared. They ran out of past. They ran out of past back into the cosmic present from which they came. They remain always 'there' but unperceived, except in rare, isolated instances. Further widespread sightings from earth are no longer possible until these intelligences discover, or are permitted to use, another stratum of the world psyche to appear in. This they will do and the contact will be more intensive.

The UFOs which hundreds of thousands of people sighted between 1948 and 1965 were carrying out a cosmic task to assist the planet's evolution by burning up vast areas of past that the earth and the human race had no further use for. Without this destruction of past by these cosmic forces of the present, time for us would have slowed down. Too much past was accumulating and choking the psyche.

Instead, time as man's comprehension and communications started to speed up.

The chief effect of this for the scientist was to make the speed of light an inadequate frame for his theoretical calculations, even though it continued to remain an absolute in his sense-perceived experience. The changes this speeding up brought about in scientific awareness as a whole were so bewildering that specialisation became the only way for scientists to preserve a grip on the almost contradictory diversity of knowledge. Specialisation will increasingly become the scientific way until ultimately specialists linking the specialist fields will be essential. Meanwhile, the masses will become further and further isolated from the esoterics of scientific knowledge while at the same time making more and more use of its revolutionary practical products. Finally, it will be realised that the scientific mind through the products is using the masses instead of the masses simply using the products. This will be a period of extreme anxiety among the more intelligent people on earth.

For mankind as a whole, the speeding up of time was responsible for the rebellion by younger generations against the old values and hypocrisy of assumed authority. Attempts to manifest more love and understanding in the face of authoritative violence and indefensible war, although many of them short-lived, combined with other liberating influences to produce today's vast movement towards tolerance, self-discovery and alternative education.

The charade

Since the earth and therefore the individual man is ultimately a cosmic being, every member of the human race has the potential in time to participate in the one cosmic consciousness shared by numerous higher intelligences in the immediate universe.

However, at the present level of race development we are still well and truly earth-bound.

So much so that in spite of our interplanetary and other space explorations we are in effect going nowhere. We are exploring an empty universe. We will not find or encounter any other intelligent life out there except perhaps in the same exasperating and inconclusive way that UFO sightings suggested the possibility of higher intelligences observing the earth — or self-delusion all round.

The entire compass of man's experience, all he can ever discover about the planets, sun and other stars and star systems, is contained in the seven levels of terrestrial mind. Beginning at the Yellow Plane of Level Three and above are the pure mind levels each of which is a rising degree of cosmic consciousness culminating in awareness of the cosmic or universal earth being, the earth idea itself, at Level Seven.

For humanity still enmeshed in the psyche way down in Level Three this has a very odd and unsuspected effect.

It means that all the scientist discovers about the planets, the sun and other stars is already contained in his own unconscious, the terrestrial mind. He (and for that matter all of us when we discover anything) merely brings or subconsciously recalls this knowledge up to the surface into his own psychic awareness, surprising and delighting himself with what he already unconsciously knows. This makes our whole existence completely subjective, tantamount to a charade in which we unknowingly and unconsciously act out each day the discovery of knowledge we already have.

The human psyche in its present distorting condition cannot know the planets as they really are no matter at what close quarters the investigation is made. While man continues to search for significance only in a sense-projected, external universe he will discover a second-hand reflection of reality, not reality itself. The planets the scientists are investigating are only symbols, and the significance of any symbol is always in the unconscious of the viewer. Whatever man deduces from his studies of the planets will necessarily be a past concept — the symbols or planets merely reflecting what he already knows and what he knew unconsciously he was looking for and going to find. The result is always materialistic, that is, it confirms his laws and theories giving rise to more laws and theories but never revealing what is really there and new: higher intelligence.

Intelligent life abounds in the universe around us irrespective of science's conclusions. What the scientists are looking for on other planets is terrestrial life; cosmic life is there, but they cannot see it. Science has even established that its terrestrial laws of physics apparently operate at the edge or beginning of the universe — a fine example of charadic delusion — but still has not seen one sign of intelligent life in all that infinity!

As man is not cosmically intelligent himself he cannot realise and cannot understand that the only purpose of space exploration is to make contact with higher intelligence. But he cannot make this contact because all he gets back is the level of intelligence he is himself employing — intellectual materialism.

Humanhood

Cosmically, man is an earthling. In the limitless cosmic interaction of universal mind or intelligence earth status merely indicates that he always retains a certain place or position, an underlying terrestrial 'bias' or obligation: his humanhood.

At present this obligation is to get his humanity on earth right. He must evolve a global system, a civilisation, which eliminates the current necessity for injustice, hardship and poverty — the fruits of intellectual materialism. He must do this by taking responsibility for all life on the planet and not just his own self-interested position.

In the meantime, no matter how many individual men realise cosmic consciousness there can be no participation by humanity as a whole in cosmic or extraterrestrial affairs.

Cosmic consciousness reveals or realises this, which is why every man reaching cosmic awareness will be found involving himself with the immediate, obvious plight of humanity as he perceives it and only then if he has the time with speculation about the universe and wider cosmic possibilities.

Humanity cannot join the cosmic club of higher knowledge and intelligence until it fulfils the basic condition of membership: it must get its own house in order. The blight of a consciousness which can tolerate the conditions under which most of humanity has to exist cannot — will not — be permitted to spread beyond this planet. Intellectual materialism and the Pandora's box of miseries it has released in its long evolutionary trail must be confined to earth. The learned doctor must learn to clean up his own mess; no orderlies will be provided.

No matter what man accomplishes in space exploration, human or public interest such as accompanied the remarkable feat of landing man on the moon will quickly fade and the achievement become just another bit of history, past. Even if he lands on other planets the only benefit for humanity will be a temporary titillation of the imagination and a plethora of materialistic information serving no real purpose whatever. And the scientists will despair at the fickleness of public support and interest, failing to see that while the fundamental aim is not right mankind is not going to be interested and that the results are not worth the effort involved except in arid intellectual satisfaction — and in the increased ability to make war, profits and comforts for those who can afford them.

Nothing endures or can endure in the public mind because the foundation, direction and priorities of nearly all of man's organised efforts are self-serving. Only the fundamental needs of all mankind matter — nothing else. Nothing can be discovered in space while there is so much misery on earth still waiting to be discovered.

19
The Draconic Transverse – Yang and Yin

The solar system is part of the myth of the constellation Draco, the dragon or serpent.

In ancient mythology the constellation is associated with death and salvation: the serpent is said to swallow up all souls that at death have not attained to gnosis (real knowledge) and to return them through its tail back to the world where they once again start a new life of struggle towards the gnosis which finally saves them from recurrence.

That is just about as far as the ancient accounts of Draco take us. The whole myth, if it has ever been told, has not been recorded in the detailed context and significance I am going to reveal now.

First let me explain the character of myth.

It is impossible to describe spirit as spirit, for spirit must communicate itself direct to the individual. But as myth, it can be done.

Myth is the only means at our disposal to describe the reality behind human existence. It is the language, the hand-writing, of the spirit, conveying the significance of things perceived.

Myth is the otherwise untellable truth behind the frag-mented physical appearance of things. So in reading what follows it is necessary to 'look through' the actual appear-ance of the part of the heavens I will be describing and to try to relate to the supporting structure of myth or truth behind it.

This is what the ancients managed to do. They did not invent the myths. The myth, or truth, was already there, as it is at this moment.

It would be completely wrong to regard the Draconic myth as imaginative fiction. This myth — which necessarily will be seen to touch upon myths of all ages, in all places — is nearer to the whole truth, THE truth, than any statement that can be made from sense-perceived experience.

The solar system is part of the myth I call the Draconic Transverse. As every myth must have its physical symbol, its appearance in the world, the Draconic Transverse is represented by a gigantic sphere in space thousands of cubic light years in volume with the constellation Draco at its north pole.

The physical extent of the Draconic Transverse is so enormous that its main stars as seen from the earth are regarded as fixed — never-moving.

As far as the tiny earth within it is concerned, the Draconic Transverse represents our field of reality, the world of myth. We can only observe and know the rest of the universe through it. The rest of the universe can have little reality for us until we at least have begun to understand the Draconic mystery or truth which, as I shall show, is so intimate to our earthly existence. The Draconic Transverse determines how we exist, evolve, perceive, live and die to exist again. At this stage of evolution we cannot go beyond it in any way whatever except as it, our reality, permits.

Draco is indeed a dragon or serpent. Its head is Yang and its tail is Yin.

Yang and Yin

The profound cosmic principle of Yang and Yin is the mythical bridge between inner and outer.

Yang is behind the apparent external created by our looking out consciously into the unconscious streaming down on to the surface of the earth; Yin is behind the unconscious within.

Together, they represent the extent of the unconscious

reality, which can only be known through myth. Myth alone transcends all conscious parameters.

Yang, the serpent's head, is 'all eyes' — a huge platform of celestial hyperception. From this vantage point in deepest space a score of light years beyond the solar system Yang, as Draco, presides over time and events which on earth are represented by life and death — the dynamic behind terrestrial evolution.

As far as the earth goes, Draco's tail — Yin — ends deep in the unconscious of the human mind, beyond the psyche, within the mind of the earth, the mind of the one earth spirit.

Between the head in space and the tail within is the serpent's body. This is man, the whole of humanity and the species both living and dead.

The character of Yang and Yin is will. Yang as Draco's head is the will in the universe; Yin as the tail is the will in terrestrial mind.

Yang is responsible for the earth's evolution as an intrinsic part of the whole evolving universe. From its towering Draco position it surveys the universe and keeps Yin informed in the terrestrial mind. Yin is responsible for seeing that the correlating evolutionary changes occur within the terrestrial mind for the evolving universe to remain conceivable to evolving humanity. Terrestrial mind and matter (sense) are so perfectly correlated by Yang and Yin that the question of causality — which comes first, outer or inner? — is purely relative.

For humanity — as distinct from other life-forms which may inhabit other planets or star systems within the Draconic Transverse — Yang surveys the universe relevant to sense perception. Also, seeing far beyond sense-perceptive evolution and to galactic factors that even our creator Sun is unable to perceive, it conveys to Yin the state of the galaxy as it affects the terrestrial mind in considerably more profound ways than we can ever be aware of.

However, Yang and Yin are not just a closed-circuit earth-to-Draco polarity. The Yang/Yin earth connection is only one of many comparable meridians linking numerous suns and their orbital matter to form a gigantic cosmic-spiritual field — the Draconic Transverse.

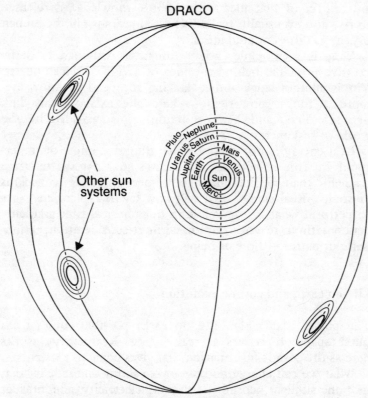

The Draconic Transverse

Within this vast evolutionary system the outer must be kept in unison and harmony with the inner. Neither must get ahead, nor behind. Yang and Yin are the principle — the will in matter and mind — ensuring this.

For us earthlings Yang is the master of the timing of substantive appearance. Yin in terrestrial mind contains all possible possibilities behind appearances, all that can ever exist in the present and future — all waiting for the moment, the exact time to manifest in consciousness at Yin's behest precisely to Yang's perfect timing.

Yin, deep in the terrestrial mind, is beyond time; it is the principle of abstract knowing attuned to the original, spiritual idea of the earth. Yang determines the time at which any aspect of that idea within Yin's knowledge is released to rise and eventually make its first appearance in the human psyche as differentiated ideas.

Yang is a principle, not a function. Although it is the positive principle behind the idea of action, it does not act. Yin is all-knowledge and in lacking the need to know any more it too is powerless to act. The extraordinary link between Yang and Yin — action — is provided by the world of real energy.

Real energy is not energy as we think we know or understand it. This is because it operates in a far swifter time gradient than our familiar sense-perceptive or conscious existence. Real energy, as I will now try to explain, manages to perform what is impossible in our physical time gradient: action-without-reaction, action-without-consideration, action-without-pause — flow or being.

Life on earth and cosmic evolution

The power that makes life on earth possible comes from outer space. It arrives as real energy. Real energy works here as the cosmic information that gives being to existence.

What we call energy and use or see acting on earth as heat, motion, sunlight, cosmic radiation, electricity and nuclear fission is reactivated energy, second-hand energy. It works as force, and there is no being, no life, in force. This reactivated energy has had 99.9 per cent of the original information extracted from it. In fact energy devoid of information is a definition of force.

By using force man imagines he creates and destroys while really he creates and destroys nothing. This is a point established long ago by science (apparently without appreciating its real significance) in the law of physics which says: matter (informational energy) can neither be created nor destroyed but may be changed (as reactivated energy) from one form to another.

Real energy acts without creating reaction. But in the

physical world, to act or be in action necessitates some kind of force: for every action there is an equal and opposite reaction, a resistance. This — Newton's third law — describes exactly the dynamic of reactivated energy.

As the energy expended in force in the physical world is equal to the resistance opposing it, no real work is ever done. This applies to every action or expenditure of energy on earth, from the exploding of a hydrogen bomb to the tapping of a typewriter key. The effects of our efforts are purely formal or cosmetic. Nothing permanent is accomplished that any individual ever sees outside of the continued existence of the human race and the world as an historical whole up to this moment. In our sense-perceptive world of cause and effect, life or information loses its instantaneity and becomes historicity or the past.

Evolution on this planet does exist, but not in the way we think. It is not the isolated phenomenon we tend to regard it as. Evolution is a cosmic movement — far vaster than our idea of it — towards cosmic consciousness, towards conscious cosmic participation.

We are seemingly alone in the universe because we have nothing to transmit to other cosmic intelligences that is not already known or available to them. Our apparent isolation will continue until we have something to contribute beyond our curiosity. We are not into space travel for what we can give but for what we can get out of it. Our cosmic ethic — what we are contributing in evolutionary terms to the whole — can be gauged at any time by the state of the world in relation to harmony, justice and the well-being of mankind as a whole.

All developed cosmic intelligences in the immediate universe are aware of our appalling lack of consciousness in these respects. And those similarly undeveloped are in no position to know any more than us about the presence of other life in the Draconic Transverse. Life is not physical — it is energetic, informationally energetic. That which is physical is only apparent. In death we are a part of energetic life and that much closer to reality.

This life that goes on and on yet seems to end perfunctorily and witlessly in death for the individual, is not your life or my life at all but the life of the planet earth appearing sense-perceptively as force — life force. Both in living and in surviving death we all combine like cells to form one single evolving terrestrial being.

It is not the evolution of life on earth that is the point, but the evolution of our planet *as* that life, together with the other planets of the solar system and any other cosmic bodies and stars within the Draconic evolutionary system.

The means by which evolution is carried on in the Draconic Transverse is real or informational energy.

Through the Yin-Yang real-energy connections of the Draconic system our sun, the earth and the planets and other stars and cosmic bodies contained in it communicate with and inform each other, exchanging and integrating their continuously changing evolutionary tones or states.

The energetic medium used to convey this information to the earth is time.

Time

Time is not what we think it is. It is not just a concept but an energy, similar to but finer than light.

The speed of light appears as the ultimate velocity in our sense-perceptive time gradient. However, our time — speed-of-light time — is not really time at all but interval.

Present scientific thinking and methods do not allow time to be isolated from interval, and so interval is mistaken for time. The fact is that time and interval are a world apart.

Time, the scientifically unsuspected but ultimate energy as far as life on earth is concerned, is the wave carrier of evolutionary information. It is not dissimilar in its function to the use, on a lower reactivated-energy scale, of a laser beam — amplified light — as a wave-carrier for conventional signals and information.

The fact that time is an energy, swifter than and yet meaningfully distinguishable from the present 'absolute' velocity of light, is an extraordinary discovery towards which science has to proceed. Relativity theory is associated with this progress, as is the scientific search for a unified field theory linking electro-magnetic theory with gravitation theory. Cybernetics is another more recent approach — but the elusive truth remains uncapturable while the search goes on in matter and not into the mind of the scientist himself.

Time, or evolutionary information, has another remarkable quality. It has, of course, numerous qualities. But at this stage of our evolution the difficulty is to comprehend even the existence of these qualities, let alone isolate them for subjective inspection. This particular quality explains how time brings about evolution on earth.

The remarkable quality I refer to is that time and informational energy are objective.

Objective here means totally objective: the subjective, which is what we regard as time and ourselves, is utterly eliminated from the perceiving equation.* It takes no time for evolutionary information to have an effect or produce an effect on earth. With no time involved, this means that the information is identical with the result; the information IS the result. Consequently there is no action as we understand action because there is no cause, no time — and therefore no force. The effect is the same as the cause — and this is total objectivity.

It means that on the earth everything that appears and happens IS the information. It is not the information acting, for to say that would imply force and interval: science would then have measured it and the world would know all about it just as every schoolboy knows about the speed of light. The information is not acting, but BEING. What we regard as being ourselves and as being the physical world around us is objectified information symbolising the evolutionary status of the earth at any moment. We, and our physical world, are symbols of reality — our own reality in another time!

The Draconic Syndrome

Really, and I mean really, man and all the species lives, dies

---

* The ethos of the word objective derives from the objective of evolution which at this time is to rid the world (ourselves) of subjective (self) considerations.

and recurs in a one-way — incoming — energy system. In fact man (and the species) IS this one-way energy system. Energy is continuously being received from the external cosmos into the three planes of human existence to form his individual body, his nature, his character, his emotional and mental responses, his circumstances and his world. But no real energy whatever is going out from him direct into the cosmos.

The informational energy which man produces — his life is a part of evolution and therefore a real energy producer — finally passes INTO the terrestrial mind after death as the residual of himself. This real-energy value of his life first passes through the death band into Level Four, the beginning of the higher abstract mind of the Earth Spirit. There, Yin, Draco's tail within the terrestrial mind, absorbs the information and passes it into the full Draconic system of Yin and Yang which unifies inner and outer existence.

In other words, we have nothing to contribute to cosmic evolution except our death. At our present level of race development only life and death — the Draconic Syndrome — produces real or cosmic-spiritual energy.

The species as a whole, and man in particular, is the chemical agency of the earth for receiving and converting cosmic energy within the frequency of terrestrial mind. Man's life is the ingestion, his living experience the conversion and his death process the distillation of the evolutionary energies received from cosmic space. These informational energies, which actually formulate man's and the species' sense-perceptive existence, he then converts to his unique frequency by the pleasure/pain of his life experience; and on death they are further refined to pass back through Yin into the entire Draconic evolutionary system.

But this is only half of the extraordinary story of the life-and-death process within the Draconic field.

The basis of astrology

As the real value of a man's past life — energetically equivalent to the outline he has made of his next life — passes out of terrestrial mind via the Yin/Yang Draconic connection, it disperses and manifests throughout the entire universe.

Because a man has always been a part of the universe his energy pervades even the most distant nebulae and is in every energetic expression originating anywhere in the universe. Every cosmic influence received on earth has to have his number on it.

For these cosmic influences to be received on earth they first have to be converted to our particular terrestrial frequency. This is performed by the sun's radiation.

Acting like a massive broom or an electro-carbon brush ceaselessly sweeping the vast area prescribed by the orbiting planets, it picks up the influences from these planets as well as from outer cosmic sources entering the solar system. These it monitors, down-grading and up-grading them to the suitable frequency for life on earth. The information is transmitted in photons or light particles to the mind through the eyes and other tissues.

This process is the basis of astrology.

It must be understood that astrology is only a partial approximation of the truth I am endeavouring to describe. Astrology is man's most successful attempt so far to formulate the mythic principle behind the Draconic evolutionary system, but due to psychic distortion in the human mind and insufficiently perceived data it falls short in its application to specific phenomena.

The new life a man makes for himself in the death world passes as informational energy through Yin into Yang to be added to the man diffused throughout the universe. Showering down on to the earth from the rest of the cosmos the new life is absorbed by his mother-to-be through sunlight as well as through the food she eats and the air she breathes. These influences — released as time by Yang — are the external factor that will at the right moment trigger the man's conception and rebirth, just as eventually they will trigger his death.

At the precise moment of his birth (or conception) the entire universe, and more specifically the sun and planets, will be in certain positions relative to the earth. Together

157

these configurations — correlating to the place, year, month, day and time of day the man is born — will present in the language of universal symbolism the nature of his self-made future.

If the positions of the cosmic bodies (Yang) can be mapped and the symbols correctly interpreted (Yin) for the moment of his birth (the earnest endeavour of astrologers down through the ages), the result will indicate not only his self-made nature or future but also the cosmic assistance and resistance he will have in endeavouring to realise the full potential of his new life.

Furthermore, the subsequent positions of the cosmic bodies will show the events affecting the man's life at that particular time.

* * *

Man is a composite of three notions of time on which the cosmic forces act.

The future
A man's future is what he constructs after death out of his power to love. This is man's real future, not his imagined or projected future, his bid to escape from death. Because it is real it has no interval, no sequence, and therefore cannot be conceptualised or thought about.

This future consists of two aspects. As Yin it is the abstract outline of his next life left by the man in the Yellow Plane of Level Three. As Yang it is represented by the sun and other cosmic bodies that convey this information to earth and trigger that life experience.

The man's self-made future will be the broad outline that his life will follow and as his inner Yin it will assert itself as his feeling of free will. But in fact it can never be lived as he intended or designed it. He will always yearn inwardly for something that never eventuates to his satisfaction. This is because the future he has made for himself will be modified from its inception by external cosmic influences (Yang) representing the evolutionary contribution of the rest of the immediate universe to his life. As he affected the universe it now affects him.

The past

A man's past also has two aspects. As Yin in the mind it is the Red Plane chemical self that forms an emotional body around the abstract Yellow Plane outline of the man's next life on earth.

This is the vital man whose involuntary self-centred motivation is to survive and reproduce itself as an emotional and organic vehicle for perpetuating the species.

It is the 'old' man in the man which will often confuse him in his new life by seeming to work against his self-made future.

The moon is the external cosmic body (Yang) representing the man's past.

Acting on the fluids of the body the moon's influence strengthens the man's emotional identification with the past of fixed perceptions, memory impressions and family, social, national, religious and racial traditions.

The present

The interplay in man's consciousness between his future and his past creates his awareness of the present. This is where beauty and the beast, the agony and the ecstasy, often seem to share the same moment in time within him.

In the mind, the present is a swiftly oscillating point between the Red Plane and the Yellow. It varies in everyone, the less evolved man living in the emotional, sensual now and the more evolved man living more in the moment. In every man's life this awareness of the present — acting sometimes as one aspect and sometimes as the other — will very often seem to be working against both his future and his past.

The distinction between these two aspects of the present, the Red and the Yellow, can be made clearer if it is remembered that in most people for most of the time one of the Yellow Plane boxes or powers of the mind is almost constantly being occupied by insurgent Red Plane self (see p. 114). Consequently, most people's Yellow Plane intellect is distorted and coloured by emotional interference.

While a man is performing work on earth or being as objective as possible (dealing only in facts) the power of his intellect is relatively clear. But the moment he thinks about the past or acts from his emotional attachments — which are as numerous as his thoughts about the past — the Yellow Plane box is invaded and he is once again subjective and unreliable.

For most of humanity nearly every thought and consideration is subconsciously tainted with past; most of the time is spent thinking or talking about the past and to a lesser degree about an imaginary future. Very little of the world is ever perceived as it is in the present moment; it is seen through the screen of past impressions and opinions, likes and dislikes, regurgitated feelings and false sentiments. These people for the most part live out of the past in the world of the senses.

Invasion of the intellect by the self is felt in its most noticeable form (if felt at all) as changes of mood (Yin) manifesting as changes of behaviour (Yang).

More widely, behavioural changes represent cosmic and planetary influences transmitted by the sun (Yang) acting on the emotional self (Yin) via the brain and glands.

As the sun symbolising enlightenment actually illuminates the moon symbolising resistance and attachment to the past, so the sun by conveying cosmic and planetary influences forces changes on the sentimental and emotional self.

As the moon's influence holds the man back by making him resist change within himself, the sun's influence goads him on to dare to dare and fulfil his potential. The moon makes him seek the safety of the herd, or the comfort of the womb, while the sun tries to tip him out into the world to live creatively, originally and individually in line with the life he scripted for himself.

Gradually, through the traumas of many lives, man's lunar attachment to his emotional organism is broken and converted into solar love — cosmic consciousness.

160

Part three

The origin of the universe

I

The two main scientific theories of the universe are the Big Bang theory and the Steady State theory.

The Steady State theory, currently out of favour, is that the universe is infinitely old, or has no beginning in time; that it has always fundamentally been the same and always will be the same; and that although it keeps expanding, as the galaxies race apart from each other, new matter is being continuously created in the space between so that the universe will always look the same from any point in space or time.

The dominant theory is that the universe began with a big bang. An infinite amount of space and matter, it is believed, was compressed into a tiny finite volume which exploded and has been flying apart as the universe ever since. Deficiencies in this theory are recognised by science and stem mainly from the fact that the calculations involved go back only to what scientists consider the first split second *after* the Big Bang. The instant before their calculations — the state or origin in which time equalled exactly zero — remains a mystery.

What happened before the Big Bang? That is the awkward question posed by the theory. And if the Big Bang was the beginning of time, as some scientists apparently are starting to wonder, what was, or is, the pre-time state?

In the following I answer these questions. I describe the state in which the physical earth and the solar system came into existence. In doing so I necessarily refer to the rest of the manifested universe and have more to say about the character of space, time, matter, life and intelligence.

Furthermore, what follows shows that *both* scientific theories of the universe are correct in their own way; and that it takes both views — or an apparent contradiction — adequately to describe the origins of the universe.

20
The creation of the universe – intellect and intelligence

The universe exists in a state of mind. Mind is the pre-existent state. Compared to mind, space is as substantial as matter.

Originally, the entire area the universe now occupies was mind, an inconceivable void empty of both space and matter.

To follow the formation of the universe as an event we have to appreciate the two distinctly different points of view involved – the mind position and the spatial position. Both of them are familiar to us all.

The mind position derives from the original state of mind in which the universe manifested. This still, pure state containing nothing – and yet subsequently everything – is involuntarily participated in by man in dreamless sleep, unconsciousness and sometimes in meditation. A version of it also can overtake people during their conscious hours producing an extraordinary feeling of wideness of vision or being. In this state, the whole natural world can seem to exist within the observer's awareness and to have a very limited or relative verity by comparison. The still-mind position is not natural for man at this stage of our evolution.

The spatial position on the other hand is the natural and instinctive viewpoint. This is understandable as it derives from the intelligence that has evolved out of the space and matter which manifested in the original void of pure mind.

Other intelligences besides man that may have evolved elsewhere in the universe will also represent a particular spatial viewpoint or form of intelligence that developed out of space and matter.

Due to the evolution of spatial intelligence as man, we can now gain some understanding of the formation of the universe by shifting between the mind and spatial viewpoints. First let us take the mind viewpoint. Let us imagine our mind is the mind which is about to contain the universe. . . .

All is still, supremely at rest and at peace. Suddenly there is the most tremendous retort, the biggest bang of all time. Immediately we are aware of something, literally jolted into knowing something. We do not know what it is except that our vision or awareness which unknowingly had been infinitely wide and uninterrupted is now cut off. Something has come across the mind, our mind. Where there was nothing, there is now something. It is a mind-riveting, mind-limiting event. The shock of knowing something where there was absolutely nothing, and not knowing what that something is, is unprecedentedly disturbing.

That something can be observed at this moment in our own minds. It is the grainy blackness, the dark lanes and pinpoints of light in front of our awareness when we close our eyes, or have them open in complete darkness. This grainy scene is present in all creatures at all times, even in the blind; and it is potentially present in every living cell. It is the *other side*, the 'mind-eye-view' of the manifested universe which we perceive so differently and diversely with our external senses. This grainy screen, closing off our pristine awareness, is the intellect.

The intellect is the obverse side of the familiar starry universe. It is a pure-energy reflective screen which by shutting off infinite mind makes intelligence universally possible.

The big 'bang' that occurred in the pre-existent mind marked the appearance of the intellect as the reflective screen that allows us to perceive and reason. It also marked the beginning — on the obverse side of the intellect — of the external, spatial universe: of time, the solar system, and the potential for intelligent life to develop there.

As physical beings we are provided by the stars, space and matter with the sense of existence; while as mental beings the intellect allows us to evaluate that experience as knowledge and to evolve intelligently.

Intelligence

Say we have our eyes closed, are observing in the mind the grainy black intellect in front of our awareness, and then open them. We are immediately spatial. At the speed of an opening eye-lid we have moved from the inner to the outer position. Whereas a second ago we were observing the intellect — not knowing anything unless we were thinking because the intellect does not reveal itself as itself — we are now earthlings, that is spatial intelligence in our own evolutionary earth world.

We can see, dig into and feel the earth, the planet that is ours in the solar system, and we can look up and see the universe of stars. What is it we are using to know this — which was not needed a second ago when we were simulating the stillness of pure mind?

Intelligence. We need intelligence to be able to know. We do not need intelligence to know nothing, to be still mind. In fact, intelligence is what we are: various degrees of it representing a gradient called life on earth. We are the intelligence that has evolved in time out of the space and matter of the solar system, and specifically the earth, on this the universal side of the intellect.

In time, or eventually, space and matter are distinguished by intelligence which arises out of them, as man has arisen out of the space and matter of the solar system. This constitutes a great truth of existence which affirms the possibility of other forms of intelligent life existing elsewhere in the universe.

Through the intellect — and I mean literally by passing through it — we have emerged to become intelligent life on earth; just as by closing our eyes and being still we can return back through the intellect to the pre-existent state. The only

proviso is we must not want, or think about, spatial existence. For that will automatically transport us back at the
same incredible speed through the intellect into intelligent
existence on earth with all its dynamically needling evolutionary traumas — and deliciously addictive experience.

Intelligence, for all its activity, is the spatial or universal
equivalent of the original still mind. To this state of stillness it must eventually return by evolving through experience of the universe via the intellect.

Motion and intelligence

According to science, the earth is moving through space
at fantastic speed. It is said to move into new space around
the sun at 30 kilometres per second, forward with the sun
at 20 kilometres per second and around the galaxy at 220
kilometres per second, all at the same time.

But on a scale of spatial existence as great as the Draconic
Transverse — bearing in mind that reality is totality and the
greater the totality observed the more the reality — the earth
is practically motionless.

In fact, the motion of all heavenly bodies is due to the
oscillation of the observing intelligence and not to any real
movement of those bodies.

From the point of view of mind — the original still
reality — the universe is motionless and has been since the
instant it manifested as the intellect. Only on the spatial
universal side is there movement or evolution of objects
in time.

The intellect has never moved, never been added to or
detracted from since the big bang that accompanied its
emergence. When we observe it in our heads it is the same
as it always has been and will be. Any apparent movement
or change is due to the unsteady state of our evolving intelligence as spatial beings.

The intellect is the stationary bridge between the universe
and mind. Intelligence, evolving out of matter and life on the
universal side, eventually crosses it to return to the timeless
and motionless original pre-existent state of mind.

It is intelligence, not the mind, which is evolving in time and space. Intelligence advances towards becoming pure, still mind by its understanding of change and motion through universal experience.

Intelligence, in this respect, can be described as an intellectual or reflective movement towards understanding of a reality greater than that suggested by the senses. Intelligence acts to know, to sort, to uncover. By reaching out through the senses and reflecting its experience off the intellect, intelligence comes to know physical existence and to give it significance and value.

Intelligence, wherever it appears in the universe, oscillates at different frequencies. The swifter the oscillation, the higher the intelligence — and motion slows down significantly. From the earthly view, the frequency of intelligence varies with the matter (the person or species) it arises in, as well as with the relative reality of the symbol or object being observed.

For instance, if a person can keep his attention intelligently focused on the intellect — that dark screen of minimal experience in front of his awareness — he will eventually lose all sense of time and motion and enter the infinitude of original still mind whence he, time, motion and all objects originate. He will remain in this state until his spatial (physical and emotional) self starts to exert its restlessness (evolutionary need of motion) and demands his intelligent participation in worldly affairs.

Intelligence, in spite of its ability to detach itself and identify with the mind in this way, is bound by time to the matter or body it arises in, and must complete that particular Draconic or evolutionary life/death cycle.

All motion on the earth is due to the relatively slow oscillation of the observing intelligence — i.e. our sense-perceptive condition — as well as to the relatively superficial significance we normally attach to it. Not much reality is apprehended in our lives; thus we are surrounded by movement and restlessness. When reality is faced or comprehended — an experience often associated with death or loss — there is a distinct slowing down both spatially and intellectually: a greater significance or inevitability is seen.

In our physical or sense-perceptive experience, the stars represent the highest reality. The greater the reality — which in relation to the furthest stars is what we apprehend as distance or time — the faster the observing intelligence has to oscillate and the slower the star is seen to move.

Similarly, the further a man is from perceiving reality in mind or sense, the slower his intelligence oscillates and the swifter and more numerous are the objects and thoughts that shoot through his mind or space and distract him.

For example, an unintelligent person would not be expected to study the cosmic reality of the heavens, or his own mind. When he did glance towards either, instead of reality he would only see the various intellectual inventions he had formulated of it or that had been formulated for him. These concepts, being unreal, would move through his mind at great speed; and being unable to slow them down or stop them with his limited intelligence the man could be said to lack the power of attention, or depth. Such people become easily bored, being addicted to the need for the constant passing of time as objects or thoughts through their mind or space around them. They desire continuous movement and stimulation.

For an intelligent observer time, like the imperceptible motion of objects in deep stellar space, is almost non-existent. The reality a man can observe at any time is determined by the stillness of his mind or his space, and this is a measure of his intelligence.

Draconic gnosis

Intelligence evolving out of matter and life eventually exceeds its life-form — its personal or planetary body — but without necessarily leaving it. It does this by speeding up, quickening. This is accomplished very slowly through evolution so that finally intelligence reaches a speed equivalent to a time-change enabling it to perceive aspects of other time gradients in addition to its own. The speed at which intelligence oscillates determines the character of the time.

The human life-form — the organic body of humanity and

the species — is fixed. But although anchored to the human body, or the earth, human intelligence can still exceed the sense-perceptive time barrier and go beyond its own gradient. (We should endeavour to think of human intelligence as a single gradient, as intelligence on earth, not as numerous individuals more or less intelligent than each other.)

In quickening intelligence towards the top end of its gradient, evolution demands that that intelligence must free itself from the ingrained habit of identifying with the particular life-form or time-gradient it occupies. It is somewhat rare for human intelligence at this point of evolution to realise it is separate from the body out of which it emerged, but it does happen. The realisation of this is identical with a time-change: automatically other life-states or worlds are then perceived direct without sense-perception and are known objectively. This is common in mystical experiences.

Because human intelligence has not yet evolved sufficiently for us to spend all our time on the mind side of the intellect, we have invented, or had invented for us, death, which is a sort of in-between world.

The world of death, or the living dead, together with the world of the dying living, makes up a wondrous whole of Draconic gnosis, the world of pure time or objective knowledge.

Draconic gnosis is a state of evolved intelligence which life on earth has achieved at the narrow higher end of its time gradient. It includes the mythical, occult and magical worlds.

Draconic gnosis is not pure mind for in pure mind nothing, not even gnosis, can exist. But it is closer to purity or stillness of mind than has yet been consciously achieved by most of humanity as the intelligence of planet earth.

21
Eternity

Reality and actuality

I am now going to present an extraordinary proposition. It requires a brand new way of looking at experience. The more we can manage this the easier it becomes. By beginning to understand it as the truth we start to enter a new time/intelligence gradient.

The Big Bang origin of the universe which science is attempting to get back to did not happen in actuality. It happened in reality — a totally different world.

The actuality is our familiar sense-perceptive world of motion and interval. And it is entirely ratio-retrospective, meaning that to know its significance we have always to think or calculate back across an interval to a supposed beginning. The naming of things is one way we have invented to do this quickly. Even to recognise a person or thing we involuntarily have to refer back. To make sense of anything means to go back. Our perception or particular time gradient demands a beginning for everything. So it is inevitable that we postulate a beginning of the universe.

However, it is impossible to calculate back to the beginning of anything, because every calculation pre-supposes a pre-existent motion or time. You can calculate back to when a bullet leaves a gun but that proves nothing about the beginning of the bullet or the gun — only the absolute presence of motion or time.

You can calculate back to the moment of your birth. But that signifies nothing about the beginning of you. If you go back further and calculate the moment of conception you are no closer to the start of you: the only answer will be in terms of motion, time — or the death sentence. You cannot calculate back to the beginning of you, or the universe, because you always arrive at motion and motion is not the beginning.

The originating Big Bang did not happen in actuality. It happened in reality when the intellect manifested in the mind as I have described. In reality, this is the only event there has been and ever will be. Whether perceived or not, the intellect is there: it is always there and always has been there. For this reason, the intellect cannot be said to have ever occurred: the question 'When?' arises from the incompleteness of its shadow, evolving intelligence, looking for a beginning or end to itself.

The intellect is the primary condition, the ever-present motionless reality that makes possible the fact of intelligence and therefore the actuality or external world.

As we proceed we must keep in mind the two sides to our existence as earthlings: the mind side which is the real side we always retain, even in sleep and unconsciousness; and the actual, external, sense-perceptive or transient side which disappears in sleep and unconsciousness.

Nothing moves in the mind, in reality. But everything is in motion in the actual world. Reality consists of mind and intellect, both of which are absolutely still; and the actuality, the ever-moving external world, consists of evolving intelligence whose restless urge-to-know is the cause of all motion.

The Big Bang theory logically postulates the beginning of motion. But there can be no beginning to motion because motion is not real. This the theory itself demonstrates by completely collapsing — failing to be able to go back any further — at the precise point where the beginning of motion and the universe is expected to be found.

Motion (and the Big Bang theory) is an effect, a condition created by developing intelligence. By trying to discover the beginning of motion we are trying to discover the beginning of our own ignorance or unintelligence: an impossibility. It is like looking in a mirror and trying to see who's looking; or trying to lift yourself off the ground by your own bootstraps.

Motion, as I have said, shows that the intelligence observing it has not evolved sufficiently to see the truth that reality is stationary.

It might be said that science will not accept that motion is unreal. All I can say to that is that science then does not represent the more evolved end of human intelligence. But I think some individual scientists do; and I suspect that through their scientific observations they have perhaps already perceived the truth of what I am saying.

It must be understood that I am not attempting to deny the actuality of our world. Our world is created as we all know by sense perception. What we do not understand is that sense perception is an evolving intelligence. And it is that intelligence, the perception behind the senses, that creates the movement of things and this passing world of ours.

That intelligence — we might call it terrestrial intelligence in the absence of any other planetary life seeming to share in it — is evolving through life on earth. Humanity as a whole, and individually, is that intelligence. That is why we all see the form of the world and the universe the same as each other.

What I am proposing, and will be proposing in different ways throughout this section of the book, is that terrestrial intelligence — us — has now evolved sufficiently for some of its individual cells — us again — to perceive this new truth that the reality behind the senses is a stationary world of infinitely greater power and significance for man.

The only intelligence that can perceive the stationary real world or universe behind the moving actuality is that which admits of no past in that moment. We all have access to this 'top end' of terrestrial intelligence because it is our planetary intelligence — if only we can surrender reliance on the past or interval. It operates now, in pure time, undistracted by the motion of things, the doubts and confusions of the past which are the waverings of the lower end of our intelligence. It surrenders the past anew every moment — memory reference, attitudes and all dependence on information outside itself — in fact dies to motion, and as a result perceives reality direct, that is, without the pause or interval that is sense perception.

Eternity

The Big Bang in the mind marking the advent of the intellect is the first cause of all motion or evolving intelligence. But the mind cannot know this until intelligence evolving out of that motion in the actual world — you — discovers that truth, as we are endeavouring to do now.

The advent of the intellect, that one and only real event of all time, *unbeknown* to the mind simultaneously created the universe, the obverse side of the intellect. Like a coin, on one side was the intellect, on the other the universe, each unbeknown to the other.

But as both sides of a coin cannot be seen together, it would be impossible to perceive or write this description — except for the truth. The truth, that most wonderful but elusive quality, lies here between the two sides, separating and yet joining them as the moment of eternity.

Truth, or eternity, is neither one side nor the other but contains the truth of both. It is the supreme abstraction, analogous to reducing the thickness of a coin so that finally it is both sides at the one time. This, eternity manages to do.

It manages it by preserving forever the moment the intellect appeared in the mind. As that moment never ends it never had a beginning. This absolute time is a discontinuous, motionless, energetic (meaning perceivable) representation of all that ever can be or will be enacted in the slower pure time of objective energy and the infinitely slower light-speed interval of our sense-perceptive gradient.

Objective energy, or pure time, is the executive power of eternity and to our perception an inseparable part of eternity. As I will demonstrate later, it is the means by which eternity is attenuated, drawn out, into a replica-in-motion of eternity: our actual, sense-perceptive world.

I have just described eternity as an energetic and therefore perceivable representation of all that ever has happened or can happen in actuality. How, then, is eternity perceived?

It is perceived as the now. The moment of eternity, the moment of truth, is now.

Now is the one and only perpetual instant from which the

world continuously — or rather discontinuously — begins afresh every moment by having no past.

The beginning of the universe and man is not some time in the past. It is now, this moment, which is demonstrably the same now as always.

What stops us from realising this is that we regard what happens as the only important consideration and dismiss entirely the continuous moment it all happens in.

If we could give equal cognisance to both we would immediately perceive the truth of the now, man and the universe.

But as it is, we are distracted from the truth by perceived events which immediately become for us fixations of the past. Each of us measures his life by those events, and so we live mostly in that past.

Actually, all we are doing with the years of our lives is measuring the past, the interval we have left behind, our distance from our assumed beginning, our birthdate. Science tries to do the same thing with the Big Bang theory by giving a date and start to the universe. But both beginnings are illusionary. Reality is neither past nor eventual; it is now. Now is the original and only state of things.

Nothing ever has happened or can happen outside of now. Although self-evident, the significance of this is extremely difficult to concede. We are involuntarily, unconsciously terrified of it for it means giving up the past and seems to predicate losing all established foundations from which we gain our psychological sense of security — but not the truth.

Through the feeling of having been, we get the feeling of being someone, something. It is a substitute for being now. It is comforting, reassuring almost to the point of necessity for most of us; but it is not the truth. To be someone or something at any time requires living in the past.

To be able to perceive the beginning of the universe and oneself as now is the beginning of immortality in the individual. To cling to any other beginning in the face of the real is for the individual to continue to calculate his own inevitable and equally unreal death.

Certainly, each of us was born as a life-form on earth. But

that proves nothing apart from the fact that each of us was born as a body. To regard the birth of any form as a beginning is totally presumptuous.

The question is, can the reader recall any time when he was not? The answer is no. But if I cannot remember, it is an absurdity to assume that there has been a time when I was not what I am now. This is the assumption of death of which most of us are guilty. Our delusions change as our past grows, but we do not.

No man feels he is 40, 50, 60, 70 — or any age. He may feel pain and the restriction of the body — his past — but the man, the pastless I in him, never feels any older. The man however old is ageless. I am not an event: not a body, a birth certificate, a memory or a bathroom mirror which by reflection on the past that is my body reveals to it its age, past or mortality. That body and all that helps to measure it by reflection and memory will die. But I cannot — any more than my birth can be my beginning.

We are beings of the now, as the universe is the expression of the now. As part of the universe we cannot be separate from it, except through the illusion of past created by our evolving earth-intelligence.

In truth there is no time but now. Now is exactly the same instant that the intellect formed in the mind and the universe began. To repeat: a Big Bang beginning of the universe calculated to have happened fifteen billion years ago, or any other figure, is unreal, illogical and illusionary. The largely discarded Steady State theory is closer to the truth in implying that the universe is ageless and the same now as ever.

In truth nothing has changed, nothing ever will, for the only time is now. The thing that does change and therefore is evolutionary, or at any moment not yet itself, is intelligence. Intelligence invented interval, the past and the Big Bang theory because it is not yet up to living in the now.

I am now proposing that it is possible for man to 'jump' his own time of past and interval and to realise for himself that eternal moment in which he and the universe are as they always have been.

This, I accept, may need a good deal of demonstrating

as such a proposition is contrary to nature and reason. However, what is natural and reasonable arises from memory and past experience and is itself part of the successional time trap that has to be vaulted.

It is universally true that any real proposition — the positing of even the highest reality — can be demonstrated through the intellect, provided the intelligence (evolutionary position) of the observer is up to it. As I will describe later, the same intellect is used by ultra-intelligences throughout the universe as well as by ourselves and the living dead, and is therefore equal to any demands that can be made of it. The intellect manifested in that original first instant which is preserved forever as eternity, and is therefore outside the successional time trap we have to vault.

22
Power, gravitation and force

I have described the creation of the universe as the instant the intellect comes across and shuts off infinite mind. I will now explain how this happens and how the intellect itself comes into being.

Everything I am about to say happens in another time gradient where there is no past, no interval. All the 'events' are happening simultaneously, now. The model and sequence I use are therefore only indicative of the essential idea.

The three first principles

Three inseparable first principles are behind the moment-to-moment existence of the universe: infinite mind, infinite Self and will.

We know very little about infinite mind and Self, but we know a great deal about will. Will is the power in the universe.

Like infinite mind and Self, the will is imponderable — except as effect. Existence of the universe is the work or effect of the will.

The will is equal in primacy to the two other principles. In fact from the created point of view (ours) it may seem to enjoy greater freedom and privilege. The will can 'travel' through infinite mind and Self without affecting either infinitude. But this is conditional on it remaining in what I have to describe as a flat and oblong shape and not starting to curve or curl around itself. This freedom of travel is symbolised in the myth of flying carpets — and I suspect the original myth, if ever recorded, is that as long as the carpet does not curl, all is well.

Will is the power of complete freedom to effect a cause. As soon as will curves there is what I call prime effect. All prime effects come from will and to us are causes. Will creates causes.

Infinite mind has to be imagined as an unending void of 'nothing'. Implicit in infinite mind is Self. This means Self is everywhere in the mind; although when Self is realised by an individual he knows it to be the centre as well as the whole. Consequently, the Self can be regarded as the centre of infinite mind from any position.

Creation of the universe began when the will, embracing the idea of the intellect, started to curve into existence in a gigantic circle around a section of infinite mind.

Curvature is the start of time, that is, the end of infinitude and the beginning of impression or past in the mind, which is the prerequisite of existence.

As the will behind the intellect curved into existence, the briefest of intervals occurred in which the Self was fully present, fully exposed or revealed as the potential centre of the piece of infinite mind being encircled.

In this briefest of moments, nothing was almost something — an impossibility outside of myth. Infinite mind and Self *are* infinite because they have no past, that is, they leave no impression. In other words, neither can have existence because they are absolute abstractions. Although for an instant the beginning of past in the will's curve actually threatened to give the Self existence as the centre of infinite mind, this could never actually happen short of the instant of Self-realisation. Infinite Self cannot be contained or encircled by existence, and therefore had to disappear.

Continuing to encircle the area, the will formed a huge girdle embodying the intellect. The effect of will-facing-will across the girdle — and this is why it must not curve — was dynamic: radial lines of power developed, focusing on the centre-point from where the Self had vanished.

Enormous power began building up both at the centre and back along the lines of power. With no outlet, the concentration of power at the centre was tremendous: at the point where the Self had vanished the universal 'I' started to arise.

Through infinite mind being dynamically focused in this way, power continued to build up in the power lines with no outlet but 'I'. (At all levels, I feel the strain of holding my world together.) Finally, under this unrelenting concentration of power, the central universal 'I' burst into full consciousness as the first expressed principle behind all cosmic idea, knowledge and existence. Without I, there is nothing.

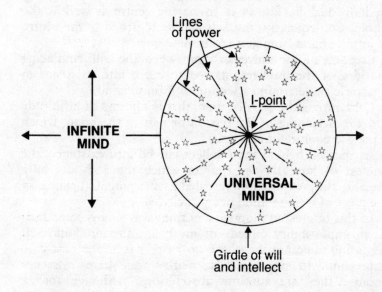

The encircled area of infinite mind had now become universal mind; what was infinite is now conditioned by having a centre, I. Infinite mind, by the power of the will, now has an expressed cosmic centre that is not absolute because it is not infinite, but which may reasonably be described as ultimate. 'I' am the ultimate truth.

'I' is the centre of the universe. I am where I am, and there is the centre of the universe as well as the I I am experiencing now as the centre of my individual awareness.

That 'I' centre can be any 'I': from I the writer or reader of these words, I the spirit of the earth or mankind, I the consciousness of the Sun, to I the almighty lord of the universe. By ascending octaves or gradients of time, all are finally united in the one mighty I.

Meanwhile, around the intensifying lines of power themselves, space — science's positive vacuum — started to form in which the universe was about to appear.

Simultaneously, the power potential continuing to build up at the centre 'I' extended back along the power lines and reached such intensity that points along the lines crystallised as stars and matter in the space just formed.

This last event, on the infinite mind side, formed ideas. In other words, on the universal side the phenomena are stars and their systems; while on the mind side they are all the ideas comprising the intellect which is completely reflective of all knowledge intelligence can ever discover and reflect on.

I repeat, all I have just described occurs simultaneously as the one and only real event and moment that has ever been. This moment is the now which also is the moment of eternity. Only in retrospect does anything else ever happen — a subjective condition due purely to the evolution of sense-perceptive intelligence through 'I'.

Stars

Stars form on lines of power. To us they are apertures or openings: each star is a different aspect, or window, to the one reality behind the intellect.

Stars epitomise power in effect. They are the nearest thing to simultaneous being and non-being as demonstrated by the paradox of light which sometimes acts as energy particles and other times as insubstantial wave effect.

In the Draconic Transverse, the manifestation of a star like the sun on a line of power is what I am forced to call the *prime effect*. This is to distinguish the prime effect from subsequent effects, as well as from cause. It may seem reasonable to regard a prime effect such as the manifestation of our sun fundamental enough to be called a cause; but it would not be strictly correct. Certainly, all effects represented by the world's existence to this moment have followed from that prime effect. But it was not the cause. The 'cause', the imponderable, is the power line.

Stars are present in the universe first as gravitation, second as sub-effects. Gravitation, as I will endeavour to show, is not a sub-effect; it is the one constant reality from which all existence arises. And it is present only in stars although it appears to be in planetary and other orbital matter. Each piece of matter takes its gravitational power from the star or stars whose system it is in.

Stars do not consist of matter such as is found in the planets. Stars in a way can be called ethereal, non-existent apart from gravitational influence which makes them discernible through their subsequent effects on matter. The universe is a gravitational field of effects provided by the stars, and principally, as far as our earthling intelligence is concerned, by our own star, the sun.

I repeat, stars do not consist of matter. What we perceive, measure and speculate on as the sun is not the sun at all but its effects on matter. The sun is not really there — all we see are subsequent effects inherent in the causal power it symbolises.

We earthlings as focuses of intelligence are eight minutes — the time light takes to travel from the sun — from that nearest solar window to reality. Spatially, we can never get much closer to reality than that: our physical vulnerability fixes our position pretty firmly. What gives point and purpose to our continued physical existence is that it offers no end to what we can discover and understand of the effects of reality without our actually getting any closer to reality in fact or truth.

We can only approach reality direct, not through its effects. And this we must do by freeing ourselves from the gravity of the past.

The stationary universe

Planetary matter manifests at the same instant as its star: prime effect.

Our sun did not manifest ahead of the planets. It and the stuff of the planets — the entire contents of the solar system — came into existence together as one complete event. Thus, original matter in the planets, including our moon and meteorites, will always be found to be the same age.

It was the sun manifesting as an effective star on the Draconic power line which gave reality, or beginning, to the solar system. But as the primary effect and therefore the only event outside of time, the sun could not manifest on its own or ahead of the other primal parts — namely the planets — which were essential to the system and all that would arise from it including the intelligent life which is ourselves.

The entire system had to manifest together; or none of it. Any object appearing later could only be a sub-effect and would not possess the original reality or permanence of that unending first instant sometimes referred to as eternity.

Time as we know it — successional time — is not a part of that first instant. That instant was and is the moment of perpetual reality. And that incredible instant is preserved forever in the unaltering, unchanging gravitational power of the solar system: our symbol of eternity.

In relation to that instant when the solar system manifested, nothing has changed. Much has happened in successional time, but nothing has changed. No new matter (energy) has joined the solar system and none has left. Any apparent incoming or outgoing is due to the action — really the limitation — of our evolving intelligence which is dependent on interval, signified by the speed of light, for the transmission and receipt of information.

If all the mass or matter in the solar system could be measured today against the original contents, exactly the same amount would be found to be present. Forms change but mass or energy can neither be added nor lost. Apart from the fluctuating frequency of intelligence, the whole universe as gravitational power is stationary.

Power lines, gravitation lines and force lines

The existence of the universe depends on three types of

energy — power lines, gravitation lines and force lines.

Power is cosmic, the supreme degree of consciousness called spirit. It originates outside the world of sense perception in the infinitude of mind which contains the space and form of the cosmos.

This sense-transcending void of original mind is a potential of power lines on which stars explode into existence to form the universe.

Our sun formed on a power line, or meridian, extending from Draco in the north to another constellation in the south.

From the sun emerge *gravitation lines*. The sun's first gravitation line is represented by the body of the sun and the remainder by the planets and their orbits. As I have explained, the planets manifested in the same instant as the sun. There was no interval.

Gravitation is of stellar origin. I repeat, planets have no intrinsic gravitational power. All gravitation is an extension of the gravitational power of the central sun or suns in any system.

Planetary matter merely serves to prescribe the real-information points at which life is possible within a star's gravitational field. Where matter is, there is the potential in time of life and intelligence. No matter can exist outside the influence of a star.

Gravitation is the property of a star, and intelligence is the ultimate property of the matter orbiting it. The power of gravitation in the star draws life and finally intelligence out of matter.

The third set of lines is *force lines*. Matter appearing on gravitation lines in the Draconic Transverse immediately polarises into force lines.

Force lines emerge from each of the planets to form discrete electro-magnetic fields of planetary intelligence. The force lines of the planet earth represent conceptual or formal intelligence.

Power lines, gravitation lines and force lines each have their own time gradient or speed of time. Power lines represent the world of spirit whose time is beyond our comprehension; gravitation lines represent the world of real time

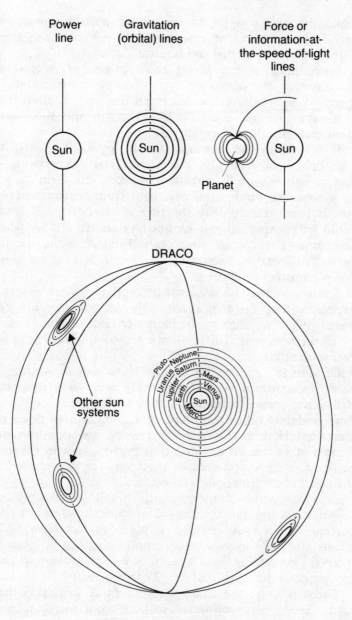

The Draconic Transverse —
Power, Gravitation and Force Lines

185

which can and now for the first time must be understood; and force lines in our case represent our physical, sense-perceptive world of past and interval.

Force lines of the planet earth consist of information travelling at the speed of light. Energy travelling at the speed of light cannot be instantaneous as real time is: it is always 'behind' the moment of origin and thus forms an interval of elapsed time or past.

It is due to the slowness of our force-line intelligence that light from the sun, the nearest star from which we receive information, is perceived to take about eight minutes to journey to earth. Similarly, light from the next nearest star is four years old by the time it reaches us. That star could have exploded and vanished yesterday and we would not know about it for four years. Even after the star had ceased to exist we would still be seeing it as it no longer was for another four years.

We can never know sense-perceptively what is really happening out there in space, only what has already happened. While we cling to the limitation of force-line thinking — intellectual materialism — we are compelled to live forever in the past.

Of course, in the intimately closed-circuit system of earth existence it works reasonably well. But associated with that same reasonable physical or sense-perceptive time gradient is the dreadful personal limitation of death and mortality. Here in this book we are endeavouring to understand and so enter the swifter time gradient in which interval or death is exceeded because that pause or past, caused by the delay of information, is eliminated.

In that swifter time gradient, it will be remembered, information and the resultant are identical, whereas to our perception information always precedes the result. This means that in the swifter perception there is no past, no interval: everything is new as it is every moment without any previous moment (past) to give it continuity.

There is only one thing that moves at this faster-than-light speed, that continues without continuity, without past — and that is life. Life is gravitational. Living, which is our conception of life, moves at a snail's pace beside it.

Life, being at the same time the information and the resultant, the beginning and the end, knows no intervening interval
and hence no death. Gravitational consciousness which observes life in this way therefore marks the state of perceived
immortality.

To individual consciousness grounded in gravitation lines
(real time), no 'time' is available for any conceptual existence
like our self-consciousness to occur in. Such a self-conscious
or self-terminating existence as ours is perceived to be unreal
against the moment-to-moment presence of all things without
beginning or end. Further, this unreal existence of ours is
seen to be a condition of the intelligence identifying with it
— in other words, the present evolved condition of the intelligence of life on earth.

Since our force-line human intelligence can only process
the gravitational information of life at the speed of light,
the residue piles up as a mighty backlog of interval or past.
While life as new information races on virtually unnoticed,
human intelligence is almost fully occupied with trying to
understand this past information. And living, as the process
of trying to sort out the past, takes over as the dominant
activity on earth.

That backlog of past has been building up since intelligence emerged out of life on earth. It has now reached such
gigantic proportions that the task of processing or conceptualising it (which was an impossible race against itself,
anyway) has become the ceaseless and wearing toil called our
way of life.

Force lines, sleep and death

Every human being is a force line of the planet earth. And
his physical body is the temporary visible manifestation of
the force line.

But an individual's force line is unaffected by the life or
death of the body. Each person as a force line and irrespective of whether alive or dead is a permanent part of the earth.

While alive in the body his force line is an active circuit
of intelligence converting into light-speed — sense perception

— the moment-to-moment information of life coming down from the spirit. When he dies he retreats down his force line into the planetary psyche. Here, unencumbered by the senses, the information he receives is more immediate and 'moves' much faster — ranging up to and beyond the present of real time (gravitation) through to the present or presence of spirit (power).

This is because behind and sustaining all people or force lines is the sun's terrestrial gravitation line represented by the body of the planet. And behind that again is the sun's spiritual power line to Draco, the serpent's head.

Similarly, when we go to sleep we recede from the body's accumulated past towards the present. Sleep is merely the need to be cleansed of the past continuously acquired through our waking penetration of the body. The further we travel up the force line towards the gravitation line or present, the more our acquired past is dissolved and the more refreshed, restored and ready for action we feel on waking. Death is precisely the same need — to be cleansed of the entire accumulated past of that particular physical existence so that we can return and create a fresh new temporary body for a fresh new temporary life.

When a person withdraws into the psyche in sleep or at death, his force line does not disappear. It remains as a current of energy or life-force representing the potential difference between the two worlds of the dying living and the living dead, the positive and the negative. In this way the force line maintains the person's connection with the world, although when the person is dead it has no manifested presence.

This permanence of force lines ensures that when a person dies he is able to return to earth by being reborn in a new body. Force lines are the means of reincarnation. They are also the means by which the dead are able to revisit the earth.

Permanence as a force line also ensures that when a person sleeps or goes unconscious he wakes up in his own body and not someone else's.

When a person goes to sleep the world disappears for him. But in spite of his absence from it it continues at the same rate to release time as interval or information. This 'lost' time or information he feels unconsciously is his 'missing' past — and his constant activity in the world is his attempt to find it. Each time he wakes he exerts himself in yet another effort to catch up with the past but eventually and inevitably it disappears unresolved into the mountain of all his other yesterdays.

This continuous daily burst of activity to find one's own missing past is the origin of man's drive for knowledge, his need to know what happened and why; and emotionally, of the impatience to get finished or get done. Both compulsions are as endless as they are futile for knowledge of the past gained through concepts and the senses achieves nothing: after he rests or sleeps he has more to do and more to find out; and after that he has to sleep which puts him behind again, creating more need to find out and do.

As a race, the ceaseless frenetic activity of humanity is an involuntary attempt to catch up with the information gaps, expendable time intervals, created by our combined lapses into sleep, death and unconsciousness. We try to do this by producing an ever-swifter output of what was lost in those intervals of lost consciousness — information as communication.

To help us keep up we invented machines, then electrical devices, and next it will be something even more swiftly productive of information — until finally in desperation we face up to the fact that it is the old story of the dog chasing its tail: that there is only one way out — to leave the world of expendable past to the robots and jump to the next time gradient.

This — until we can manage it ourselves while alive — death does for us now. Death is temporary respite from the hopeless human race.

The reducing speed of light

The speed of light in a vacuum is officially given as 300,000 kilometres per second. But then no vacuum is possible in the physical universe, or in any other. Even light cannot

189

travel on nothing. Every so-called vacuum — even the theoretical kind created in the scientist's mind for him to theorise about such things — contains gravitation lines.

Gravitation lines are the medium along which light travels as information to form force lines. And the nature of gravitation lines is time, real time: the motionless, actionless, interval-less energy of pure consciousness.

Scientists are currently searching for what are called gravitons, the particles or waves they believe are concerned in gravitation. If they ever find them — true gravitons and not some functional reflection in their minds — they will be face to face with my principle of time and the certainty of a realisable, discontinuous, individual immortality.

Meanwhile, the existence of gravitation lines as something entirely new called by the old name time, may be difficult for materialistic scientific consumption. But that does not alter the fact of it. What science and the world have called time to date, is interval, which adds up to historicity or theoretical concept which cannot go back to the truth of the 'beginning'. As I have endeavoured to explain, interval — the total gradient of our sense-perceived existence which is merely an accumulation of past — moves like wave-motion in the medium of time. Time — real time — is no more affected or involved than the carrier or principle behind the waves of the sea, or any other wave phenomena. In fact all wave phenomena, even the wave of humanity, are carried on time. Time is the continuum that not only carries light, but carries life. Light and life both move in or through time like waves. Time is not subject to cause and effect — time is both at the same time. Time is present presence.

To date, science as a whole has shown little understanding of real time and none at all of power or spirit. It recognises one time only, our time, and that is not time at all, but interval or past. This omission occurs because the body of scientific intelligence is currently grounded in the inferior planetary force lines rather than in gravitation lines. Although the intelligence of individual scientists rises continuously to gravitational levels of inspiration and genius, the body of scientific opinion continues to cling to the conceptualised past.

A drastic global revolution in the body of scientific knowledge is pending. It will be the biggest upheaval ever in science — and possibly in world history. A fantastic breakthrough will follow, opening the way to a completely new system of physics for the twenty-first century. It will involve events that give a wide-spread appreciation of real time as I am describing it and force a complete break with past force-line thinking and present intellectual materialism.

* * *

Science has also yet to realise that the speed of light is getting slower in relation to man. This is because man is getting imperceptibly closer to reality. As science proceeds in the future that is left, the discrepancy between light-speed and man's intelligent capability will begin to be noticed more and more. More and more compromises, intellectual inventions such as virtual particles, singularity and the positivity of the vacuum, will have to be made to avoid facing up to the simple truth of time as I have described it with its enormous significance for man of a realisable immortality.

When life as intelligence first appeared on earth, the speed of light was almost identical with time. Light moved so swiftly in relation to intelligence that like time it was almost stationary and as a result there was barely any interval or past in the world. But the evolution of intelligence on earth has put the interval in time and slowed down light-speed so that now it is well separate from time.

As intelligence developed (speeded up), the gap or interval between time and light-speed increased. Today light-speed is a relatively slow phenomenon compared with the oscillation-speed that intelligence on earth has reached at the top end of its gradient: hence the emergence of relativity and quantum theory. And it is becoming notably less satisfactory (if only some scientific authority would admit it) in meeting the demands of intelligence on earth.

Time and the speed of light are now a good way apart. And science will have to realise this, and face up to the implications, to enter the new-century physics.

23
Induction and deduction

The creation order as I have described it is: intellect, lines of power, universal mind, space, stars, matter and force lines. All of these 'events' occur simultaneously and together represent the moment of eternity after which nothing else ever happens except in retrospect, or by deduction, which provides our idea of time and the sense-perceived world.

It would be impossible to describe or understand such events were it not for induction. Induction is the state of seeing the now; deduction is the method of seeing the past.

Induction is probably the most poorly defined and least understood word in the philosophic glossary. This is not surprising, as induction is the act of seeing the truth or, in the context I have been describing it in, of being able to observe eternity.

Induction, being a state, cannot be learned. Deduction, being a method, is learned. The deductive process begins naturally in the now as the means by which we are taught as infants to evaluate our entire knowledge of experience in the sense-perceived world. We deduce everything from past information, even the existence of ourselves and the world around us.

Deduction means arriving at a relative whole, or a conclusion, from a consideration of parts or details. A detective practises deduction by drawing together the clues of a crime into an all-embracing picture that hopefully points to the culprit.

Even so, is the culprit ever the whole, the whole cause? Never: he is still only a part. The whole arrived at by deduction is only a relative whole, a partial whole that is no bigger than its parts. The process is selective, taking only what it thinks to be significant and rejecting everything else. Deduction is a process of individual intelligence in which the results can be as varied as the levels of intelligence and self-interest.

Induction, on the other hand, is a state of mind, a state of intelligence, in which the presence of the individual cannot affect the results. The results are implicit, invariable, precisely the same for everyone who enters the same state.

Anyone able to observe eternity or the now will understand my description of both, as I will understand their descriptions. They may see other aspects as well, but those I have mentioned will be there. It is because of this that we are able to perceive, love and appreciate the truths seen by Socrates, Plato, Buddha, Christ and other great philosophers of the past.

Intuition is a familiar instance of induction: in that moment I am aware of knowing a truth without having had to deduce it or infer it. But as soon as I think about it, doubt it or need to check it I am back in the past – back in deduction.

To observe the now, eternity, the myth or the truth of existence as a whole and not partially, one has to be inducted into pure, objective time: a state open to every man as soon as he can perceive the truth of deduction and the past. The state then implies the parts; the communication is immediate; the whole IS the parts.

Deduction is the other way round: from a series of parts or details one tries to infer a whole and yet can only reach a conclusion which is another sort of part.

I cannot arrive at eternity, or the whole truth, by inference or deduction. I will always fall short of it as the Big Bang theory so amply illustrates. I must begin by knowing or entering the whole *now* – and its parts will then be implicit as my knowledge.

To demonstrate this in a worldly and therefore partial sense: If I enter a room (the now or eternity) and describe what is there at that moment I am not deducing or inferring, not relying on past clues. What I see is implicit in my being (there). Because I am inducted, introduced into the state (the room or eternity), there is no distinction for me between the whole and its parts. Is the table in the corner not a part of the room I am describing? The weakness of this worldly parallel is that I am relying on my senses. If one of them fails me I may be in trouble, perhaps back in the dark, in ignorance. The observation of eternity does not require senses.

Induction, as the dictionary shows, is another word for initiation. When we are able to discern the now or eternity, in other words see the truth of existence and describe or appreciate it, we are indeed in an initiated, privileged state of mind or intelligence. One is then not dependent on the past or the interval required for reasoning or deduction.

Induction is supposed to be the way that laws are formulated: by inference from particular experience or observations. But laws — for instance, of gravity — are not inferred; they are observed, discovered in the moment. In the moment the law is perceived, the truth of the whole of it is present. What comes after is deduction, resurrection — and always partial.

As soon as a law or principle is used deductively — that is, remembered, thought about or believed — it is no longer a whole but a part: a part of my experience, a part of my past world. There can be no whole in the past, or coming from the past. The whole is directly experienced in the moment now — and then there is no need of deduction or parts because all is implicit in the whole being observed.

At the everyday level induction operates with the same unerring and unarguable straightforwardness: it is the act of seeing what is there in front of us now without the complication of classifying or comparing it.

For example, no one can tell us we are not seeing the words on this page: the truth is implicit in the looking. All the truths of our existence now are implicit now in what we are doing and seeing. The only limitation is how clearly we are perceiving.

The error creeps in as soon as we try to interpret what we are seeing, or put it in some other context outside of the now where it is. An example is when we tell another person what we think they are seeing or should be seeing — in other words, give out our opinions. The fact is, there can be no argument with what is true now in a person's own experience: it is with his deductions (opinions and inferences) that we disagree, as that person will disagree with ours. All normal people will agree that the sky is blue if they are all looking now; but whether it was blue yesterday will be invariably disputed by someone.

We all use induction throughout our day but mostly it goes unnoticed so that we are unable to appreciate the freedom it gives. We are in the state of induction when we are enjoying ourselves or working happily or normally oblivious of any personal problems. But when in such a state we suddenly remember a problem and start thinking, we lose our freedom and spontaneity: that is deduction, inference, establishing our identity by past reference.

To make the point of induction clearer: say I am in a place where I describe by telephone some of the objects around me. The game is to guess where I am. Is the game deduction or induction? It depends on which role you identify with.

If you identify with the detective role, the person at the other end of the phone, it is deduction: he starts off in the dark being forced to rely on reasoning from the clues or parts given to try to arrive at the truth of where I am now.

But if you are I the observer inside the place giving the clues, it is a clear case of induction: I am in the room now, in the know, in the light so to speak — in the truth. I do not need clues or interval for laborious consideration. I am at the beginning and end of the game.

Going back to the first detective example: the question is, can the detective by deduction arrive at the truth?

He might find the guilty person but he cannot find the truth. There will be other such culprits, other such relative truths: that deduction game never ends, as life shows.

What the detective is really trying to find by his life experience, and not merely by his deductive detective job, is where he himself, the man, is.

Once that truth is induced, or he is inducted into it, the deduction game is up — or over.

24
Man

As it is, the universe is stationary. As we conceive it, it is in constant motion.

In this chapter I intend to explain a number of facets leading up to the actual mechanics of how evolved intelligence makes the universe move. First, let us get the stationary side clear and how it relates to man.

Eternal man and reasonable man

The stationary, pure intellect with all its truth and power is implicit in the moment of eternity which is in every individual man's awareness now.

All that prevents any man from inducing eternity in his own mind at this moment is his evolved intelligence, that is, his habitual reliance on his reasoning and deductive faculty. He cannot induce eternity because he cannot believe it, or deduce it, first. His approach is back to front.

That deductive faculty has no place in eternity, nor any hope of ever perceiving or knowing it, let alone entering it. Fortunately, that deductive faculty or self has evolved independently of the real man that every man is. The first task now at this stage of intelligent evolution is to leave the deductive faculty in the world where it belongs and to discover the real man behind it.

The real man of every man is in eternity now, is an implicit part of eternity. The real man of every man on earth is his intellect. As every man has this intellect, every man is real in so far as he is conscious of his intellect now in the same

196

distinct way as he is aware now of his intelligent deductions (such as his thoughts and feelings) and his body. He has to discover and become familiar with the character of his intellect.

Let me make it clear what I am implying. The real man in every man is his intellect which never changes. The unreal man is the constantly unsteady intelligent faculty or self, the thing that thinks and reasons and that has evolved out of life on earth.

The real man, the intellect, does not evolve. It is the same now as always; eternal. It is so real, close and intimate now to each man as himself that he takes it for granted, confusing it with his evolving human natural self whose existence is completely dependent on it.

Without the presence of the intellect, intelligence and intelligent life are impossible; the reasoning deductive man could not reason or deduce; there would be nothing to bounce his perceptions off, no space in which to think, nothing to make the world real, knowable.

So we have this extraordinary situation: man's intellect is real; his intelligence is not — not until it is evolved sufficiently to give up its dependence on the past, its notions and motions, its inferences, itself. Immediately intelligence does this, it induces the now, eternity, the intellect, the real man; immediately, intelligence and intellect are conjoined: the part that somehow appeared by reason to become separated is once more implicit in the whole, and the deductive interval — cause and effect — is dissolved or bridged.

The principle of the other, or the eternal paradox

But life or the motional world as we perceive it still goes on. How?

By means of self-reflection, which we call sense-perception.

Let us return to the coin example of the stationary intellect on the mind side, and the motional, evolving universe on the other side. As we shall now see, they are not a world apart but a world together.

Self-reflection on the mind side, is sense-perception on the motional side.

On the mind side, the intellect is reflecting itself. And the effect of self-reflection, or self reflecting self without an observer or monitor being present, is nothing. The observer or monitor, here, is our deductive, evolved, intelligent self who is always getting in the way of the truth or the moment of induction. Hence, mystics and others who realise exalted truths declare that the highest truth is nothing. In that moment they have eliminated or overcome their motional intelligent faculty, the monitor, and are self-reflecting on self — the intellect, nothing.

The effect of the intellect reflecting itself without the self-conscious monitor being present can be likened to the inside of a mirrored empty sphere: the reflection there is of nothing. This example, because it excludes the monitor, has to be incomprehensible to our deductive reasoning. But strangely and splendidly we can get the idea of it quite simply and easily. We do this through the intellect, through induction — by disengaging the logical and pedantic deductive monitor and by just being, just listening to the words, just being there.

I was saying that self-reflection on the mind side equals sense-perception on the motional side. How this is so, and how I am able to know this, is contained in the principle of the idea of side, or other.

One side of a coin (or anything) implies the other.

Narcissus did not know he had fallen in love with his own reflection: it was his assumptive self that had not yet become deductively self-conscious which, in its unevolved one-sided ignorance, caused the beautiful youth to pine away and die from lack of love, not love. One side of a coin — even a mirrored reflection in a pool — implies the other; but only to intelligence that has evolved to the level of self-consciousness, the point in evolution on the motional side where man started to emerge from the rest of the species. Narcissus was on the assumptive first wave of man. We are on the deductive second wave going into the inductive third.

One side of anything implies the other.

What is other? We assume, here, it is side, that is, something having characteristics of 'this', this side. But we do not know that. Neither that other side nor its character can be deduced from this side. The other side is implicit.

Further, two sides of a coin, or anything, cannot be perceived simultaneously — or so it appears to deductive reasoning. Implicit in one side alone is the other. What is implicit is by induction intrinsic, inseparable in character from the whole. This means one side of anything is induced or real, and the other side is deduced or assumed.

This I call the principle of the other.

The question implicit in the principle of the other — and which arises with the self-consciousness Narcissus did not have — is which side is real?

This is what I call the paradox of eternity, or the eternal paradox. It can only be answered or the answer perceived by intelligence that has evolved to the next stage after self-consciousness.

The question I am asking is this: can we now, at this moment, from the principle of the other, perceive and determine which side of the universe (or anything) is real as well as the character of that reality?

The answer is yes. So let us do it. At the same time we will start to get the idea of how our world comes into being.

I have said that one side of anything is induced and real, and the other is deduced or assumed.

If we look at a coin or anything now, which side are we looking at, the true or the false?

We are looking at the false, the unreal, because the side we are seeing implies the other; and the other, as we can perceive it now, does not exist: it is as nothing. This is a stupendous perception.

We must not be misguided into thinking that by turning the coin over we are seeing the other. Doing this, we are still looking at the same side, the sense-perceived side, which is our habitual perception, the not-too-swift deductive faculty that is always on this side and never sees the other side. The other side, it can be clearly seen, is nothing; it does not exist from this side and non-existence, or nothing, is its immediately-presented implicit character.

So is it true that the other side of the universe, or the

intellect reflecting itself which produces nothing, cannot be seen? No. It is being seen now, not by deduction, but by induction, the direct self-presenting truth of the now which demonstrates that the other side of anything does not exist: it appears as nothing as can be seen now.

The truth is crystal clear. The world is completely lop-sided, one-sided. The other is nothing! One side of the world does not exist.

Implicit in this are several other great truths.

As the other side, nothing, is implicit in this side but cannot be deduced from this side, then to perceive that nothingness must demand an induced or inducted state of mind. In other words, anyone seeing that nothing as the other side of this side, is not on this side but is in the other. That, of course, is a description of the intellect observing itself, or reflecting itself, with nothing at all being produced or nothing in between. Anyone seeing this truth no matter how fleetingly to begin with, is looking into eternity. In that moment, they are the intellect. They are as nothing.

Another truth arising out of this is that the false (side) always implies the true (side). In other words, what is true can only be seen through what is false.

The implications of this are amazing as we shall see; and it brings us back to the world of sense-perception — not that we ever really left the world, but we did have to utilise a different and stiller state of perception which literally saw the truth by looking through this world.

Sense-perception, this side, is the false and yet it is only through it or because of it that above we were able to see the truth of the other, the nothing, the character of eternity which shields the intellect from our direct vision.

Why is it necessary to perceive the truth through the false?

Our problem as earthlings is that evolving human intelligence cannot stand to see the intellect or man's real being as it is in its stationary state. The race intelligence has not yet evolved sufficiently to face the full blast of its truth and power.

This is both our human limitation and our protection.

As humans, we cannot take the intellect as it is. The naked truth and power of it is too much for us. Even at the higher end of human intelligence which we just induced, we can still only look at it through the protective character of eternity — nothing — and receive its truths through implication, or myth. So, in the sense-perceived world the infinite truth and power of the intellect is broken down into objects and movement.

This, terrestrial intelligence has managed to do through evolution by developing a very complex and amazingly ingenious sense-perceptive screen. The vital intelligence we are looks through the eye-piece of the senses into reality and the senses plus the perception attached to them break down the power and truth of it into interval, that is, into a succession of pauses so that we receive only small sequential doses.

While the senses and the evaluating perception behind them make the truth and power of reality bearable to our state of development, they also make the reality appear to move, giving us an attenuated, moment-to-moment experience of it which we call time and motion.

The questions implicit in this are, how is it done? And what are the mechanics of it?

On the mind side it is all very simple: the intellect is observing, reflecting itself, as we have seen. Being all, it is completely self-contained, self-sufficient, the supreme truth or great self. As only the false implies the true and never vice versa, it is oblivious of any motional universe or other (side) existing outside its own omnipresent self.

There is no movement or time in the great self. But the moment of its appearance as the intellect induced the moment of eternity and that one and only moment continues forever as pure, objective time.

That event, the only real event ever to happen, caused what I can only describe as an echo, the release of an eternal succession of implicit ideas that continues as the now. (Now is the only real event of all time, there being no other time but now for anything else to happen.)

Unbeknown to the great self, the echo carried through the power lines to eternity. That eternal echo is now being 'listened' to and translated into life on earth through an incredible terrestrial apparatus called sense, matter or sensation (sense plus intelligence).

This vital apparatus — the sense-machine — was developed by terrestrial intelligence working behind the scenes of matter through the psychic brain, as I have described at the beginning of this book.

Further, through the sense-machine and the earth idea in matter, terrestrial intelligence translates the eternal echo of the great self into myriad sensations of little-self — us.

Hence the earlier statement that self-reflection on the mind side is equivalent to sense-perception on the motional side. For self, read vitally intelligent selves.

Now we come to the location of the intellect relative to the senses.

Behind the sense-apparatus is our vitally intelligent or sensuous self and behind that again is the intellect.

One might perhaps have thought that the sense-apparatus would be facing 'out' towards the intellect in the same way as we deduce we are looking out at the motional universe. But it is not.

The sense-machine's operational function is not unlike the human astronomers' largest telescopes which have a small angular eye-piece through which the final image of the object is presented after numerous refractions within the instrument. The eye-piece image does not indicate in which direction the main lens is facing, nor is it material.

In the head of the observer using the eye-piece is his brain and within the brain, way, way back, is the intellect.

Similar again to the idea behind a telescope or camera lens, intelligence on earth has a moveable linear depth of focus. Either it can be hard up against the eye-piece as the vitally involved sensuous self, or it can be way, way back, sensationally stilled and almost one with the stationary intellect behind or within.

In this last condition or when approaching it, a man is able virtually to look back over his shoulder away from the machine and implicitly perceive the presence of the intellect, the character of which, as we have seen, appears as nothing.

At other times he can become so sensationally stilled, that is vitally detached from a surfeit of looking or living through the eye-piece of the senses, that he is able to look back not only direct at the nothing but through the nothing to reality. He then enters eternity, is conjoined with the intellect and perceives all the power and truth of it as his real self that his present evolved level of being or intelligence can absorb.

* * *

Now we come to the mechanics.

The sense-machine and the vital perception attached to it which together make up the sense-complex work at the speed of light. Everything relies on the speed of light for its finite or sensible existence.

We must break with the habitual thinking that the speed of light refers only to the external world. Light-speed is the maximum velocity at which any information or data can be transmitted, not only in physical space but also in the human mind.

It has been a fundamental error of science and reason to place our senses outside the laws of the universe and to ignore sense-perception as the critical factor still influencing all observations and experiments. Data is data and in a force-field such as the earth's there is no distinction between external space and mind because our minds are in that field or that field is in our minds. All data in and out of the mind travels at a maximum velocity of around 300,000 kilometres per second.

The mechanics of intelligence and sense perception

Intelligence is the action of reflection.

For us it consists of sense-information moving at the speed of light back through the psychic brain to the deep-seated intellect off which it is reflected and returned to our physical brain.

Two levels of intelligence operate simultaneously in our awareness: terrestrial intelligence and individual intelligence.

Terrestrial intelligence, the superior level, is the combined intelligence or intellectual reflection of life on earth. Terrestrial

203

intelligence operates through the sense-apparatus described above. After converting the ever-present reality into sense-information, the sense-machine pulses the image back to reflect as terrestrial intelligence off the deep intellect and return to the individual brain, thereby creating the physical world which every human being sees as the same.

The second level, individual intelligence, consists of the same terrestrial intelligence being re-reflected off the intellect to become each person's evaluation of the physical world. This time the reflection passes through the vital double to the intellect and then back through the vital double to the brain.

Individual intelligence gives personal significance and meaning to our terrestrial perceptions and in the process creates the person. Individual intelligence varies enormously, being determined by the evolutionary state of the individual's vital self or double through which each reflection must pass and be conditioned or coloured on the way back to the physical brain.

In the following I am going to deal mainly with terrestrial intelligence and reveal facts about it that one day will be the basis of a whole new way of observing and regarding the world scientifically and philosophically.

The truth of sense-perceptive existence follows:

The solid in which we live

Gravity is the presenter of reality to the sense-machine; the sense-machine then translates the reality at light-speed into the physical world. Gravity is the ever-present medium or presenter of reality to the planet or terrestrial intelligence in the same way as light-speed is the carrier of that information to our individual brain.

Being real, gravity before conversion by the senses contains no parts, no separation and no interval — therefore no space. Reality is total and complete togetherness.

If we look closely at the physical world in front of us now we shall see that in the whole of what we are apprehending no separation exists — *provided we see space as part of the whole*.

So, the reality is indeed repeated or reflected in sense in our physical world except for the perplexing addition of space which does not and cannot exist in reality!

How, then, does space originate?

The origin of space

The image of reality which the sense-machine pulses back to reflect off the intellect moves at the speed of light. By the time the image covers this double distance at light-speed, the moment of the brain's apprehension of it is a micro-interval behind the moment of sensing.

This discrepancy between the real and its sense-reflection is tiny but intolerable, and has to be compensated for under the universal law of conservation of energy. This compensation is made by a shrinkage of the sense-image. Thus, every object we perceive in the world is 'smaller' than it really is.

The combined shrinkage of the whole picture at any moment is the space we see. Space is sense devoid of image.

Why objects at a distance are smaller

In reality, as I have said, everything is not only immediately present; it is undifferentiated, meaning everything is 'joined together' and the same 'size' as the whole.

But in our physical world things appear to be larger in size when closer and smaller when distant.

I have explained that the double interval or distance covered by the image of reality in travelling to the deep intellect and back to the brain has to be compensated for, and that this is done by a shrinkage of the sense-image. What actually happens is this:

The reduced image and the space created during this double passage are projected 'outwards' by the sense-machine, thus producing the visual appearance of distance or depth and the phenomenon of distant objects being smaller.

But here another factor comes into play.

This is the degree of reality that has been attained by the

image being observed as well as by the observer. Evolution, cosmic and terrestrial, is the process of things (ideas) and observers (intelligence) becoming more real.

In cosmic evolution — I am talking now of evolution outside life on earth — the only real objects are, first the stars, and then their planets or other orbiting matter in which life is potential or already exists.

By us looking at the sky and stars the correlation between size, distance and reality can most easily be demonstrated.

The greater the reality of an object as seen from the earth, the smaller it appears and the more space is created between it and the observer. This is because the reality (gravity) represented by a star exerts such an enormous pull on the sense-machine (which is hard up against it, not distant) that it prevents the full energy of the image-carrying pulse escaping back to the intellect.

The result is that even though the speed of the image as it moves away from the reality remains constant and does not slow down, *the pulse is less energetic.*

The effect of this is an even more drastic constriction of the image received by the brain and a correspondingly acute creation of space. As image reduces, space increases.

Thus, near a real object of great gravity or mass, space (distance) appears to be intensified and very different in quality to the space near a less real object such as the earth or an earth observer: 'less real' because stars are more real than orbital matter and its intelligence.

Also, for an observer studying the stars there is a sharp intensification of time, producing a greater awareness of immediacy, swiftness or presence. This is demonstrated by the scientist's use of the speed of light — the ultimate finite measurement — as the basic unit of time in astrophysics and the main component of relativity theory.

Science has yet to recognise or even start to understand that cognisance of such space/time intensities near a star or real object is due to the interval, or past, being taken out of the earth observer's awareness or intelligence. This is done by the observer's intelligence literally being pulled out of the past by the gravity or reality of the object being perceived. At a certain point of pastlessness his intelligence can reach equivalence, or enter and become real time or reality. Einstein's intelligence in perceiving and defining Relativity reached that point of pastlessness.

Thus, although stars appearing to be at the greatest distance in deepest space have the smallest image or effect on the brain, the effect on intelligence, the evolving state behind the brain, is inversely tremendous.

Intensified space and intensified time as I have just described them have distinctly different and recognisable roles in the evolution of intelligence such as developed on earth and culminated in man.

Intensified space, or stellar gravity, is the universal power that draws life in the form of intelligence out of surrounding orbital matter. (This is what happened to create life on earth.) Then, as the life-form develops sufficient intelligence, intensified space around the stars attracts the attention, then the interest and finally the wonder of intelligence (in our case man) which begins to reach out, to speed up or attempt by investigation to travel back intellectually through the interval of the past and space towards reality.

Simultaneously, *intensified time* – the reduced interval or past that occurs in the vicinity of stars for someone approaching reality – releases the truth or inspiration to allow intelligence to discriminate between the motionless reality it is trying to approach and the force of the distracting incoming light-speed stream of information against which it must persevere to remain still, detached and undisturbed.

In other words, intensified space draws out intelligence, and intensified time provides the self-knowledge (immediate knowledge) for it to resist being engulfed by the incessant onslaught of sense-information and weighed down by the past.

Where the past and memory come from

I will now explain what the past is and where it comes from.

We have seen that the delay involved in the sense-image travelling from the sense-machine to the intellect and back to the brain means that when it returns to the brain as a perception it is always old. Due to the finite speed of light a micro-interval occurs between the original and the perceived image.

As image interval creates space, so it creates past.

The past is a very tangible thing for intelligence. It is created, with space, by the shrinkage of the sense-image. Each piece of space carries an indelible impression of the original image 'erased' from it by shrinkage. The resulting accumulation of these permanent spatial impressions through endless, countless perceptions since 'time' began, or since the first perception, is what the past is.

The enormous interval or past that has built up (like space) since the first sense-perceptions by life on earth began creating it, is self-evident in the history of the world and our personal memory.

But also, and far more significantly for man, the accumulated indelible impressions together sustain a record of every moment of the past since life began on earth.

This record is the virtually unsuspected and undiscovered racial memory.

The racial memory is our own living past, stretching back as I have just explained to the very first life-forms on earth. Man can only begin to understand this living past, or have access to it consciously, to the degree that he succeeds while alive in uniting with his vital double in the world of the living dead. This is done by endeavouring to clear his own personal psychic space as I have described earlier in this book.

Although the racial past or memory with its enormous range is beyond the recall of man as he is, he reflects off the substance of it all the time to affirm his external sense-impressions. For instance, if he sees a tree now the external image is reflected off the image of 'tree' in the past and he then 'knows' he is seeing a tree. This is what is called 'being objective' and 'sticking to facts'.

Without this interval of past we could not reflect as individuals. Self-consciousness would be impossible — we could not cognise our own existence. In fact, without the past there could be no life as we know it.

So, due to the accumulation of this racial interval or memory, our brain now not only receives and perceives the physical sense world but is able to reflect back the other way on to the permanent racial record of it — something like another world — and by comparisons between the two evaluate the present, reason about the future and deduce the past.

Within the same racial memory the individual man gradually builds up his own personalised impression of events in the space of his earlier perceptions, thus producing his personal memory.

While he remains 'objective' or factual he keeps this at the level of the racial memory and it works fairly well and efficiently in his personal life. But when he reflects exclusively on his personalised memory the result is emotional reflection containing hardly any intelligence. The necessary false through which the truth can and must be seen degenerates into blind ignorance which can see neither the false nor the true.

The source of ignorance

All sense information is past and represents the false through which the truth has to be seen.

But the false is not ignorance.

Even terrestrial intelligence or reflection which provides us with the physical sense-world has to be termed false because it consists of past images of reality. But compared with the deluding information we receive from reflecting exclusively on our personalised memory, terrestrial reflection is valid and real.

Reflection as intelligence on personalised memory consists almost entirely of ignorance moving at the speed of light. The consequent error and distortion are so enormous for self-conscious intelligence like man's that they create most of the tension and confusion in the world. The result for the individual is spasmodic worry and severe emotional instability which the unself-conscious species do not have to contend with.

The cosmic truth

The Big Bang theory assigns to the beginning of the universe a time, as an event, billions of years ago. It says, in other words, that the universe started billions of years before now.

The theory is derived from scientific observations made now being arithmetically tacked on to the non-existent 'other side' of the legitimate (experienced) past which began only with life on earth, as I have just explained. The result is pure fiction.

In what follows I am not attempting to deride science, but am drawing attention to an area of conjecture into which science is unknowingly straying from the boundaries of realism. In doing so it can unintentionally uphold and perpetuate a method of reasoning in cosmic physics that is not only invalid but has false premises. As the erroneous reasoning employed looks like being repeated for a long time, it is appropriate and essential to refute it now before it infects the new generations of mind. The alternative, the real, must be stated.

Man has not yet realised — and it is at the root of the whole problem of his reasoning — that he cannot calculate or deduce back beyond his own past, beyond the beginning of the species. To do so as science does in pursuing an external cosmic beginning is like solving a murder that never happened.

Beyond the unique past of life on earth, there is nothing to go back to. The cosmic truth and reality are all in the now. The past is the sole, unreal creation of earth intelligence evolving through the sense machine. This is the fundamental truth of existence that has to be realised for man to jump to the next, the real, time gradient.

Only the past — that intelligible record of the evolution of terrestrial and human intelligence — can contain differences, changes; not the now. Once intelligence understands this mighty truth that there is no cosmic past apart from what man himself has created with his perceptions, the past and the value of it will be seen in an entirely new light. All past is man's; the cosmos has none.

The scientist making his calculations that endeavour to

exceed the human past is like the spider that spins a self-supportive web out of its own secretions. The web holds up nothing but what is essentially its own survival. In relation to the spider the web is a completely subjective structure. It is all his own making. In both web and past there is no truth, no reality, except the man or spider – intelligence – shed of subjectivity.

The proposition that the cosmos has no past is naturally unacceptable. Man, as evolving intelligence, is bound to accept the unreal in all its forms until the real is explained to him and he has the chance to discriminate, or until he seriously begins the approach to reality in himself for himself.

The Big Bang error

Through the Big Bang theory science implies it has reached the end of the measurable universe. It cannot get back any further even if it appears to because every calculation persists in ending a split second before the beginning is reached.

In other words, the Big Bang theorists calculate back to a point fifteen billion years ago – fifteen billion years before now – and at the same time present it as a split second away from that which demonstrably is the ceaseless origin of everything – the now.

How can the beginning be fifteen billion years and a split second away at the same time? The proposition would be rejected as ludicrous if the erroneous thinking involved was not the universal norm. Now is now. Anything away from it or short of it is palpably unreal. By just one influential scientific mind glimpsing this truth a whole exciting new para-scientific epoch could begin.

The Big Bang error starts with the assumption that a 'past' cosmic now can be inferred from this now, in other words, that there can be two nows: one fifteen billion years away, the other a split second away. And just as startling is the further assumption that one now can be different from another now. The one self-evident quality of now is that it never changes; it is always original, always the beginning of everything.

Among the theorists' several basic mistakes in applying the Big Bang theory is the assumption that change or motion is a verity and that the universe is at any time different to what it is now.

Such an approach would be legitimate if the theory were concerned with events within the human past, the past of the species. But it is not. The theory is concerned with the cosmos — which has no past and therefore is the same now as always, as the alternative Steady State theory suggests. Now and the universe are cosmically identical: the universe is now, and now is the universe. So to have any chance of being valid the theory has to be applicable to now.

That clearly eliminates any supposed cosmic beginning fifteen billion years ago. But what of the split second? Is that, even though a fractionally minute interval, also an event relatively distant from the now?

No. That split second *is* intelligence and is the interval in which the universe is apprehended. In other words, the split second is the action or condition of terrestrial intelligence itself ceaselessly pursuing the pre-emptive unknown or the originating nothing as science and all mankind are doing in one way or another. Science has unknowingly discovered the point in time of its own intelligence: a split second away from the now.

As the scientist's application of the theory shows, no calculation (that is, movement of intelligence) has succeeded or can succeed in getting beyond the split second to the nothing because any calculation (movement of intelligence) is itself the problem. In other words, the theory shows correctly that intelligence has reached a point where it is chasing its own tail.

This tail-chasing action is due in the first instance to the false assumptions by science which I am describing. It is false assumptions, or ignorance, at every level which make intelligence move or race. Where cosmic principles are involved, any movement of intelligence is always away from the truth. Cosmic truth is implicit in the stillness of intelligence, which then becomes the pure intellect. Cosmic truth cannot be calculated or deduced. It is always intuited, even by the scientist, and then by implication applied to formal structures. Lesser minds then deduce from these formal structures — and invariably arrive at wrong conclusions.

The extraordinary thing is that essentially the Big Bang theory is an esoteric description — or in this philosophy a para-scientific description — of the true origin of the universe, *provided it is applied to the universe and the observer now* and not to a supposedly different universe in the past. But when the theory is applied historically to arrive at a supposed physical explosion creating everything out of nothing, it is hopelessly misguided and misleading.

The Big Bang theory proceeds to telescope the universe as it is perceived into a pin-point, literally to squeeze the whole physical existence of space and matter down to the size of a speck to make it all-but disappear back into the 'nothing' out of which the theory correctly intuits it must have come.

It is a fantastic feat of calculative wizardry which would be really effective, and an astonishing scientific advance, if the theorising observer realised that as intelligence he was reducing all he is seeing and imagining, including himself, to within a split second of the non-existent now-point in his own brain, the point of reality and the emergent point of the whole extant universe as far as man and sense-perception go.

Then the theory would be absolutely correct. The scientist would not be concerned with a fabricated beginning fifteen billion years ago but with himself, intelligence, being only a split second away from the pre-emptive state, his own and everything's source — the motionless pure intellect. Universe and man as intelligence would then unite in one sublime realised truth — and the way would be open for para-scientific entry into the new epoch of time and knowledge beyond light-speed, sense and past.

The rational justification for mentally reducing the universe back to a dot is that it has changed, moved or expanded since the beginning. But that is absolutely irrelevant to the cosmic objectivity; it is a subjective distortion by the observer having no meaning outside the evolution of human intelligence whose subjectivity is creating the illusion of a motional universe. The theoretical scientist is substituting the condition of his own intelligence that has created the idea of an expanding universe — that purely calculated process — for the now.

The truth behind the theory which the theorist himself has not realised is that it works perfectly when applied to the scientist himself. Then there is no need mentally to change anything or to go into the past. Repeating the analogy already used, what the scientist is doing without knowing it and without any need for calculations is merely reducing the wide end of the telescope he is looking through to the dot of his own intelligence behind the eye-piece at the other end — which somehow, until he gets the point, annoyingly continues to persist in existing as the split second of interval between the man himself and reality.

Man's being — not his intelligence — is that non-point, the pre-emptive state of the universe. His intelligence — the only moving evolving thing — is one iota or dot into existence from the non-being point.

That infinitely reducible, minute 'distance' or interval is represented by the split second intelligence surmises it is short of the ultimate. Intelligence is the split second endeavouring to eliminate itself. That it can only do internally by reducing itself to the stillness of the intellect — being without intelligence or the need to know any more because all is implicit in being.

25
Objectivity

What is it to be objective — really objective? How can we perceive the world in an entirely new way, for that obviously is what it means.

Normally, to be objective means being able to perceive a thing 'as it is' without the observer allowing emotional considerations — his subjectivity — to alter the result.

That is sufficient to arrive at and deal with the facts and practicalities of life. But to arrive at the truth of both life and death — to realise and participate in a greater reality than is normally experienced — requires a more fundamental objectivity, what amounts to a revolutionary change in the individual's way of perceiving.

Anyway, when we are being normally objective how can we be sure there is no subjective factor already distorting what we are seeing?

We cannot. In fact and truth, everything we see — the whole physical world — is already subjectively conditioned when we apprehend it.

For one thing, as I have explained, no object in the world is its original 'size': all is hugely diminished by conversion to sense, which simultaneously creates space (another distortion), also past (a further distortion).

Moreover, the initial intelligence in us which cognises the sense world — terrestrial intelligence — due to its present evolutionary status creates the false impression of movement: another distortion. Our normal perception is like a four-dimensional movie that embraces and encloses us, and we cannot get out of it except by a very special way — realising objectivity.

What humanity regards as being objective, even at the professional and scientific level, is still a phase in our innate subjectivity. However, in the planetary consciousness, behind our normal extrapolating awareness, is an objective point, and it is this that we have to discover, reach and realise.

Objectivity is so subtle and elusive to our subjective comprehension that it defies definition: we cannot be told in advance what we are looking for. Hence the need for it to be individually realised, in the same way as being in love or any other sensational state has to be self-realised before it can be known intellectually.

The first step towards realising objectivity is to understand subjectivity — the almost total subjectivity of human perception. This we will now attempt to do.

Three subjectivities are at work in the human psyche. They are: first, the senses; second, the egoic naming process; and third, the vital or emotional self.

Subjectivity No. 1: the senses

The senses present precisely the same physical world to all humanity. Here there is no thought or calculation, no re-arranging of context or significance outside of what is; no 'this' or 'that', no 'me' or 'mine'.

Here is the impersonal human condition where all humanity (the observer) is fundamentally one in the one world or perception. Mountain or tree appear the same to all.

At this point of human awareness, no persons exist. There is no evaluated difference in what is seen or who is seeing it; no adopted position or attitude. The observer could be anyone, is anyone. Here, in fact, we are the impersonal intelligence of humanity observing the world as it is from a myriad of individual positions in the human psyche — hence, terrestrial intelligence.

However, as straightforward as this initial sense-perception seems, it is still, as I have explained, subjective.

Subjectivity No. 2: the egoic naming process

Subjectivity No. 2, the almost instantaneous egoic naming process which follows, is where humanity – the intelligence of the earth – starts to divide into persons. Here our individual or divided self begins. The world having been perceived as the senses present it to all humanity, our individual perception then takes over and starts the attribution, orientating and naming process.

This process is the mental dynamic of existence. Although not a part of the senses, or sense machine, the ego attaches itself to the senses and by naming of objects and repetition starts constructing the subtle or intellectual memory. By ceaselessly re-identifying things through language or thought it creates a conceivable, considerable, reflective world. This intellectual world is the basis for our reasonably presumed professional and scientific objectivity.

Naming requires past. For a thing to be named or recognised it must have been previously cognised. That initial cognition and essential past are provided by the senses (subjectivity No. 1) which act first by conveying and reducing reality down to our perceived physical world.

This shrinkage of the sense images in the human psyche provides the necessary space and past for the ego to set up shop in and start work. The work of the ego, which begins even before birth in the womb, is to fill the child's psychological space with its own images or personal impressions of the perceived world, thus gradually building up the subtle memory.

In this task the ego is assisted by the parent's (and the environment's) continual repetition of naming and reaffirmation-by-experience of identifying words. Thus language and thought gradually become substitutes for objects – and the intellectual world is created.

In other words, the original reality converted by the senses to the world of what is, is now further converted into the world of what was – the memory. Here the ego lives and operates ceaselessly as thinking, calculating and dreaming.

The ego, being outwardly attentive on the world, has

— in spite of popular misconceptions — a minimum of self-centred identification. It is only very faintly dependent on the emotional or vital body, subjectivity No. 3. The ego is like the flame at the tip of a wick that will continue to burn with very little wax (body or emotion).

Subjectivity No. 3: the vital or emotional self

The virulence, potency and violence behind all human subjectivity is in desire coming from the emotional self and expressing itself through the physical body.

As the ego is the self of awareness and thought, this emotional self is the self of feeling and sensation. It is the real weight behind self-centredness. By pressing up on the ego it uses it, forces it to express its desires in words and thought in the same way as the wax of a candle 'forces' the wick to keep burning.

The emotional self creates the personally exclusive and highly viscous memory of 'me' and 'mine'. This memory is not intellectual — ungrounded — like the subtle memory but rooted in sensation.

The emotional self, as I have explained, is formed out of the psychic reservoir of past and self created by all life that has ever lived on earth. This vast reservoir of past — the racial memory — is pathological, and I use the word in the sense of the original Greek root 'pathos': suffering. It includes the original, experiential memory of all the species which is preserved in the deep unconscious of the terrestrial psyche and is expressed in the intermediate levels as man's emotions.

The racial memory is incredibly residual, immemorially ancient. Through each person's emotional self the whole mortal past of the species, its sufferings, dreads and fears, influences the behaviour of humanity in the now.

Backed by this immense force of sensuous past, antedating thought and enlightening knowledge in the species, the emotional self compels the ego, when its desires are opposed or crossed, to name, accuse, judge and argue with vehemence. Words and thoughts are used as weapons or

218

lures, depending on the kind of sensational or physical gratification this emotional subjectivity demands at the time.

* * *

Those are the three subjectivities separating us from reality or objectivity. And yet, paradoxically, they are the only means — life — by which we can attain to it.

In what follows I will be speaking to the first and second subjectivities in the reader because the third subjectivity, the emotional self, unless quiescent has no chance of or interest in understanding or participating. Only in the ego's realisation of objectivity does the emotional self start to become enlightened. Even then it is a very long process to bring the power of realised objectivity down into the emotional self and into the body — which is the very point of life after death and life after realisation.

Association

As our divided self, the ego, we are unable to make sense of anything in isolation. Each of us perceives individual objects not as themselves (as the senses present them) but in association with other objects, that is, partially and historically. Everything is placed in a context of the past, grouped in the subtle memory with other objects previously named and remembered which themselves had been subject to the same time-slotting process right back to our earliest infantile perceptions. Everything is strung out along the line of time, in the past, so as to be understood. That means giving each object or condition a selective relationship to other objects which the thing itself does not have. By doing this we create reasonable significance — one thing pointing to another, cause and effect, continuity, or in other words, historicity.

Whether we are awake or asleep the divided self is ceaselessly active in our memory, slotting and re-slotting even the most trivial perceptions into some 'reasonable' context, so much so that with the habit of years it gains an insane sort of tempo like a chattering idiot whose aimless jabbering is often heard on the edge of sleep — and outwardly in the aged and senile when the restraints and need of practical performance have broken down. For all of us, what began as the necessary business of establishing a functional memory degenerates sooner or later into an involuntary nightmare — the uncontrollable restless mind.

To begin perceiving objectively we have to release ourselves from this instinctive associative and grouping habit. We have to start observing objects without subtle connecting thought to the past or future, and without being afraid — for if we succeed even for an instant we are on the edge of eternity where nothing familiar in time exists and awful loneliness or emptiness can be sensed. It will be obvious from this that thought, as the associative function, is time.

To start being really objective we have to learn to interrupt the automatic naming or thinking process. We must thrust our intelligence in between what the senses present and the normal aimless, egoic reaffirming of what is seen. The ego must no longer be allowed to identify things habitually and think indiscriminately in the subtle memory as it does all the time when we have nothing particular on our mind.

This means that for a long while ahead we can never relax as we have in the past. We must be uncompromisingly vigilant, not allow one aimless movement of thought in our heads. We have to stay in the now: see only what the senses are presenting every moment without judgment or subtle discrimination, and denying any memory reference whatever unless it is to find a fact to carry out a practical action. We must commit ourselves to not discussing or relating past events.

We will fail frequently. But we must not be discouraged, for even to be discouraged is a sign of egoic interference, reference to the past. Life is now and for the purpose of discovering its objectivity, its deathlessness, we will never run out of time. We must be patient and resolute, never naming failure but forgetting it by staying in the now and trying to do better next time which is now, anyway.

To start being objective we have to be very honest with ourselves. We seldom need to refer to the past, even to yesterday: if we do we are probably fooling ourselves – or the ego is fooling us. In the first twenty-one years of our life we have done most of the naming we ever need to do. What we have to do now is dissolve the thick layer of past that has built up over and obscured the impersonal point in our psyche through which we must go forward into increasing objectivity, or reality, finally to arrive at the one real undivided and undividing self that each of us is.

Perceiving objectively

To be objective in any instant we must be free of thought or evaluation. We must resist the pressure to run the instants together to think about or consider what our senses are reporting. We must see with our senses without naming what we are seeing, without imparting historicity to the object. We will then deny the object subjective continuity and thus remove it from the past and future as well as from ourselves. We will then be perceiving it exactly as it is.

But to try being objective with any object or person in our daily lives is extremely difficult. Each has too much habitual association. The familiar world around us, as a result of our constant, reaffirming, associative thinking, has solidified into blocks of time from which it can be agonising for us to try to pry ourselves free. Even to lose one piece of it, such as an old friend, someone we love or a valued possession or position, can produce great distress and grief.

It is the memory of things lost that pains us so much. This memory reflex extends down into the cells of our bodies. Addiction is a cellular craving for repetition or continuity of the familiar, the known, the past.

To start to perceive the objective reality of existence we have to exclude those things that are sub-effects, that is those things that are not cosmic, that were not present in the first instant of eternity. This includes all man-made objects as well as people as they represent successional time or interval and, to begin with, are almost impossible to perceive objectively.

If we go outside on a clear night and observe the stars without any reference to the earth, or speculative thought, all that we see is what manifested in the first instant that never ends. As the universe we are looking at is now, is as it has always been. It is the beginning and the end. It is there when we are born; there when we die. It is eternal.

If our perception is very swift, we will realise that this instant of observation is identical with that first eternal instant, and that each instant in which we fail to see any motion in the heavens is the same timeless, eternally present instant. By looking at something that has no past, such as the cosmos, and seeing it as it is, the observer himself sheds his past, loses his subjectivity.

If, on the other hand, he thinks, calculates or draws a conclusion, he has awarded it a past it does not have; he has imposed his functional self on it, given the timeless a piece of his own limital intelligence, and therefore rendered the objective subjective. Inasmuch as he thinks and calculates, he is seeing a function of himself; and the reality remains as distant and elusive as ever.

The universe is a mirror, an intellectual reflector, until a man learns to see through appearances. Later, when he can look at any object or person without subtly imputing past to either, the same universal reality will be perceived.

If while observing the heavens our perception is very swift we will see that the universe is as it always is irrespective of sub-effects such as people, objects or circumstances which may appear to come between. Objectivity is to hold this timelessness of the universe, or the now, irrespective of what else may be going on 'below' in human affairs. If in our daily lives we can remain identified with a timeless object like the universe, or the now, we ourselves are similarly timeless and therefore similarly objective, eternal and real. A man is as mortal or immortal as the idea or time he identifies with.

If when looking at the heavens we are tempted to surmise that the starry scene we are observing has changed since the first instant, we are speculating and thinking successionally. Now is the first and only instant. Whether or not the objects we are seeing have changed appearance or position is irrelevant and dependent on thought and time as interval. Such reasoning requires two instants to be run together as now and then — and we have entered the time-trap of subjectivity.

Let us say we are observing the heavens and we become aware of movement such as the twinkle of a star. This twinkle is a sub-effect caused by the earth's atmosphere — really, our own subjectivity — and as such is not part of the wider universe. We have to look through the twinkle, through the effect, the sense-appearance — and see the star.

The starry heavens we are observing are the field of objective reality. What they consist of — matter, energy or whatever — is irrelevant and to attempt to name it even scientifically is to fall into subjectivity.

That field of reality cannot and does not change. The condition of the field, its sense-appearance at any time, is secondary, a sub-effect, created by the oscillation of evolving terrestrial intelligence.

That evolving intelligence, it will be remembered, is behind the initial point of sense-perception — before we individuals come into existence — and is the evolving intelligence of humanity as a whole. It is the relative unsteadiness of this intelligence — its relatively unevolved state compared with the finest intelligences in the universe — that creates the moving sense-perceived world.

To higher intelligences, motion as we see it hardly exists; and where we apprehend relative motionlessness such as in the perceived heavens, higher intelligences are aware of fantastic activity. Our intervals of centuries — which are measures of past, not time — to them pass in seconds.

The uncomfortable but unarguable fact is that any change or motion we perceive in the cosmos occurs in the past, in ourselves. And of course the past cannot be the present — let alone the eternal instant, or objective reality.

When humanity evolves into higher intelligence the sense-perceived world will not necessarily disappear. We will just elect to spend less time in it, as in dying we involuntarily spend less time in it now. We will then not merely be able to see through movement and sense-appearance but will begin to 'pass through' both so that they are no longer barriers to a greater, more universal existence.

26
The mythic universe

There was no one big bang beginning of the universe.

Each star system in which intelligent life is to develop manifests with its own big bang in the mind. And within each star system is the universe. The universe is contained within each star system, through which the intelligence of that system must observe the universe. Without a star system to observe the universe through, there would be no universe.

The only part of the universe that ever manifested in the mind as far as we earthlings are concerned is the solar system, our star system. To this and this alone do we belong as past or emotional beings.

To us, other parts of the universe can exist only as myth — as the solar system and humanity can exist only as myth to those other parts until they are able to enter our system as intelligent beings, or we theirs, via the one common intellect shared by all intelligent life in the universe.

Myth has no before or after existence. Myth is ever-present in the intellect; it is the truth that as information has exceeded light-speed to become power. Myth symbolises presence of mind when it is understood.

Any visitors from outer space first have to enter the solar mind through the myth of the Draconic Transverse and then through the solar system myth enter terrestrial mind — our mind. This is why so many thousands of respected people claim to have seen UFOs and communicated with other intelligences involved but none can produce evidence that all can believe. The myth which UFOs are at this time can only be demonstrated 'now' in the mind and not by historicity or calculations based on the past, as in scientific method. One day it may be possible. But at present, as imagination cannot materialise objects, so intellectual materialism cannot detect the reality of the myth, or its own presence of mind.

The unity of life

The solar intellect, as the obverse in the mind of the solar system, is incapable of reflecting the circumstances of its own birth or beginning for the self-evident reason that it was not present in any intelligent life there to be able to do so. The sun and planetary matter were all there but no life was present to affirm the fact of their existence through the intellect.

However, the contradiction of the solar system existing and not existing at the same time which would make it impossible for life to develop in it was prevented by one simple though profound fact. The spatial big bang, the apparent explosion in which the solar system made its appearance in matter and time, was observed by intelligent life existing elsewhere in the universe.

One extraordinary cosmic rule is that what has not been observed by intelligent life in the universe cannot exist. Nothing can just appear and be held in a sort of limbo until someone gets around to seeing it for the first time. An observer must be present initially to allow or affirm existence.

This, unknowingly, is behind our speculation about intelligent life existing elsewhere in the universe. Intelligent life had to exist elsewhere for us to exist. If life is here, life is there. It is as simple as that.

Ultimately, all life is the one life. And ultimately, all life anywhere can succeed in achieving is to observe, know and finally realise itself, its own inseparable oneness — even across the apparent vastness of the physical universe.

The impediment of intelligence

When intelligence as thought, calculation or speculation is absolutely stilled, that is, when it becomes the pure stationary intellect, life is realised as unity. Distance and the universe as separating factors then vanish: all is life, this ineffable being that I am.

So, between life elsewhere in the universe and life on earth lies the refracting impediment of intelligence. If we look closely at this statement and what I have been saying we will see that the universe itself is the massed condition of intelligence which separates life from life.

The physical universe itself is in fact a vast intelligence concealing the unity of life — the mystery of life — from all its cosmic parts until each unit-part evolves sufficiently to realise this truth for itself. When it realises that truth — realises life — it is truly intelligent and that is the start of cosmic consciousness.

Man's cosmic body

In spite of our inferred individuality, intelligence is a cosmic factor.

In this part of the universe where life exists on earth as humanity and the species living and dead, it combines to form terrestrial intelligence, or the intelligence of our cosmic body, the planet earth. Each of us is an intelligent cell in the brain of that great cosmic being.

Thus, we can see that wherever life develops intelligently in the universe it is really the intelligence of the life of the cosmic body out of which it emerged, and not of any apparent individual part of it that happens to be present such as ourselves. And yet, in consciousness the part is as great as the whole — is the whole — when the whole is realised.

Looking out at the vastness of the universe from the earth's position would be an extremely chilling if not devastating experience for any individual who for a moment connected up with the whole terrestrial awareness and realised the planet's cosmic isolation in space. This awful, inspiring aloneness is sometimes realised by man. But when it is, the man in that moment exceeds the limited individuality of the part and shares in the compensating cosmic self-knowledge of the great terrestrial being which includes hyper-awareness of its own place in the beauty, precision and rightness of the universe.

Thus, between life 'here' and life 'there' lies the vastness of the universe, or of universal intelligence, posing or masquerading as distance and separation — maya, the Hindu concept of cosmic illusion, or lilah, the divine dance.

The fully-formed appearance of the solar system

The advent of the solar intellect in the mind was not accompanied by a simultaneous physical event; that is, the solar system did not suddenly appear 'here' in this part of the universe. It could not appear here for there was no life here to observe it.

It appeared 'there' on the other side of the universe to other intelligences in the same way as we observe distant star systems. And it was fully formed as it is today; there was no gradual build-up. Moreover, its fully-formed appearance occurred only after an inconceivable interval during which it had absolutely no physical existence!

The solar system did not evolve physically out of cooling gases into blobs of matter. That all happens in the mind where it is still happening now in the psyche — intelligence plus past — of the scientists and others who calculate and imagine these non-existent events.

The physical existence of the solar system can be seen in its cosmic entirety only from astronomical distances away. But this is not due to the obvious reason of size or distance. A far more profound rule governs such things and is in fact behind the concept of distance. It is this: the interval in light years which the light image of the solar system takes to reach distant intelligences is proportional to the interval between the advent of the solar intellect in the mind and the start of life on earth.

This is no quirk of reality; it serves to demonstrate its impeccable consistency. That gap, or non-interval of non-past before life began on earth, cannot be known by other intelligences as an event any more than by us: their observation of the physical fact of the sun's and earth's existence had to be delayed until life started here or until the beginning of time on earth. Nothing out of the past can be seen before its time.

Similarly, the solar system had to appear or manifest fully formed – although, it must be said, discernible only to the extent of life's development here. The delay in light-speed ensures that the perceived image of the solar system always correlates to the state of our intelligence now. As life and intelligence developed and develop here, so do the appearance and knowability of our system in outer space. In other words, as we evolve, our intelligent effectiveness expands or travels further into space as the solar light-image. This means we have already started to travel to other star systems; but due to our psychic limitation we cannot realise it until we rid our perception of the past.

What makes all this possible is the fact of the unity of life ... divided only by the conditions of intelligence or existence. Those conditions in each case are the condition of intelligence itself which determines the appearance of the universe and the apparent distance between life wherever it may be.

Towards cosmic consciousness

As I have just explained, the solar system can be seen in its cosmic entirety only by intelligences a certain number of light years away in deep space. It is not visible as a reality to life within the solar system or even to life immediately outside it. To us and those immediate observers if they exist the solar system is not yet complete, not yet real: it is still mainly in the mind, only very fragmentally existent. We have to observe most of its planetary parts in isolation, never as a whole, and we depend on our imagination – intelligence working in the human psyche or past – to put it together for us.

This limitation of our perception, correlating to our physical position as observers, is the measure of our place along the long line of cosmic evolution. We are cosmic babes.

Although able to observe the formal reality of other star systems — able as cosmic observers to give them existence — we are forced to settle for a subjective, mainly calculated or imagined scheme of our own reality. No man has ever seen the solar system as it is. We cannot see our place in that reality until we can 'travel' outside of it to other star systems by transcending the confining human psyche and its past. We can do this only by learning to see life more objectively, without self-reference or past-reference; that is, to see through the impediment of our evolving intelligence which is so concrete and narrowly materialistic, or past-bound. When we manage this we will be cosmically conscious, able to participate in the knowledge-without-past of the cosmic reality from which we come — a mighty advance for human intelligence.

Meanwhile, it may help us to remember that anything which has another side to it that needs to be seen or known — whether it is a star system, a planet or a point of view — is still partly unreal, still a subjective part of the human psyche, still bedded in our own past.

At the edge of the human psyche, or from our point of view on the 'other side' of it, is the cosmic or spiritual consciousness of the Yellow Plane in which there are no sides to anything, nothing is hidden and nothing needs to be known but what is being revealed now — in other words, the goal of life.

Cosmic or spiritual consciousness is liberation from the past. It does not mean that the sense-perceived world or universe changes; it merely enables one to see through them to the other, the reality.

The mystery of the intellect

Through this section of the book I have endeavoured to explain that the obverse or mind side of the physical universe — the 'inner' side of it — is the intellect. Although as physical creatures we are on the 'outside' of the universe, as mental beings we are on the inside. When we look up at the starry sky at night we are literally seeing the universe and the intellect at the same time.

229

Just as there is only one mind so there is only one common intellect used by all intelligences in the universe: one universe, one intellect. However, each intelligent form of life is able to use only that part of the universal intellect represented by its own star system until such time as it outgrows the system by evolving into higher intelligence.

I will now explain the dynamic of this evolutionary process. In doing so I will try to give some indication of how terrestrial affairs are based on cosmic principles.

Being the obverse side of the manifested universe, out of which all intelligence arises, the intellect contains every possible possibility that evolving intelligence can ever reflect on or know.

It can be said that the character of the intellect is idea and its nature is intelligence. In it is written in ideal energetic form all that ever will be known and can be known by intelligence in the universe. It is the repository, the affirmational source of all knowledge in experience.

However, there is a profound mystery behind the continued presence of the intellect itself.

Although supreme in the whole scheme of existence it is still subject to a process of activation and partial dissolution. That is, if an idea in the intellect is not used by intelligence the idea starts to fade and lose luminosity in the same way as a star might be said to grow old and begin the process of stellar decay. When a star in the heavens is dying it means an idea is dissolving from disuse in the setting of the intellect. Or when a new star is forming it means a new idea is being activated somewhere in the cosmos. This deactivating and activating of ideas in the intellect is behind the actual movement of the universe, and is the dynamic of intelligent evolution.

Let us take the human intellect, which really is inseparable from the solar intellect represented by the obverse side of the solar system.

First we must understand that the intellect is not a personal thing. If it were, ours would be a world in which sleep and unconsciousness were unknown. A person who slept (or died) for the first time in such a world could never return to it as we do to ours. He would find no place – no interval maintained as a force-line — for him to re-enter by. He would find his past position had disappeared in the succession of information about him: he would be a non-being in that world through having lost his place or continuity, and would be forced back to find his own world. But no man has a world of his own as no man has a personal intellect — which shows the impossibility of that situation. The only personal thing about a man is his intelligence, and the strength of that is determined by a great many factors all of which depend on the existence of the one common intellect.

Our continuance as physical beings is due to the fact that all humanity uses the one intellect. Each individual while he is alive continues to reaffirm his place in the world, or his particular part of the common intellect, by waking up and using it; and others do the same for him by using the intellect to reaffirm his existence through recognising and considering him.

Similarly, humanity's ceaseless daily intellectual reflection on objects prevents the world itself, or parts of it, from starting to disappear.

While one individual, one intelligent being, continues to use the intellect in this way, the world as he knows it holds together. But if he alone existed while the rest of humanity went to sleep for a thousand years, they would awake to a very pale and scarcely recognisable replica of the world they used to know. Through non-use the world ideas would have faded in the intellect and almost returned to a state of pure potentiality. But as it is, with less than one-third of humanity asleep at the one time, we all wake up from sleep (and, one day we may discover, from death) to a world that has continued in our absence in a solid, sensible way.

When the solar intellect crystallised to shut off or contain the part of the mind that is humanity's (and the rest of the species') none of the intellect was activated. No life being present to reflect on it, the intellect remained wholly potential.

Nevertheless, this potential is the positivity, the power, in the universal mind. By shutting off infinite mind and containing the power of it by reflecting it back on itself, the intellect provided the pre-tensional dynamic for life on

231

earth to begin to develop. Without such intellectual potency the life impulse emerging from within the matter of the earth would have disappeared 'out' into infinite mind and never have been reflected intelligently so as to be known to exist.

Evolution of terrestrial intelligence is simply the process of making the solar intellect functional. To become functional, each potential iota of it has first to be activated by intelligent reflection. Man does this by seeing the truth or fact in life; the energy of his perception then activates that iota of the intellect.

All the familiar objects and conditions around us were not always familiar. Each had to be cognised, activated in the intellect by some man's original perception for other men to be able to re-cognise it. Each such original perception activates the corresponding potential part of the human intellect and it becomes just that little bit 'wider', and the potential of intelligence that little bit more profound. The new idea, although very faintly actuated, is from then on more positively available — in fact compellingly so — for reflection on by all humans whose perception can reach or relate to it.

At first, such an idea may be completely incomprehensible to most of humanity and remain dormant for centuries. But having been actuated, the certainty is that sooner or later it will recur in man's perceptions and enlighten him.

There are numerous examples of this. One that comes to mind is the Copernican idea that the earth revolves around the sun, an intuition that occurred as an activation of the intellect 1800 years earlier to the Greek philosopher Aristarchus. In AD 1633 — two thousand years after Aristarchus and two centuries after Copernicus — this great truth was still not luminous enough (or conversely, human intelligence was not brilliant enough) for it to be received by humanity and Galileo was forced to recant and deny it as a heresy in order to save his life.

An idea actuated in the intellect can be said to become more luminous with use (or, intelligence more brilliant) and more accessible to more of humanity until it becomes an 'obvious' truth to all. Unfortunately, this usually means that it is superficially known but seldom understood with the brilliance that such splendorous ideas as the Copernican insight should evoke in man.

Man has now activated — made functional — enough of the solar intellect for him to be capable of using a much vaster section of the intellect than that represented by the solar system.

A life form that begins intelligently to exceed its own star system automatically expands its intellectual capacity to include that part of the intellect represented by one or more adjoining star systems. This means the intelligence then has access to much more abstract knowledge and information and is potentially capable of understanding the forms of life or intelligence existing there, and finally of communicating.

As this philosophy and this book show, man now has incipient access to that vast and exciting area of the intellect represented by the Draconic Transverse, a section spatially hundreds of light years across, which as I have explained contains and controls the informational syndrome of life and death, human existence, and the spiritual evolution of the planetary beings under the aegis of the sun.

It is extremely doubtful whether any form of intelligence in the universe as we know it is capable of using the entire common intellect. However, some intelligences in outer space are so mighty that they are able to use vast tracts of the intellect represented by whole galaxies extending far beyond their formal, spatial position in the universe.

With the spatial appearance of the solar system (and every new star system) the common universal intellect was 'enlarged' or extended in scope to include the potential of the human sense experience as well as of any other intelligent life-form existence on the other planets.

This extension or enlargement of the universal intellect means that every cosmic system is intelligently observed as it comes into existence, and can in time be further explored and understood by life forms able to evolve in intelligence beyond their own initially limited area of intellect, or formal and spatial position.

The solar intellect has never changed nor been added to since it first occurred in the mind. But as humanity becomes more intelligent we activate more of it. And eventually, as I have explained, we will have access to wider or extra-human sections of the intellect by means of our more mature intelligent reflection on life and death and other realities behind the perceived universe.

In other words, man will one day exceed the human intellect and this will be synonymous with some extraordinary inter-stellar discoveries, events and achievements.

The timelessness of the solar system

Man cannot truly begin to understand the wider universe — and enter a greater reality — until he has grasped the timelessness of the solar system, or the difference between the cosmic and the cosmetic.

As I have said, the advent of the solar intellect in the mind did not coincide with a physical event. As with the universe, the temptation is to imagine that there was a physical, evolutionary beginning to the solar system. But evolutionary beginning implies past and the solar system, being intrinsic to the universe, has no past except that which life on earth has created with its perceptions.

Anything that is not now as it was in the beginning, has past.

Certainly we can see evidence of innumerable changes that have taken place on the earth since the start of the species. That, in fact, is the trail, the past created and left by our intelligent evolutionary passage. But the earth, the planet earth, has not changed cosmically; with the other planets of the system it continues to circle the sun with the same unaltering precision. The sun pours out its heat, its gravitation; all that is cosmic is majestically untouched.

The changes we know or see are purely cosmetic, transient, the reflection or reflections of life-on-earth's evolving intelligence. Even these changes change again and keep changing. Nothing within our purview is stable, predictable — except the timeless rhythm of the solar system that has no past and therefore knows no change.

The solar system's physical existence is part of the

phenomenon of terrestrial life. It did not precede life. It was not 'here' before life started. Life 'brought' it with it. Take away life, and the physical solar system and universe disappear. I say again, the sun and planets did not evolve out of gases and dust. They are as they always have been in reality. It has been life's evolving intelligent ability to sense, perceive and then conceive of their significance that has created any apparent changes.

The sun and planets we see, like the rest of the visible universe, are projections by the psychic brain of the reality deep within the unconscious, behind the racial past. There the real universe, as the intellect, exists as it is, and not as we sense it, conceive it or change it.

As life on earth evolved intelligently, the solar system and the universe 'kept pace' by appearing or being present in ever greater detail or knowledge. It was life's intelligent ability, not the solar system, which evolved and took clearer form or made form clearer and more intelligible.

Like the universe, the solar system has always been the same in character and that character is completely responsive and sufficient to the evolving, ever-expanding demands of intelligence for more knowledge. What intelligence needs to know next is always there in any moment — but not necessarily what it wants to know.

For man today, the universe is still not as it really is: it is only as clear, as complete as his intelligence can conceive it and that perception will be different again for future generations.

The perceiver, intelligence, changes, not the objectivity perceived.

*　　*　　*

I will now sum up this section of the book and add some observations.

The universe we see, we are simultaneously reflecting on from the inside in the mind as the common intellect shared by all intelligent life in the universe. Supra-intelligent beings existing elsewhere in the universe are reflecting on or off the same intellect as us, only more of it which, I repeat, is the obverse side of that mighty energetic canopy of light, power and clarity we see above as the universe of stars.

Each star is an idea, a concentration of information; each piece of matter represents life and intelligence in time.

The universe of galaxies is the spatial or intelligent-life view of what in the mind is the stationary universal intellect. The indicated motion of stellar objects is due solely to the action of the observing intelligence, motion's reciprocal.

As our human development demonstrates, intelligence wherever it appears in the universe eventually, or in time, comes to reflect on the stars which stand for all the ideas of reality.

As intelligence observes the stars (and obversely, reflects on them in the mind off the universal intellect), the ideas in the stars devolve into information which is transmitted back off the intellect at light-speed to become man's perceptive awareness.

The speed of light, being a finite yet absolute velocity for the transmission and receipt of sense-perceptive information, is the factor that creates the impression of motion, or interval, giving rise to historicity or our concept of time and past. Motion — intelligence — is only possible within a stationary matrix — the intellect.

Thus the universe is not expanding, as science suggests. What is exploding or expanding is knowledge of the stationary intellect which absorbs and always will absorb the attention of intelligent life wherever it arises in matter until it realises the truth of life within itself.

The scientific Big Bang theory of an expanding universe requires a centre for the bang to have occurred in. But there is no such centre to the universe. The only centre is the position of the observing intelligence and from that point the universe as knowledge is always seen to be expanding.

Thus, wherever intelligence (the observer) is, that is the centre of the universe. And the nearest point of reality for such an observer is the star of the system to which he belongs — or, in the case of 'travelling' higher intelligences, the star of the system he happens to be in. Supra-intelligences use star power to journey or swing from system to system on the mind or intellect side of the universe — a means of being informationally swifter than the speed of light. Ultimately you only travel in your own being.

There was and is no first or last, oldest or newest, in relation to the instant in which each section of the universe appears. Such concepts of time are gained from the spatial point of view which in man's case arose as intelligent life out of the big bang that produced the solar intellect.

Hence, as far as our earthling intelligence is concerned, the manifestation of the solar intellect was the beginning of the entire universe. An intelligence in another star system would have had the same precise moment of beginning in that perpetual first instant of all manifestation, but not necessarily so if the interval could be measured in succeedent time which is our time alone, or our way of perceiving at this time.

Nothing in the universe is expanding except knowledge. Nothing is moving except intelligence. The universe is exactly the same as it 'was' in the first instant except that stellar information or knowledge has been transferred to matter by way of subsequent effects/events or succeedent time.

Stars devolve, knowledge expands, while intelligence increases.

II

27
An introduction to reality

This is the spiral girdle of eternity.

It is all there is.

It consists of the intellect, consciousness, and the six worlds and minds of existence, the last and least of which is the human mind at the bottom of the spiral.

The cone-shaped axis is a zone of limitless intelligence differentiating into levels of 'I', one for each world.

The top first loop of the spiral is the outer gallery or ring of eternity and endless consciousness.

Within and below that is the second gallery or ring of eternity, the universe, containing universal mind. Then there are two spatial galleries: the stellar gallery containing stellar mind, and the solar gallery containing solar mind.

Next is the solid gallery or ring of the planetary world containing terrestrial mind.

Within and below that is the spatial psychic gallery, or world of the living dead. Then, finally, there is the solid sense-gallery containing the human mind.

The entire spiral girdle is a massive, self-sufficient, objective system of being and existence in the infinitude of mind, powered or fuelled internally by the substance of eternity, the now.

Its cosmic, spiritual name is reality.

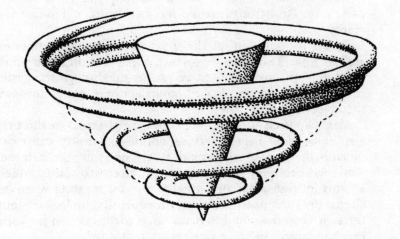

The object of reality

With our imprecise knowledge of the human psyche and even less of the minds above, it is not easy to conceive of reality as a precise and definitive structure.

Being spellbound by our seemingly external world of the senses it is extremely difficult to realise that everything including the universe is actually in the mind and that in turn all is contained in one single idea/object called reality or the spiral girdle of eternity as it is depicted above.

Here on earth man is at the bottom end of the spiral of reality. And from here he has two ways of looking for reality.

One is to look 'out' at the apparent reality of the universe around him. The other is to turn the attention inward and look back through the human psyche up through the girdle towards the solar and higher minds above — that is, through the object of reality itself.

Man has been looking out through his senses in the first way since time began. But as nothing in reality can exist outside the end of the spiral where he is at, the external world he perceives is only apparent, a relative reality which affirms its transience or unreality by disappearing when he sleeps or goes unconscious. Consequently, in looking out through the senses he has never succeeded, nor can he hope ever to succeed, in perceiving reality that way.

This raises the question: how does the sense-perceived universe — if it is not real — appear at all, and appear with such reality?

The answer in the first instance is due to the extra-ordinary quality of the infinitude of mind which surrounds the spiral object of reality and in particular the point where man exists at the bottom.

The infinitude of mind around reality cannot be 'seen through'; it defies perception. It is totally, absolutely reflective. It turns the observer's vision, the eye or I, back on itself so that the observer perceives his own place in reality at that moment. As man's place is at the bottom end of reality, when he looks 'out' at the infinitude of mind he sees a reflection of the reality 'behind' him — which then appears to be in front of him. It is like holding up a mirror and looking into it back over your shoulder. The scene in the mirror appears to be happening in front of you when really it is only a reflection of what is happening behind you. Further, what is approaching from behind seems in the mirror to be actually coming towards you from in front.

Within the girdle 'behind' man who is looking 'out', the stream or current of reality is from the higher minds down to the bottom end of the spiral where he is. Thus, looking into the mirror of infinite mind, like looking into a mirror and seeing over your shoulder, produces the illusion that what is approaching from behind is actually coming at you from in front.

This means that when we are looking 'out' — looking into the mirror of infinite mind by seeing with the senses as you are now — the apparent or reflected reality of the universe is streaming down on to the earth and through us (humanity) into the psyche like an endless energetic shower or current.

The principle is this: while the senses are being used — and they are in ceaseless use except in sleep or unconsciousness — the mirror effect is in operation, and everything happens and has to be explained in the relative reality of that reflection. In other words, the reflection of reality — the energetic universe streaming in towards us — is the reality of the mirror effect.

This stream of (relative) reality makes the miracle of sense perception possible. I will explain.

When man looks 'out' he (or rather the sense machine) is projecting the sense data *against* and on to the incoming stream. The dynamic meeting of the outgoing sense data and the incoming current produces the effect of the visible or sense-measurable universe. So he is actually seeing and experiencing what he or the sense machine is projecting — images of *the* reality behind — with the reflected current providing the necessary matrix or sense of reality. Nothing, not even a stupendous psychic illusion like the universe, can exist without the presence, reflected or otherwise, of reality.

The other way man has of looking for reality — turning

his attention inward and going with the incoming mirror current — gives a completely different result.

Although in this case the sense machine continues to operate outwardly so that he retains his sense-perceptive existence, it is powerless to project inward. The sense machine needs resistance to produce a positive creation or reflection such as the external universe, and a man going with the incoming stream fails to provide that resistance. The result is that the man begins to have two simultaneous perceptions — one of the projected sense world around him, and the other a growing awareness of reality itself within.

His inward-going attention, although still a part of the mirror effect, has in essence neutralised the sense machine and is travelling with the reflected stream into reality itself. His attention continues to refine until finally it becomes the impersonal universal energy of the ingoing stream itself. At this point it 'meets' with the downcoming current of reality itself — the infinitely obscure point where a mirror image and the reality it is reflecting meet or begin. The outcome is not dissimilar to how the sense world is created by the projections of the sense machine: the dynamic meeting of the incoming universal attention with the downcoming current of reality gives a perception which in this case enlightens the perceiver with the truth or knowledge of reality itself.

Reality itself is not a creation, not an effect like the universe around us. The universe in spite of its grandeur is only the sense machine's partial, projected approximation of the inner reality which never changes and is absolutely self-sufficient in its own right. Take away the senses, the universe itself, and reality is quite unaffected.

We earthlings while alive and awake must always remain sense-perceptive beings; in short, mirror beings. However, in time we can and must introduce the perception of reality itself into our sense-existence. This is done by the inward-going journey of the attention. We must remember that reality is always going within, that it cannot be registered outside through the senses. It can be reflected through the senses, through the universe, which accounts for the beauty and wonder we perceive. But it cannot be held as an enduring awareness until the attention is refined enough to be able to focus on, or join, the point of reality itself — where the mirror meets the real — within the individual.

*　　*　　*

In continuing this approach to reality I ask you to keep in mind that as sense-perceptive beings we are looking out into a mirror reflecting reality behind us.

As reality is behind us, so must the mirror image that is the world appear in principle in front of us. Let us now confirm this in your experience.

In the object of reality behind us, the universal mind at the top of the spiral is reached through the solar mind; the solar mind is reached through the terrestrial mind; and the terrestrial mind is reached through the psyche at the bottom by the attention being turned inward.

In the mirror image that is the world in front of us, the universe representing the universal mind is seen through the solar system representing the solar mind; the solar system is seen through the planetary orbits representing the planetary, or in our case terrestrial, mind; and the entire mirror-image of all that is, is seen through our individual awareness representing the human mind, or the psyche turned outward.

So man, looking out into the mirror from the bottom end of the object of reality, is at the tail-end of the downcoming higher minds in reality behind, and at the tail-end of the incoming stream of perception of the universe in front of him.

In other words, the whole universe — representing the reflected reality of the higher minds behind the psyche — is streaming down energetically through the solar system on to the earth and into his outward-focused psyche. This energy, for the purposes of man and life on earth, is represented by sunlight. Sunlight or starlight represents the solar or universal stream of consciousness against which the sense machine projects its data to create the sense world.

The incoming solar or universal stream of consciousness which returns the projected sense images to the psyche, is responsible for man's notion that reality is infinite. In the mirror image that is the universe he sees infinite form and possibilities. But reality is only infinite in its projections, not in itself. Reality in fact begins with a finite, complete state of being in the observer – the result of man's intelligent attention being directed inward with the stream to where it meets its downcoming source.

Although every man's life on earth is of short duration, while it lasts it is almost invincibly persuasive that outward into infinity is the only reality and the only way to proceed. But the fact remains that the source, where the depth of the reflection meets the reality it reflects, is in the opposite direction to what the senses suggest; and that that is where man must look to find it.

In terms of the seven levels of mind, he must look 'back' from Level One where he is on the earth's surface, through the psyche (Levels Two and Three) and the higher levels of the terrestrial mind (Four, Five and Six) towards Level Seven.

Level Seven, although the end of the terrestrial mind, is also the beginning of the solar mind; and the end of the solar mind is in turn the beginning of the universal mind.

A man looking inwards through the minds in their correct order is actually looking 'up' through the girdle's central axis of intelligence. Then the minds and each 'I' function like a series of resolving lenses and enable reality to be seen as it is.

On the other hand, when man looks out from the earth's surface and perceives the external universe through the senses he gets precisely the opposite effect, like looking through the wrong end of a telescope. The cosmic bodies seem very distant, removed, remote, when in reality they are not.

Looking out this way, or through astronomy or space travel, into the incoming stream of consciousness, he can never hope to get back to the beginning, reality itself.

Probing into the incoming stream like this is the beginning of infinity. Infinity – represented by the formal universe – arises when one perceives against or travels out against the stream. In truth as well as by definition infinity can have no end in itself: it is endless. Having no end, infinity as the universe also can have no beginning — outside of the man searching for it there. Such a man is looking for the reality of himself and finding only the endlessness of the world.

All of this means that as a physical being on the face of the earth at the tail-end of the incoming solar/universal stream, man actually occupies the last outpost in the infinite energetic universe. Wherever in the future he travels to in outer space, that place will still remain another reflected part of this reflected end and therefore continue to be part of the endless journey into infinity. He just cannot escape from infinity the external way he is pursuing.

However, man's assumption that he should be able to take the obvious physical route straight out from the earth into the reflected solar mind, or solar system, is understandable. But the error in this reasoning is that man is not really a physical being. His very brief life on earth, and the fact that the same physical man is never seen again, are pretty convincing evidence of this.

Man is a feeling (psychic) and mental (higher terrestrial) being. He is not yet a cosmic (solar) being. If he were he would not be at the tail-end of the solar reflection confronted with nothing but its infinite forms and concepts. He would have a knowledge of reality. He would be at the beginning within himself where the one idea of reality is complete without concepts.

Man's physical occupation of this tail-end of the universal mirror image — or the beginning of infinity — is not unlike his having invaded an alien cosmic territory scourged by a disease called death. To retain a hold on the earth as a race his individual physical parts must keep on dying and then returning to comply with the external infinity's demand for endless cycles.

But by discovering the reality of himself within his physical being, man can bring this beginning in the shape of immortality into this physical life and make this otherwise alien territory his own. Death the scourge will then be conquered, overcome. Immortality is his own real state, anyway, and by bringing it consciously with him into his mirror-life on earth he will complete the mysterious, sacred circle, the linking of the beginning (reality) and the end (infinity), Yang and Yin, as foreshadowed by that most ancient of spiritual and occult symbols — the ouroboros, the serpent swallowing its tail.

An amazing life lies ahead of the human race when physical life on earth will no longer be interrupted by death or made superficial and self-serving by the dread of it. Man will then be responsible for this part of the cosmos — and his life or lives will be filled with extraordinary new purpose. Eventually when he dies and comes back to the 'place' that has been kept for him on earth he will consciously 'pick up' where he left off. He will be a true cosmic being making a conscious contribution to cosmic life with which he will then be in continuous contact.

But for now man has to be told and persuaded intellectually that immortality exists for him to start breaking down the barriers of attachment and preoccupation with his external mirror-self and mirror-world.

When a man dies he does not go out into solar space, into the infinity which he strives so hard to penetrate while alive. He withdraws back into the psyche, into the earth, into his own real world of Level Three behind the outward-going drive of matter and sense. There, right beside him, is Level Four, the beginning of the higher terrestrial mind and the resplendent centre of the psychic world of the living dead.

Depending on how much he has managed through his lives on earth to clear his psychic space by going inward with the stream, he can then look straight through the higher levels of the spiral girdle to the solar/universal minds and see reality as it is — as the whole or some aspect of what I describe in this section. It was from such splendid inner visions of reality by the great prophets while alive that the concepts of paradise, heaven, nirvana and the rest derive.

The spiral object of reality as I have described and pictured it above is the home of all intelligence and life in the cosmos. This ranges from God — the highest principle of intelligence above the universal mind — down through the great spirits of the stellar and solar mind to the terrestrial mind and man, who for the most part at this time is floundering in the inner and outer, life and death dilemma of the psyche at the bottom.

Nevertheless, the object of reality is *our* reality, no matter how lowly or tentative our position in it may seem.

Very swiftly the individual man's (or woman's) intelligence can rise up the central cone. As he starts to ascend out of the misty subconscious of the psyche into the clarity of the terrestrial or planetary mind, he begins to realise that reality is indeed his, that time itself is at his disposal, not against him, and that reality is a wonderland, a substantive objective idea through which he can wander at will because it is his home.

When a man's psyche is clearly and correctly aligned with the higher minds he gains access to the terrestrial gallery of the spiral. Each of the minds in reality has a gallery. Each gallery is a unique world as well as an observation port from which the individual intelligence can look out at the surrounding infinitude of mind as from a space station.

The gallery of our physical world — the sense-gallery — is the projection of the sense machine. Its observation port provides the familiar view from the surface of the earth. When we look out we see the reflection of nature — rich and beautiful but mortally ephemeral for the dying living. When we look or go in behind the sense machine we discover the reality of nature which is shared with the living dead. Together, these two hemispheres form a whole, representing the incredible future fullness of immortal life which it is humanity's evolutionary task to bring about.

The next gallery up is the terrestrial gallery. This connects with the inner radiant world of the planet, the life splendid — immortal life already realised. Looking out from here into infinite mind, or contemplating the void of nothing, one sees reflected like in a mirror the object of reality itself, the entire spiral girdle of eternity as it is pictured above.

When observed through the terrestrial gallery as a reflection in infinite mind, the girdle of eternity has an astonishing quality.

Not only is it possible to perceive reality as it is now — it is also possible to see how it began, and all of its constituent parts still in the act of forming. This, I will now describe.

The story that follows — like this book as a whole — is literally a journey into the reader's mind.

Other than finally perceiving reality for himself, the only verification he can have that what is written here is true and that there is such an amazing object as reality in the mind is if, as I describe it, he is able to discern in himself a feeling of correctness, rightness or recognition – in other words the ring of truth. The ring of truth is none other than the ring of eternity, the sound of reality itself.

In this journey and story each man is truly his own authority.

To follow, the reader does not need to understand all that is being said or to have to try to remember any of it; only to listen with an open mind. The truth in him will do the rest. It is the reader's own mind-structure I will be describing and he should recognise at least parts of what is in it. It is, however, a necessarily complex exposition.

The fruit of such a journey is self-knowledge. By voluntarily going with the stream into the structure of reality through an open mind the reader or listener releases powerful new energies in his unconscious. To the degree that he is enlightened by such energies man grows in understanding towards the state of conscious immortality when the inevitable moment arrives of his physical death and he disappears back into the psychic reality whence he came not so long ago.

28
The beginning of reality – the echo or the 'Word'

Reality began to form the instant the intellect came across infinite mind as described in the previous section of this book.

Nevertheless, the intellect itself could not cause existence: the intellect is too abstract, meaning pastless, and as I have explained, all existence has to occur in the past.

The means of existence was provided by the echo or percussion of the intellect's sudden appearance in infinite mind. This was the mightiest and most enduring bang of all time. It continues in the mind for us today as the now-that-never-ends – and the sensation we never cease to feel.

The echo was a complete reproduction in sound, percussion or vibration of everything the intellect contained, therefore, everything that ever could be. In some ancient religious philosophies it is described as the 'Word' or Logos and in another as Aum, the sacred sound of creation. All existence to follow in succeedent time or past would be merely a reverberation in a lower octave of this one eternal instant which by us must be regarded as absolute time – eternity.

Although this continuous moment, the now, is to us the optimum point of the present (being the absence of any perceived past), as the echo of that one and only event, or the advent of all time or any time, it remains a reproduction, therefore a past expression. Hence, as everything to follow would have to occur within it, all existence happens in the past.

The now as it emerged in that original first instant was similar in character but very different in nature to the now of today. Now, as then, retains the same absoluteness in that it cannot be lost, delayed, outdistanced or avoided. It pours on inexorably in life, death and unconsciousness. It is the one demonstrable constant of all time.

But in that first instant before any worlds existed or any 'I' was present to perceive them, the now in its absoluteness contained all space, all time and all matter. It was all there was, an inconceivable singularity. And it was *absolutely substantial*.

The space we perceive in life and the universe today is that original solidity of absolute past rendered insubstantial by reality's extraction from it of all existence to date. Reality, as stated earlier, 'runs' on the fuel of the now; existence is the resultant and space is the remainder. As more and more existence (knowledge) is extracted every moment from the now, so proportionately does space increase.

Consequently as we discover new matter such as stars, or extend our knowledge to include considerations of the moon, planets or the subatomic microcosm, we become aware of more space and time (or interval) in the universe. Similarly, as we add to existence in the form of time-saving technological advances we again create additional time or space for further activities of existence. We cannot help making more space and time (interval) because space and time are our existence.

Moreover, every day the solidness of the individual's own existence is minutely eroded and replaced by more space. This he feels as a certain emptiness in his life or himself, often inducing him to question or fear the purpose or uncertainty of his existence.

The fact that man is more and more busily engaged in trying to fill the world's expanding space, or his own apperceived emptiness or aloneness, is incidental. The truth remains that space (universal and personal) is growing as it has done ever since existence first began in that all-substantial moment of eternity.

But for man it is now compounding at such a rapid rate that there is less and less fabric to existence: what was yesterday considered the established norm of social or civilised interaction is today found to be disintegrating and evaporating. Deep personal uncertainty, which is impossible to allay by communicating or sharing with others like the old emotions of the past, is affecting all but the very young and the very insensitive. The need for real solutions, original foundations which only the truth can provide, is felt to be crucial. Materialism — the intellectualising of matter or the world — is no longer enough for most of us to retain an adequate sense of being.

Intellectual materialism is also becoming too tenuous and abstract to support those more frequent moments when the pressures of spatial existence and personal emptiness are upon us. Rational thought is merely mentalised matter and it is useless as a support against the expansion of space and the personal diffusion we feel.

The primary proposition of existence

The idea of the world or universe coming into existence necessitates nothing to manifest as something.

In the approach to reality this can be called the primary proposition of existence. Implicitly, it demands a demonstration. The quest for that demonstration is the perennial search for truth and origins by science and true philosophy.

Traditional science's most favoured recent attempt at demonstrating how nothing becomes something is the Big Bang theory. But having virtually completed the course backwards by shrinking the universe down to a starting point the theory stumbles at the last hurdle. Although succeeding in describing events back to a split second after the primordial bang it falls down this side of existence after existence had begun. The jump back over and into the nothing remains uncleared.

Theoretical physics, the relatively new esoteric wing of science, has been somewhat more successful. Its way of demonstrating nothing becoming something was simply to invent something where nothing apparently had existed, and call it a 'virtual' particle. Although admitting that the virtual particle has no existence the physicists have found its presence essential for the articulation of the latest black hole theory of the creation of matter.

Nevertheless, the virtual particle does now exist. It exists because the physicist has made it exist by discovering or perceiving it in the mind. At the edge of reality and existence where nothing is continuously becoming something and something continuously disappearing into nothing, all is occurring in the mind of the observer who is able to penetrate to this region. The more one-pointed his attention the deeper and more confidently he can penetrate into the clear abstract areas of mind and the more originally, profoundly and necessarily mythically he perceives.

Thus science itself has had to resort to myth, the final articulative bridge for all who would seriously attempt to demonstrate the truth behind existence.

None the less, although serving to demonstrate very simply the point of nothing becoming something, the theoretical physicist's method still does not reveal the enabling principle behind it. Like a man demonstrating running by running he merely demonstrates invention by invention and discovery by discovery — all aspects of existence — and takes for granted the enabling moment in which the demonstration occurs.

The fact is that nothing can become something and something nothing only because of the now or moment in which these and all events occur. Any demonstration, even the demonstration of existence as living, is secondary in the approach to reality unless it reveals the truth of the now.

The now is the point of reality behind the something. It also is the point of reality behind the 'no thing', that is, behind the space or positive vacuum that remains when something disappears. In short, space as well as the objects and demonstrations appearing in it are all phenomenological, existent, on the material side of nothing. The task is to get behind space itself and into the nothing; and the only means is through the now.

Consequently, the next crucial step in the approach to reality by both science and ourselves is to penetrate the now, to go into or look into the heart of the myth: into the moment of eternity. The moment of eternity lies between existence and reality, the intellect. There, and only there, in this never-ending moment, can what is behind 'no thing', space, the positive vacuum or existence, be perceived.

In this endeavour the scientist presumably will stick to his adopted language of mathematical calculus and, for reasons I will explain, advance further into the endless maze of discovery without finality — existence.

We, on the other hand, will use plain language, human language, the universal medium of the common man — with one decisive addition: we will be using right or objective words. This will lead us to the end, the beginning, finality.

In the approach to reality there is a series of words that actually stand for the original events occurring at the beginning of existence. The events these words represent are forever 'recurring' in eternity — in the mind of us all at this moment, now. All we as individuals have to do is to get there in our own consciousness by absorbing these words, and perceive for ourselves what is happening there.

A right or objective word is a word which retains its original cosmic, spiritual or pastless energy, therefore its correct signification. When correctly received, right or objective words do not allow the play of subjectivity.

However, today's language has invested these words with meanings totally out of character with their original significance. As a result they have lost their power to inform fundamentally.

From the beginning of language, human subjectivity has gradually attached itself to words and spawned generation after generation of derivatives until few if any are registered for their original content. This blanketing subjectivity derives from imprecise usage arising out of assumptions, ignorance, aimless chatter and considerations of the market-place, self and personality. Language as now used is mainly a record of man's subjectivity and no longer a demonstration of the original truth. Any such truth in it is well and truly buried.

The impact of most words in all tongues today relates to human experience that occurred long after the events which created words or the impulse of language. In the passage of historical time away from the truth of the beginning of man and his language, right words have become encased in layers of subjective and relatively meaningless meanings. Meaning is meaningful only inasmuch as it relates to origins.

Mathematics, the alternative language favoured by science, developed during the very early evolution of human language. It emerged in response to the increasing disappearance of right words and the proliferation of conceptual or subjective words.

Men who could be called the first scientists, or the first to demonstrate the scientific consciousness, determined to try to trace their way back to the historically receding truth, the original event or moment of existence. This they essayed to do through using external symbols rather than through themselves as was the inclination of other men demonstrating the divine or true philosophic consciousness.

Casting around for an objective system, these original scientists seized on number which was then emerging from language as an abstraction for measuring the environment. Impartial, non-subjective number they reckoned would substitute for human language. They were right – but not quite all right.

Originally, human language was not just a tool of convenience or conversation. It arose out of the need to preserve in existence and to communicate to all generations the original truth or original events which gave rise to existence. These events were all present in the mind, in its pre-existent nucleus – the moment of eternity.

A word at that time did not symbolise an event. It *contained* the event. The effect of a word on the recipient's mind was to produce an insight into the moment of eternity where the event the word signified was (and is) continuously being 're-enacted'.

Every word was some aspect of eternity. Instead of merely having a meaning, each word provided a miniature demonstration in the man's own awareness of its eternal significance. What today is called understanding – knowing without memorable knowledge – followed. This now-forgotten, almost extinct process of systemic comprehension existed before subjective memory developed in man. Today, subjective memory is the principal obstruction to this amazing original way of apperceiving and demonstrating the truth.

Psychedelic drugs such as LSD represent the externalisation of objective words. When taken into the system they produce equivalent effects.

Since original objective words related to the beginning of existence, the start of the world, all of the world's chief languages necessarily begin with creation myths.

The difficulty today in relating to the myths (and to the drug-induced images) is that our interpretative faculty is subjective whereas the original words or ideas of the myths were, and still are, objectively present in our consciousness. Stripped of our acquired and contrived subjectivity we would immediately perceive and comprehend their meaning.

The all-powerful deterrent to this comprehension, however, is that when correctly interpreted the creation myths (and the drug images) are demolishing of the rational subjective world we have erected with our conceptual language. Man can rarely perceive the truth of the myths — let alone live this truth — without seeming to lose touch with his reason and his world.

Original language was sparse. Words that comprise most of today's language were unthinkable, utterly unnecessary. To the intelligence of man at that time they would in fact have been unworthy of being included in language because the import of such words was already obvious in the action and process of life itself. Tree, for instance, was not a word for the reason that it was a living fact: words were only for the signification of ideas that had not yet manifested as objects. The idea of tree had externalised as a living objective fact for all men to perceive for themselves.

In short, objective language demonstrated in the mind ideas that had not yet externalised, and life, as nature and activity, demonstrated those that had externalised. Thus the need for other words was non-existent. All existence was self-demonstrating, interiorly or exteriorly. There was no artificial world which language has since created. Original ideas had not become conceptually adulterated — sophistry — for the reason that tomorrow, the first word signifying escapism or man's flight from death through the artifice of invention, had not been thought of. There was no death so no fear and no need of any tomorrow or an unreal world built on words or concepts.

To the intelligence of man at that time language as it is today with its host of inferior words would be regarded as completely redundant and serving only to demonstrate that men using it had neither correctly perceived nor understood life as it is. Such men — ourselves — would be regarded as completely subjective creatures, living inside a word-spun hypnotic dream. The language of all races today is almost entirely superfluous to the truth of life. This is a mighty thing to realise.

Even so, those later scientifically inclined men who determined to find their way back through number to the beginning of life were doomed to failure from the start. Although number had evolved out of language at a very early stage in human history, already the rot of subjectivity had set in and become part of man himself. The original truth, simplicity and purity of man and his original language had already been substantially overwhelmed. Number was only relatively objective and therefore liable to subjective distortions of time and position.

Consequently, the numerical offspring of language could only ever lead back to the point of existence where numbering had begun. All it could get back to was near the beginning of phenomenal existence — and that was not the beginning of life. Thus, as the Big Bang theorists' calculations confirm, science by using number cannot get back to the moment before existence externalised out of nothing. The zero and one minus one or something minus something merely represent the concept of 'no thing', that is, space and time — both of which to us are still within the subjective conceptual play. Right words are not symbols like mathematical signs. They are the real thing and, as I will now show, they go back to the state before the beginning of existence: the moment of eternity.

29
The forming of reality

We will now look into the moment of eternity, the state in our own minds before the beginning of existence, and see the truth of the beginning for ourselves.

We are looking into infinite mind, into nothing, immersed in it. We do not know or need to know whether we exist or do not exist. The state is like being alert in the stillness and silence of deep dreamless sleep.

A tremendous crack of 'sound' fixes our attention on a point somewhere in the void.

Unknown to us this is the echo of the intellect, the now, approaching or expanding towards us at absolute velocity. Absolute velocity means absolute mass which is equivalent to absolute substantiality or solidness – primary energy or matter at its unimaginable densest.

The effect sense-perceptively of the now emerging from the void like this would be similar to the faintest distant star suddenly expanding or approaching at such incredible speed that in one single instant it fills the entire field of perception and engulfs the observer.

But this does not happen.

In the peculiar causal world of the instant of eternity whose phases we are observing produce the total effect of subsequent existence, what does not happen is as real as what does happen.

So what does not happen – inasmuch as it does not happen in subsequent existence although it happens in eternity – is that the solid point of the echo or now expands in a flash filling or engulfing the whole void including our watching Self in an incredibly dense mass of energy – original time,

257

past or matter — that makes any further existence impossible. Although the observing Self remains completely unaffected by the enveloping energy of solid time, the energy can be said to be apprehended by the Self as unspeakable blackness, darkness or oblivion. Nothing exists or could exist in such primal density of matter. Apart from the presence of our observing Self, all opportunity for further existence is past in that one single instant.

What does happen, however — inasmuch as it happens in subsequent existence as well as in eternity — is that the point of the now emerges at absolute speed as a solid line or extension without expanding. The reason it does not expand is that the watching Self, being infinite like the void of infinite mind in which it is implicit, cannot continue as infinitude in the presence of any thing; so it instantly retreats, withdraws, at infinite speed. The effect is similar to a spaceship suddenly accelerating away from an approaching, apparently expanding planet and by its superior speed 'reducing' the planet's size and maintaining it at that of a dot.

By exceeding the absolute speed of the now, the Self escapes and transcends the absoluteness of time.

This induces the first time-change in eternity out of which arise the three principles behind subsequent existence: intelligence, space and energy (matter).

Intelligence. Out of the vanishing point into which the infinitude of mind as infinite Self retreats and disappears, arises 'I'. 'I' am the first condition of all existence — intelligence. While Self alone is non-existent yet ever-present in the oblivion of original time and what does not happen, 'I' who arise out of Self am the first effect of time out-distanced or transcended: hence, 'I' am the beginning of existence. Stated another way, Self is the presence in the non-existent stillness of what does not happen; and 'I' am the presence of existence in all that does happen.

Primal Space or the Negative Vacuum is the second principle of existence arising out of the eternal time-change. It determines the subsequent character, the 'no thingness', of universal space which is the positive vacuum in which existence occurs.

Primal space, or the negative vacuum of eternity, is

created by the absolute expansion of the now — that which does not happen but happens in eternity — being made abstract by the Self's withdrawal. Into this primal vacuum — which may be described as the interval or interstice of eternity — the point of the now emerges as solid line or extension.

In short, the line of solid time travels in its own abstract space: what happens travelling through what does not happen. This abstract dimension of primal space is equivalent in negative volume to time's own absolute non-existent mass — which is simply the dimension of eternity.

Energy/Matter. Having emerged from the void, the solid line of the now prescribes and forms the entire spiral girdle of eternity in its own abstract primal space. It completes the girdle containing all worlds and minds of existence in one instant. That instant is equivalent to time's own substantive mass: energy/matter. In that instant nothing becomes something as we have seen, then becomes everything and then disappears back into nothing while everything as 'I' continues.

So far we have observed the making of eternity out of nothing. We will now observe the other phases of eternity leading to the creation of the universe and finally of the human psyche at the bottom of the spiral where the now disappears back into the nothing.

The initial gallery of eternity and eternal mind

The solid line of the now emerging at absolute speed does not follow a 'straight' trajectory. Instead, it is drawn down and inward towards the contracting centre into which infinite mind is disappearing. This forces the line of original time, space and matter into a huge spiral trajectory — establishing the curve and spiral as the fundamental 'shape' of subsequent universal time, space and motion.

The first enormous spiral circuit completed by the now forms the absolute or initial gallery of eternity. This gallery, on its outer or 'other' side, is completely abstract and non-existent — the intellect. On 'this' side, the inner side, through which the endless echo of eternity reverberates, it is absolutely

solid, impossible of existence — therefore completely unknowable to our intelligence. Where infinite mind has withdrawn
is now eternal mind: endless consciousness.

Universal mind and the universe

By the time the first spiral gallery is completed, infinite mind
has contracted to a point of infinite Self — and vanished.
(Infinite Self like infinite mind cannot abide even the negative presence of eternity.)

Between the centre where the Self has disappeared and the
surrounding girdle, power lines arise like innumerable fine
wire spokes to create universal mind within eternal mind.

Simultaneously, due to the enormous concentration of
power at the centre, where the Self has disappeared the
universal 'I' starts to arise.

From the arising 'I' a backsurge of power sweeps out
towards the girdle in the form of gravitation. Gravitation is
the velocity at which the universal 'I' travels, as our perception travels at light-speed. It is also the communication
power intrinsic in stars.

But although gravitation — universal perception or star-
intelligence — has for us the quality of omnipresence and is
thus far 'swifter' than light, it is still finite. Although ultimate, it is not absolute like the now. Therefore the 'I''s
perception is taking time to cross the huge stretch of universal mind out towards the girdle; in spite of its enormous
speed it is falling behind absolute time.

Also, there is no world for 'I''s perception to reflect
on when it does arrive. The initial gallery is too abstract
and the 'I''s perception would pass straight through it into
infinitude making existence impossible. Without a world or
gallery to reflect on, 'I' cannot exist.

So where is the world to come from? How can a solid,
reflective universe be created out of nothing in this infinites-
imal interval?

The answer lies in the absolute speed and ceaseless flow
of original time.

In this minutest of intervals the now is completing a

second circuit — around the central arising 'I'. This second gallery, less abstract than the first, is crystallising in time at the wavelength of universal mind. (The now always crystallises at the wavelength of the mind it is enclosing.)

This second gallery of crystallised time represents the section of original time — of the original echo or word of creation — which the 'I' has missed due to the relative slowness of its perception, and which is now lost to it forever.

This second gallery, the universal 'I''s unknowable past, is the stationary universe.

Immediately the 'I' perceives the stationary universe the universe begins to move.

It moves because the intelligence of the universal 'I' is less than absolute. Since its knowledge of reality, or all time, is incomplete due to the gap or barrier created by its unknowable past — the solid universe — it must hereafter share in the apparent universal process of motion or change towards the rectification of that ignorance: evolution.

Although a superb, universal and therefore relatively selfless intelligence, the universal 'I' has sufficient subjectivity (positional bias as the centre of a system) to create the perception of 'this' side whereas before there had only been the completely abstract 'other' side, or nothing.

Although the knowledge of this first part of creation is preserved for all time in the form of the starry universe, it can never be known so as to be understood by perception.

This is because the world immediately perceived or occupied by any 'I' — including this sense-perceived world I the reader occupy — must always remain unknowable. Each such world, to the 'I' and mind in phase with it, is absolutely substantial in time, meaning completely unfathomable because that particular world consists in each case of eternal time or echo absolutely lost to the knower 'I' while arising to consciousness of that world.

In short, I am always separate from what is substantial or unknowable — the world I occupy. I can know *about* this world, or about parts of it, but I can never know it as it really is apart from myself. This is because the world I occupy, or perceive as being apart from myself, is not really my world at all. I assume it is my world — and that is the most fundamental, time-consuming, self-perpetuating blunder of all time.

In man's case, his world is not the external world he perceives but the inner natural world he feels. One can never perceive one's own world, one can only be one's own world in the same way as man *is* his feeling and not his perception or concept of it. This state prevails in life after death when man actually experiences the death world as his own emotional, feeling self. This is the state that while alive he yearns for as the sharing quality of constant love, but which persistently evades him while he looks for it in the unknowable matter of the external world that is not his.

Really, my world is my Self, out of which I arise in every case. My Self is before I am and is present when I am not. My Self alone can I know, or do I need to know to know all. I and my world are implicit in my Self. This world on the surface of the earth which I, as man, assume to be mine must therefore remain the source of my confusion until I die to it in one way or another and realise the subtle infinitude or truth of my Self.

Stellar mind and solar mind

Immediately the universal 'I''s perception reaches the new gallery the first system of existence in eternity is complete: 'I', mind and world (the universe).

Simultaneously, the universe stops forming.

It stops forming because the 'I''s perception, having reached or caught up with the now, the present, is no longer accumulating unknowable past; therefore no more solid universe can be created.

So where is the solid matter of the now now going?

It is being consumed by the new universal system of 'I', mind and matter to sustain its own existence. As the now flows on it makes two more circuits beneath the solid universal gallery. These appear as two loops or galleries of universal space. Universal space — the reality behind the scientists' positive vacuum — is what is left when the solidness of the now is extracted to create universal existence.

The top solid gallery of the universe and the two of space immediately below together enclose the three minds of the universal system: the universal mind within the solid gallery of the universe; the stellar mind within the first gallery of universal space; and the solar mind within the second spatial gallery.

Furthermore, as the now makes its first spatial circuit the stellar 'I' arises, and as it makes its second spatial circuit the solar 'I' arises. As I cannot exist until I have a world or something to perceive, so no world, gallery or anything else can exist without I being present to perceive it. I am then the present, or the presence of the now, in which existence continues to continue in the absence of my Self.

Terrestrial, planetary or orbital mind

As the now completes its second spatial circuit, the newly-arisen solar 'I' emits several *ideo-rings* into the surrounding space/time of solar mind.

An ideo-ring is a cosmic or divine idea expressed by a star, in this case our sun.

One of the ideo-rings is the idea of the planet earth, not as an orb of solid matter as our senses present, but as a ring of consciousness (spirit) containing the life-principle of man.

Terrestrial consciousness is actually the consciousness of man, not man as we understand him but man in his pre-conscious, pristine and august state where he is one being, a real and objective character/idea. In terrestrial consciousness, which is the higher mind behind and supporting the human psyche, there is no earth as such; the earth is a ring of consciousness — symbolised by its physical orbit — encircling the central solar 'I'. Terrestrial consciousness is the principle of intelligence behind and in all life on earth — the terrestrial 'I', the one and only Man, the lord-spirit of the earth.

Ten or twelve ideo-rings encircle the solar 'I'. Each represents the consciousness and governing principle of a planet, and together they form a single band of ultimate orbital consciousness or spirit within the solar mind.

Each planet or ideo-ring has a different ruling principle. The consciousness of all planets is identical but the principles vary. The ruling principles of all the planets influence in turn the ruling principle of each planet through any life expression that may form there.

The ideo-rings represent the real shape of the planets and their real significance relating to human immortality and the grand scheme behind the information provided by the short-lived narrow-visional senses.

The planets perceived by the senses are very limited, formal versions of the ideo-rings and by comparison are very uninformative. The senses only present variations on the point or orb of a planet which is in fact the shape of all matter coming into existence as determined by the emergence of the now in the first phase of eternity. In other words, all cosmic bodies whether distant or near take their shape from the original point and expansion of the now.

From the point of view of the human psyche, the ideo-rings are abstract, meaning pastless, in character. They can only be intuited. This is not difficult; it is merely a matter of recognising the truth of them as they are described. Furthermore, they are incredibly potent or real, consisting of spirit — pure idealised energy — and thus are divine principles or incontrovertible laws governing existence. Together, as a single band, the planetary ideo-rings permanently occupy the first, finest and most central region of the solar mind. There they form the radiant planetary or terrestrial world of spirit and life — paradise, the seventh level of mind or seventh heaven.

Release of the terrestrial ideo-ring into the solar mind starts another chain reaction.

The pastless ideo-ring immediately reacts to the gravitational field of the solar mind into which it has been emitted. This induces a new field of dynamic tension around it — the terrestrial mind.

Simultaneously, its pastless consciousness — the terrestrial Self — vanishes. In its place arises the terrestrial 'I'. The terrestrial 'I''s perception starts speeding out towards the stellar universe at the speed of light using the medium of solar space/time and gravitation lines now being incorporated into the terrestrial mind.

Light velocity is the speed of planetary communication (except when the sun or the spirit of the planet is involved, in which case 'instantaneous' gravitational communication occurs). Once again, due to the finitude of light, there is a delay as the 'I''s perception traverses the terrestrial mind.

In that interval the now forms a solid, smaller gallery beneath the two spatial stellar and solar circuits. This gallery is the lost or unknowable past of the terrestrial 'I'. Immediately the 'I''s perception reaches it the gallery stops forming and exists as terrestrial or planetary matter: the original substance of the earth.

However, this original earth matter is completely 'dead', inconceivably dense and lifeless and unlike anything perceivable in our external existence today.

Today, all the matter we perceive possesses past: can be described, analysed, named. Hence our external view of the earth and its matter is always of some form.

But original matter has no form, only absolute density. That is because it has no past. Past is the track of life, and original earth matter is utterly devoid of any vestige of life — something beyond our life-given comprehension.

Also, our view today is from the externalised surface of the earth, but in this original phase of eternity there is no surface, just as there is no life. Today, nowhere on the earth or within the earth which we explore or manage to dig out is there a place where life cannot be found to exist in some form or other. This is because life is now 'here', has actually penetrated and permeated the original, lifeless girdle of earth matter from within in the form of nature and the species.

Nature is not life itself but it is the life process of this planet. Life itself is cosmic and it manifests on earth and to earth-man in the process and forms of nature.

Nature itself originates from a second terrestrial ideo-ring which is now emitted by the solar 'I' in the next phase of eternity. This is the ideo-ring of the moon, the lunar principle. This glides out through the first terrestrial ideo-ring of man or intelligence and stops adjoining it, adding a brilliant nature-ring to the radiant band of terrestrial spirit.

This order of ideo-rings in the mind – intelligence surrounded by nature – is symbolised in the external reality by the moon, the nearest cosmic body, orbiting man and the earth.

As man represents the first terrestrial principle of intelligence so the moon represents the second principle of natural or organic life. The lunar principle determines natural or organic life as a fluid or liquid process expressed in flow and rhythm. Essentially, it manifests as juices, acids, sap and blood.

Since life on earth is determined exclusively by our moon it is most unlikely that the nature of life on any other planet is the same as that here. However, the form as distinct from its nature could be similar because all forms of planetary life in the solar system are determined by the combined influence of the planetary ideo-rings.

For example, we on earth may have a dream or see a vision. Although the form may be recognisable, the inner chemistry or life-process of the form is beyond our knowing because it is not natural, meaning, not of our moon. Anything without organic properties is lifeless to us. Life on Mars will be influenced to some extent by the intelligence of the earth and the nature of the moon. But the essential character of life there, whatever it is, will be determined by the Mars principle or ideo-ring and this has yet to be discovered.

As the first principle of terrestrial life is intelligence manifesting through the idea of man, and the second principle is organic nature appearing through the idea of lunar ebb and flow, so the third principle is form determined by the combined planetary characters or ideo-rings.

Forming of the human psyche and the externalising of life on earth

Once again, the release of the pastless lunar ideo-ring into the terrestrial mind opposite the girdle of terrestrial past causes a sharp reaction. A new field of tension – vital force – charges the surface of the mind between the two.

The stage is now set for the final phase of reality: the forming of the human psyche and the externalising of life on earth.

This begins with the ideo-ring of man or intelligence — the terrestrial 'I' — emitting a ringed replica of itself. This replica can be called the psychic 'I', the original empiric or evolutionary soul.

Here begins in eternity what religious tradition calls the journey of the soul. This is the original journey which the souls of all men on earth are making through life and death and whose final solution all must eventually emulate.

On release, the ringed replica of intelligence is pastless like its alter-self, the terrestrial 'I'. Gliding out still pastless through the radiant world of spirit it receives from the lunar ideo-ring an abstract impression of the lunar nature. It now has the character of intelligence and the nature of the moon, although both are only potential due to the replica still having no past.

However, immediately on leaving the world of spirit and entering the vital field the replica begins to gather vital energy and past — psyche. Pushed along by psycho-spiritual waves and pulses emanating from the ideo-ring world of spirit, the replica expands slowly as it moves out towards the girdle, every instant leaving its alter-self further behind. Past or psyche accumulates around and behind it in direct proportion to the distance it has travelled from its source.

At first, due to the absence of psyche or past, the replica's awareness registers no existence beyond the level of dreamless sleep. But proceeding deeper into the vital field it amasses sufficient psyche — sufficient past for reflection — to start to dream.

These most obscure of dreams, including vague possibilities of future life, arise within the replica itself from the earlier impression of nature received as it passed through the lunar ideo-ring. Mixed with them is the intrinsic urge, radiating from its alter-self, to make life or the replica more conscious. Man today still has these distinct and vaguely prophetic dreams seeming to require the performance of impossible tasks.

Finally, after what in our time would be vast aeons, the

replica comes to a stop hard up against the terrestrial girdle. The replica has now gathered a fat body of psyche around its original ring of intelligence and is shaped like a puffy ringed doughnut. Further, the whole area behind it back to the world of spirit now consists of its unknowable psychic past.

On the journey out across the vital field the replica received virtually no information from the waves carrying it. But now, jammed hard up against the girdle, it is being bombarded with waves of information psychic and spiritual. Amongst this data, made very obscure by psychic distortion, is the ceaseless urge to pursue the task of intelligence — to make life or itself more conscious.

From deep within its acquired psychic body the replica's true identity of abstract intelligence — soul — starts responding to this call of the spirit. Between the pressure from within and the waves pounding it from without, the dreaming replica awakes to ego consciousness, the awareness of being I. However, this egoic 'I' identifies only with the replica's acquired psychic body, its immediate position — not with its eternal state, the soul.

Trapped beneath the lifeless earth girdle, the replica can go neither back nor forward. It is like a pocket of air trying to escape through granite.

Somehow the replica's organising ego representing life and intelligence has to penetrate the lifeless girdle of earth matter in front of it. Somehow, it has to find a way out — or, as it would seem to us today with hindsight, to put on the surface vital life in the form of the species, and then self-conscious life in the form of creative man. No more formidable task ever confronted the ego.

The great ear and brain

Two simultaneous events now occur. The first involves the replica's psychic body. This, pressed hard up against the terrestrial girdle, is reverberating to the dynamic of the now coming through the girdle — the echo or word of eternity out of which all existence comes to mind.

Under this influence, and at the imperceptible pace of evolution, the psychic body goes through a metamorphosis. The outer region of it touching the girdle evolves into a great ear — the original ear of which all externalised ears are copies. Inside the ear a bony structure forms, resonating to the vibrations coming through the ear from the girdle. Deeper in again, and influenced by the developing intelligence of the ego due to the ideo-waves sweeping in from across the psyche, an embryo brain section starts to form. Slowly this organises itself into a chambered system for interpreting and evaluating the inner ear's reproduction of the eternal sound. This is the original brain on which all subsequent brains are modelled.

The outer body of the replica is now an ear and brain, a complete, independent system for translating the echo of the now into the psychic frequency we experience today as sensation.

But the brain's perceptions of reality have no life. The effect is one of complete mechanical detachment as though the brain were a camera registering the images of reality without in any sense being a part of it. Also, at this stage the whole brain/ear apparatus is purely a receiver.

Meanwhile, deeper within the replica's psychic body near the point of its abstract consciousness, the other major evolutionary event is in progress.

Here, at the root of the ego, far removed from the mechanical ear/brain function, great pressure is coming from the spiritual ideo-waves. These, as a solution to the replica's psychic entrapment and to further the task of intelligence to make life conscious, are demanding and forcing an inward-going spiritual awakening corresponding in magnitude to the psychic evolution of the ear and brain.

For a cosmic principle like life as we know it to start, requires a cosmic trigger. The cosmic trigger of life is the sun. But in this phase of eternity there is no sun as there is no external earth or world — because there is no external life. For external life to exist requires the external sun and for the external sun to exist requires external life. It is a deadlock that can be broken only by a spiritual or cosmic initiative in the mind. The ego must be made to realise the true sun within — the sire of the idea of the earth — by achieving reunion with its alter-self the terrestrial 'I' in the ideo-world. For this its deeper awareness has to be induced to journey back across the psychic field — the equivalent of its subconscious — to the radiant light. This means in a sense having consciously to undo all that has so far been psychically or psychologically accomplished.

So, against the full onslaught of the psychic waves of past, and unknowingly guided by the spiritual pulses, the ego now starts by psychic dissociation to force a line of consciousness back across the psyche to its alter-self.

We must try to appreciate the enormity of this effort because any of us who venture to realise the truth will have to make the same journey with the same invincible persistence. It means that the ego first has to disengage its habitual attention from the overriding importance our brain (and the brains of others) attaches to the external sense world. It means that the ego literally has to roll back time — its unknowable past — and shatter the familiar, comforting psychic cocoon of dreams that has spun around its intelligence since the ideo-world was left behind.

As the ego pursues this path of psychological self-immolation it is assailed by near-irresistible psychic illusions, blandishments and enticements to go on dreaming and to forget the effort of becoming radiantly conscious.

But by sheer strength of character derived from its intelligence — the same admirable spirit that man displays today in any noble determination or restraint — the ego dissolves its identification with its false psychic body and its past enough to make direct contact with its alter-self and the radiant inner world. In a brilliant burst of light the ego realises the true sun, the spirit of life — and in the same instant is obliterated.

In its place, shimmering phoenix-like with terrestrial consciousness, is the enlightened psychic 'I'. Through the psychic 'I' cosmic power — and along with it the realised lunar principle of vital life — streams into the outer brain from the radiant inner world. The cosmic connection has been made — the trigger for life on earth. 'I' had actualised the sun.

Immediately, through the great ear pressed to the girdle, the brain begins to register sensations of the external sun and moon. Hazy perceptions of other 'outer' conditions also start to occur. But most significant of all, among the sensations being received through the girdle are the first signifying life on earth.

Survival after death and the return to earth

After an interval an extraordinary development occurs, extraordinary because even today the outward-orientated brain or ego cannot comprehend it.

Behind the brain a peculiar pressure is beginning to build up within the psychic field. This unconscious pressure consists of myriads of vital impulses corresponding to forms of external life that have ended or died. In other words, as sensations of life-forms on earth cease to exist (die) in one sense (compartment of the brain), they are recurring in a new, more potent and enduring sense (compartment) behind the brain — in the psyche or the brain's unconscious.

The psychic world of survival after death has begun.

Up until now the brain has had no retention, no memory of any of the signals coming from the girdle; all have just 'passed through'. But with the new vital back-pressure, information is gestating, no longer passing through. The effect for us would be like the shock of feeling our memory starting to come alive.

The brain itself now comes to life. The back-pressure of surviving life causes it to identify with the similar sensations of 'outer' life and conditions coming through the girdle. This pressure, compelling the brain's almost exclusive attention on the outer, is due to the vital life-force pressing to return to existence through the brain.

No longer is the brain an impartial, mechanical listener. It is beginning to have feelings. Every sensation starts to have significance for it: all impressions of the sun and moon and other 'outer' conditions start to be evaluated against the ultimate 'good' of life — outer life's continuance as a sensation or feeling in the brain.

271

Some outer sensations are felt as good and helpful, others as bad and threatening. Anxiety and conflict enter the brain – and a new psychic ego, responsive to the survival needs of the new life-sensations, starts to evolve.

Up to this point the psychic 'I', invested with the task of making life (more) conscious, has had no direct control over the brain. But now the situation is entirely different. The 'I' is now in a position to exert its will or influence through the new medium of surviving psychic life forming as the unconscious around it. It does this by imbuing surviving life with the simplest and most fundamental form of intelligence: instinct.

The 'I' is the genius, the consciousness, behind and within instinct. Instinct is the vital aptitude for survival arising from the experience of having lived and survived. The inner psychic life now pressing on the brain has already survived both life and death: instinct is this knowledge plus the desire to live again.

Experience – that is, first-hand knowledge of earth existence – leads to instinct. This experience is now the crucial bond between the 'I' and surviving psychic life which the brain and ego do not have. The 'I' has realised the sun and the potential of conscious life it offers, while psychic life has actually lived and perished under the influence of the sun on earth. But the brain's and ego's knowledge of the external world is all second-hand, obtained mechanically from 'listening' to the girdle, not through their own experience. The ego is the brain's attendant – mythically a dwarf who must be content to stay forever in the infernal underworld compartments of the sense machine. When he ventures 'up' to the surface as emotion, there is invariably trouble.

At this stage, surviving life in the psychic world behind the brain is undifferentiated. The life-forms living and dying on earth are too elementary to support individual consciousness in the death-world or to sustain disparate psychic identities there. Surviving life can only mass into a pool of nebulous but vitally determined desire demanding one thing: re-experience of living. Life that has experienced living, naturally or instinctively wants more. And with this mighty unconscious urge or longing the enlightened psychic 'I' deep in the new unconscious is totally consonant.

The first obstacle to life returning to the surface is the brain with its one-way incoming system.

As life continues to die on earth the internal pressure mounts. During this protracted period life on earth (or signs of life coming through the girdle) remains extremely simple and seemingly tenuous in its hold — out of all proportion to the sudden, accelerated development soon to occur.

This happens when finally the inner intensity peaks, probably causing the severest headache of all time. Vital life, unbeknown to the outward-looking ego, bursts into the brain from behind.

Flooding through the evaluating compartments of the sense machine it absorbs the sense (or condition) of existing life on earth coming from the girdle — and emerges as a stream of brainwaves carrying sensory 'messages' and mutations for the survival and evolution of life on earth.

The brainwaves then travel up through the ear to the girdle — now no longer an impervious barrier. The pulses of life on earth coming from the girdle represent life's legitimate or knowable past and form actual life-lines, capillaries, through the otherwise impenetrable unknowable past of the girdle. Along these the returning vital lifewaves surge to the surface to renewed sensory existence.

This momentous breakthrough by instinctive intelligence results in the sudden tremendous burgeoning of life on earth referred to earlier in this book, which will be confirmed by fossilised evidence or any correct scientific reconstruction of the evolution of the species.

The whole episode is a manoeuvre of unquestionable genius that has left the world of sensation behind in the brain or sense machine and put consciousness in the slender form of unconscious instinct in life on earth.

'I' — the one consciousness in all earth-life which all men instinctively refer to as I — has made remarkable progress in its task of making life more conscious. Through instinct it now controls both inner and outer life independent of the brain and ego which have no knowledge of the psychic reality behind them. As far as the brain is concerned, with

its mechanical conversion of the incoming signals into sensations of life, these will go on the same forever as the incipient
senses of the species.

The real triumph is that the 'I' has now consciously
exceeded the senses (a fact demonstrable to anyone who has
observed how much swifter and more reliable are the responses of instinct). And this in spite of the fact that it will
take some two billion years for the 'I' in instinctive life to
become the 'I' in self-conscious life — man.

From now on, evolution will centre on the endless cyclic
stream of life on earth and 'death' in the psychic world, with
the psychic 'I' deep within the unconscious in complete
though covert control.

Through the life-signals entering the brain from the girdle,
the 'I' can now perceive exactly what is happening to life
anywhere on the surface of the earth. Conversely, through
its control of the instinctive reincarnating lifestream travelling up to the surface via the brain or sense machine, the 'I'
can maintain or alter the intensity of life and initiate changes
as required.

Thus evolved the impeccable psychic network controlling
nature as described at the beginning of this book.

30
Lunar enlightenment

Every object in the sky has been placed there by man. Man is forming the external universe.

The real universe — beginning with the ideo-world — is deep within his unconscious and, as I have already explained, man has been slowly projecting it through his senses via the intellect since time began for him. If it were possible to return to a point before man became self-conscious, most of the exterior universe would be seen to be missing.

The universe manifests in proportion to man's ability to perceive it and define it.

Yet it cannot be said to be his creation for it already has total reality within the radiant world of spirit in the mind. None the less, man is under unremitting pressure from the central core of intelligence to give the universe ever clearer sense-perceptive and rational existence, which is precisely what he is doing via his telescopes, rockets, films, space journeys, writings and imagination.

Using the example of the moon, I will now demonstrate how man is forming the universe.

The moon is the first cosmic body out from the earth and the nearest object in the sky to man. Its proximity is of great significance, no accident or coincidence. The moon was the first cosmic body to illumine man's brain.

The story goes back to millions of years before man became self-conscious.

Earlier in this book I described the rending of the veil of opaqueness, the psychic membrane that lies behind all animal eyes; and how this rending enabled sunlight to penetrate animal-man's unconscious, thus allowing him to fork off from the rest of the species on his lone, long journey towards becoming a self-conscious human being.

It was lunar enlightenment that rent the veil.

In a number of sub-human primates living in the east a stunningly brilliant light suddenly blazed in their individual brains. The illumination would have appeared to them like a great hole of light in their consciousness. These sub-human primates, who had no self-conscious existence, were vitally 'blinded', rendered inoperative for quite some time, our equivalent of being made unconscious.

However, at that time there was no external moon in the sky. The 'sky' consisted of the dark awareness of the species which for these particular sub-humans alone was now almost nothing but light. There was no sense-perceptive moon. The only moon was the real moon infinitely deep in the unconscious mind — and a replica of it that had been moving across the vital field of the preconscious since life began several million years before.

What had happened was this. The lunar replica emitted into the vital field by the real moon — the lunar ideo-ring — so long before had at last reached, entered and enlightened the psychic brain with its psycho-spiritual energy.

The psychic brain is the governing brain of all the species — the speci-al brain. The special brain is the nucleus at the centre of every individual physical brain on earth; the original of the ever-recurring individual reproductions. Being the one brain behind each man, it also contains the sense-complex that creates the sense-perceptive world the species sees and evolves in.

Lunar enlightenment of the special brain was not able to be registered by all the species. The resultant illumination occurred only in the individual brains of the most evolved sub-human primates then alive.

After a time the dazzlingly brilliant light in the sub-human awareness reduced in extent and power to the size, intensity and reality of the full moon. Finally this faded in phases and returned to the full in phases to light up the sub-human awareness over a period equal to our twenty-nine and a half days. Without physical eyes to see it, or cognition to know it, the moon indubitably shone brightly in the sub-human awareness.

This was the same moon we see today. But our overt intelligence or self-consciousness, which came a long time after, has seemingly exteriorised it, transferred it 'outside' as an object of sight in the same way as man has materialised himself as a sense-object outside his inner awareness.

When we lose our self-consciousness, as in sleep, the external world disappears and we remain either unconscious of anything or sub-conscious in a dream world; and this continues off and on until the day we die physically or sense-perceptively. Our awareness then passes back through the sense-complex or the special brain — and into the original sub-human awareness where the moon first shone. This, the former preconscious, is now the teeming psychic world where the moon still shines and the human awareness of sky and space is filled with all the wonders of the world that has been made by man.

The moon was the first cosmic object to be intuited by the human mind. At the time of the lunar enlightenment animal man could not yet perceive the moon in the sky; but his brain, his future intellectual instrument, was illuminated by the idea of it which meant the moon could now start to be projected sense-perceptively and seen with eyes. Scientists and others still follow this routine today: the individual intuits the existence (say) of a new sub-atomic particle and then he discovers what he intuited. In other words, man forms his universe out of what is already in his brain.

Nothing can be perceived or discovered in the external world that has not already been intuited or preconceived in this way by man in his inner awareness. However, that inner awareness is not individual, and the man who intuits is not necessarily the discoverer of a particular phenomenon. Frequently the same discovery is made simultaneously by different men in different places — due to the cumulative intuitive vision of many men before.

The point is especially important that an original idea such as the lunar replica enlightens the special brain and not the individual self or man. Individual self, or man himself, has to evolve to the point where he can realise the original ideas in his own personal brain and thus change its constitution and power. Until he does this, he is forced to use old cells in his own brain that have been superseded in the special brain, and in that respect he can be said to be operating below his potential as a human being. When an individual man realises an original idea or replica of an ideo-ring it is rightly called realisation — the realisation in his personal self of the illumination in his personal brain of an enlightenment that has already occurred in the brain of the species.

Lunar enlightenment produced the most radical changes in brain cells that had occurred to that date. But even so, those changes — like the enlightenment itself — were the climax of a long process stretching back several million years in time to when the lunar ideo-ring first emitted the replica of itself into the psychic field.

Each replica consists of a set or series of precise characteristics representing the cosmic principle of the originating ideo-ring. Characteristics derive from a principle being devolved or differentiated — considered — in the human psyche; that is, by a psychic replica (an idea) moving out (as consideration or thought) towards matter or the conscious world of physical action. In this way principles deteriorate psychologically into characteristics and characteristics manifest sense-perceptively as nature. The lunar principle is flow or rhythm and this is characterised in organic life and the appearance of nature.

As the lunar replica moved across the psychic field of the unconscious it projected its characterising influence ahead of it until finally it entered the special brain and enlightened the cells totally with the idea it represented.

The emission of the replica into the vital field coincided with the first appearance of life on earth. The first characteristic of the replica being organic life, as soon as it entered the psyche the first life-form started to appear on earth.

The further across the vital field the replica moved, the stronger was its influence and the more pronounced and complex became its effect as the species. In this way the replica's characteristics became the characteristics of the species — a series of biological, hereditary facts determining how our bodies from that point on will function and react, and even how we will think.

It was the inexorable approach of the lunar replica that provided the ideal power, the irresistible pressure behind evolution up to the point of its arrival in the psychic or special brain. Its closing proximity forced continuous changes in the brains of the species and other mutations corresponding ever more faithfully to the ultimate lunar characteristics.

The first of these was the idea of mammals released shortly before the lunar enlightenment. This produced the warm-blooded creatures that suckled their young, culminating in the primates — apes, monkeys and earliest man.

It was in a number of these sub-human primates that the veil of opaqueness, the psychic membrane behind all animal eyes, was rent as described above. By destroying the psychic membrane in the man primate, the lunar illumination raised him to incipient human status. It also had the effect of reconstituting the relevant brain cells of each of these sub-humans — old cells that had been in disuse since the early days of the species — with the ultimate characteristics of the lunar replica.

As lunar enlightenment was effective only in the human branch of the species, the final higher functional and behavioural lunar characteristics were to appear only in man, thus completing the irrevocable division between him and the rest of the primates — and starting the final run-up to homo sapiens.

The lunar influence on life was responsible for the female menses. Various female primates of breeding age menstruate every three and a half to five weeks and it was the approach of the lunar replica that caused this. However, the subsequent lunar enlightenment of the brain was responsible for the menstruation period peculiar to woman, as well as for changes in the coupling habit and numerous other uniquely human idiosyncrasies and inclinations.

Lunar enlightenment also engendered in man the capability of a unique sympathetic feeling response which would eventually manifest as the power to care and be concerned for. This sympathetic response, as against purely instinctive response, prepared the way for the human memory and imagination based on emotional recall or reliving of the past as a later visualising medium. From here on man learned to feel, cherish and nurture beyond the hold of instinct.

And as a compensating release for his new-found but more demanding humanity, he developed the power to sob and cry tears of pain — incipient compassion.

31
The source of the human unconscious

The human past is the non-stop succession of conceptual knowledge which has continued to arise and gather in the mind since the first spark of life on earth.

That knowledge is added to every moment in the continuum of the now or what might be called the stream of time: the human past, as knowledge and events, grows and keeps on growing at a furiously compounding rate.

This past, stretching back to the first point of life on earth, forms the collective unconscious of the species – the racial memory. Out of all this unconscious past come the survival instincts of the species including ourselves.

This can be called the accessible race past, or the accessible race unconscious.

Behind this, within the mind and therefore beyond any sense- or time-reference, is the terrestrial memory.

The terrestrial memory stretches back beyond time, or the past of life on earth, to the arising of the terrestrial 'I'. Its correct spiritual or cosmic name is the Vast Memory. Man, the highest intelligence, when evolved sufficiently can have conscious access to parts of all that vast memory, right 'back' (if it serves the race purpose) to eternity itself.

Nevertheless, underneath or behind this vast memory is another more fundamental area of the mind which is not accessible as knowledge. This is the terrestrial non-past, the terrestrial girdle, the substance of eternity itself.

The terrestrial girdle, it will be remembered, is part of the moment or ring of eternity which started or sounded the instant the intellect came across infinite mind, and which continues for us today as the now that never ends.

This girdle forms the rock-bottom foundation of our psyche as well as of the clearer terrestrial mind. Through the human psyche we can have access to the girdle now as understanding — but not as knowledge. For, as I have already explained, the girdle's peculiar consistency is unknowable past.

Knowable past is the substance of existence. But unknowable or non-past is the substance of eternity — and as such it is completely impenetrable, impervious to mind.

Fortunately however, in spite of our worldly conditioning, we do not need to know in order to understand. In fact, if we were dependent on knowing we would not understand half the things we do. In the most important matters in our lives it is enough for us to understand. This, in the matter of eternity, the girdle at the base of our psyche allows us to do without our needing to know anything outside our own existence. If we can listen — easier said than done in a knowing world — we can understand.

In what follows we are going to observe the girdle through our own psyche. This is necessarily a very restricted view of it. The girdle itself of course remains unchanged. It is our ability to see or appreciate it that diminishes. The human psyche from the ordinary outgoing self-conscious point of view is a very murky lens to look through for the truth within. The self-conscious human psyche mostly believes that the only real truth is what the newspapers and other media busy themselves with. Myth, or the truth behind our beginning as a race, is either incomprehensible or nonsense.

Nevertheless, as the rock-bottom foundation of our psyche, the terrestrial girdle makes its presence felt even to the most insensitive of us: sooner or later we apprehend it; we 'know' it is there. And it is not a pleasant sensation.

Everything else in the human psyche from instinct to memory consists of legitimate past extending back to the start of life itself and — given the effort and inspiration — is knowable, or recognisable. But the girdle is totally devoid of such past, which is to say it is something so dead or absent for us as to be virtually non-existent or non-distinguishable.

And yet, although deader than dead in this sense and therefore literally non-sensical or unable to be known, it persists in being apprehensible at the self-conscious surface of the human psyche — a fact which gives it an extremely sinister and frightening quality: it exists but it should not exist (our sense-based knowledge tells us); it is 'there' but instinctively we know it should not be, for its presence challenges the very validity of our perceived existence.

If the legitimate past is to be called the unconscious, meaning knowledge of life that has once been but is presently unrealised — and we all know how mysterious and elusive the unconscious is — the non-past is for us the complete absence of consciousness itself, that is, of 'I' the knower and the known. In other words, it represents the ultimate dread of all self-conscious life: extinction.

The non-past is sometimes sensed in dreams, in the imagination and in delirium. The effect is of terror, of monstrous, impossible demands being made on the individual. To try to visualise nothing can bring it on. It is the rock on which sanity perishes and madness survives. Its demands or presentation of the impossible is how it will best be identified and remembered by those who have met it. It is a tangible horror never to be forgotten once experienced.

Although inaccessible to knowledge, meaning knowing can never enter it or recall what is in it, the presence of the non-past as a state in the mind is demonstrable not only in individual experience but also in that most reliable of all human records — myth.

The Stygian darkness

The non-past or girdle at the bottom of the human psyche is the Stygian darkness identical with the Greek mythical stream Styx, considered to be the chief river of the subterranean world of the dead. Hence the word 'stygian' means 'hellish, infernal, characteristic of death'.

This hellish portent of the non-past is responsible for man's dread of death. But remarkably, the non-past has nothing to do with death. Death is part of the legitimate past. The non-past lies the other side of the legitimate past, beyond, where it can never interfere with life or death.

In other words, man's dread of death is a case of mistaken identity. The non-past at the foundation of the psyche is infinitely *worse* than death. But as I say, it cannot touch us, except as a threat or fear.

Death, on the other hand, is merely the unknown. The unknown is only tomorrow and that is not enough to create our dread of death — otherwise we would all be running around hysterically morbid at our inescapable fate. In fact we see through death, are actually looking through death now and do not realise it. It is as harmless as that. Death is merely the other side of life; it is familiar, intimately known by every one of us in its benignant essence. No one at the moment of dying fears death; most welcome it. To all, it is the most natural thing in the world. The sad thing at the moment of dying is that the living do not understand.

Only while we are in the moment of living do we see through death, through the middle region of the psyche, and glimpse the awful, lifeless, non-past foundation behind it. That — understandably — is what man dreads. All conscious life apprehends the primal non-past as the ultimate horror. It is felt to be the absolute end — when in fact it is the absolute beginning.

The primal non-past is the mind equivalent of matter out of which life emerged and out of which in turn intelligence evolved.

Man's position in relation to the non-past is represented by the human body. Intelligence, the head, balances on the body of life which is up to its neck in Stygian matter.

When man as much as moves his intelligent head to look down, or apprehends the primal matter out of which he came, he is petrified by his predicament. Since he fails to see death as his protector — for if he lived as long as he chose he would gradually fossilise and disappear back into matter — he is terrifyingly aware of being fractionally above the impinging primal darkness.

Man cannot fall back into matter. Death compassionately sees to that. But this does not prevent him from mistaking death for the vulnerability he feels in the presence of the primal source out of which, through the ceaseless now of life and death, he has struggled to emerge and be free since time began.

Index

Index

Index

Other works by Barry Long